Global Challenges in Res

Corporate responsibility has gone global. It has secured the attention of business leaders, governments and NGOs to an unprecedented extent. Increasingly, it is argued that business must play a constructive role in addressing massive global challenges. Business is not responsible for causing most of the problems associated with, for example, extreme poverty and hunger, child mortality and HIV/AIDS. However, it is often claimed that business has a responsibility to help ameliorate many of these problems and, indeed, it may be the only institution capable of effectively addressing some of them. *Global Challenges in Responsible Business* addresses the implications for business of corporate responsibility in the context of globalization and the social and environmental problems we face today. Featuring research from Europe, North America, Asia and Africa, it focuses on three major themes: embedding corporate responsibility, corporate responsibility and marketing, and corporate responsibility in developing countries.

N. CRAIG SMITH is the INSEAD Chaired Professor of Ethics and Social Responsibility at INSEAD, France.

C.B. BHATTACHARYA is the E.ON Chair Professor in Corporate Responsibility at the European School of Management and Technology, Berlin.

DAVID VOGEL is the Solomon Lee Professor of Business Ethics at the Haas School of Business, University of California, Berkeley.

DAVID I. LEVINE is the Eugene E. and Catherine M. Trefethen Professor of Business Administration at the Haas School of Business, University of California, Berkeley.

Cambridge Companions to Management

Cambridge Companions to Management is an essential new resource for academics, graduate students and reflective business practitioners seeking cutting-edge perspectives on managing people in organizations. Each *Companion* integrates the latest academic thinking with contemporary business practice, dealing with real-world issues facing organizations and individuals in the workplace, and demonstrating how and why practice has changed over time. World-class editors and contributors write with unrivalled depth on managing people and organizations in today's global business environment, making the series a truly international resource.

Global Challenges in Responsible Business

Edited by

N. CRAIG SMITH
INSEAD

C.B. BHATTACHARYA
European School of Management, Berlin

DAVID VOGEL
Haas School of Business, University of California, Berkeley

DAVID I. LEVINE
Haas School of Business, University of California, Berkeley

CAMBRIDGE UNIVERSITY PRESS
Cambridge, New York, Melbourne, Madrid, Cape Town, Singapore,
São Paulo, Delhi, Dubai, Tokyo

Cambridge University Press
The Edinburgh Building, Cambridge CB2 8RU, UK

Published in the United States of America by Cambridge University Press, New York

www.cambridge.org
Information on this title: www.cambridge.org/9780521735889

© Cambridge University Press 2010

First published 2010

Printed in the United Kingdom at the University Press, Cambridge

A catalogue record for this publication is available from the British Library

Library of Congress Cataloguing in Publication data
Global challenges in responsible business / [edited by] N. Craig Smith ... [et al.].
    p.   cm. – (Cambridge companions to management)
Includes bibliographical references and index.
ISBN 978-0-521-51598-6 – ISBN 978-0-521-73588-9 (pbk.)
1. Social responsibility of business.   2. Corporate culture.
I. Smith, N. Craig, 1958–   II. Title.   III. Series.
HD60.G556 2010
658.4'08–dc22
2010011226

ISBN 978-0-521-51598-6 Hardback
ISBN 978-0-521-73588-9 Paperback

Contents

Figures

Tables

Contributors

AURÉLIEN ACQUIER is Assistant Professor at ESCP Europe in the Paris campus. In collaboration with various national and multinational companies, his research focuses on the relationships between sustainable development, corporate strategy and institutional change. Aurélien Acquier is the author of various articles in French and English, and co-author of the book *Organizing Sustainable Development* (forthcoming).

PAT AUGER is an Associate Professor of Information Systems and e-commerce at the Melbourne Business School (MBS), the University of Melbourne. He is currently the Academic Director of the Executive MBA programme at MBS and teaches Information Systems and e-commerce in the MBA and Executive MBA programmes. Pat's research focuses on ethical decision-making by consumers and managers, and on the strategic use of Internet-based electronic commerce in business. He has published extensively in leading academic journals in a variety of disciplines including information systems, marketing, business ethics, international business, and strategy.

BROOKE BARTON is Senior Manager of Corporate Accountability at Ceres. She is responsible for advising Ceres member companies on sustainability strategy, reporting and stakeholder engagement. In this role, she facilitates dialogues between companies and their stakeholders to foster corporate sustainability. Brooke works with companies in the food and beverage, oil and gas, and airline sector. She also leads Ceres' work with companies and investors to address the growing business risks posed by water scarcity. Prior to Ceres, Brooke was a researcher for the Harvard Business School's Social Enterprise Initiative, where she wrote case studies and articles on the CSR strategies of multinational corporations in developing countries. While at Harvard, she co-edited *Business Solutions for the Global Poor: Creating Economic and Social Value*, a book examining over twenty business models for serving low-income consumers. Brooke's other professional experience includes communications and advocacy work with ACCION International, a microfinance NGO, and project evaluation with Catholic Relief Services in Bolivia. She holds a master's degree from the Fletcher School of Law and Diplomacy, where she studied corporate social responsibility and development economics, and a BA in economics from Duke University. She speaks Spanish and Portuguese.

IDA E. BERGER's research interests are invested in social identity, ethnic diversity, social alliances, consumer behaviour and advertising. Professor Berger earned BA, MBA and PhD degrees from the University of Toronto and has conducted extensive academic research, authored and co-authored numerous papers, presented many papers at conferences, given numerous addresses and refereed many papers, and presented special conference sessions on subjects related to marketing, branding, advertising, consumer attitudes and consumer social responsibility. Her work has been recognized with awards from the American Marketing Association, *Journal of Consumer Research* and the Marketing and Public Policy Conference.

C.B. BHATTACHARYA is the E.ON Chair Professor in Corporate Responsibility at the European School of Management and Technology in Berlin, Germany and Everett W. Lord Distinguished Faculty Scholar and Professor of Marketing at the School of Management, Boston University. Dr Bhattacharya received his PhD in Marketing from the Wharton School of the University of Pennsylvania in 1993 and his MBA from the Indian Institute of Management in 1984. He has served on the Editorial Review Board of the *Journal of Marketing*, *Corporate Reputation Review* and *Business Ethics Quarterly* and has also served as editor of special issues of the *California Management Review*, *Journal of Business Research* and *Journal of Public Policy and Marketing*. He has published several articles in journals such as the *Journal of Marketing Research*, *Journal of Marketing*, *Journal of Applied Psychology*, *Organization Science*, and many other journals.

SANDRO CASTALDO is Full Professor of Management at Università Bocconi and Chairman of the Marketing Department at Sda Bocconi School of Management. He is member of the CSR Unit at Università Bocconi. His research interests include relationship management,

trust and corporate social responsibility, customer-based intan-
gibles, and shopping behaviour. His recent articles have been published in the *Journal of Business Ethics, Business Strategy and the
Environment, Business Ethics: A European Review, Industrial
Marketing Management* and *International Journal of Electronic
Commerce.* His recent book, *Trust and Market Relationships*, was
published in 2007.

PEGGY H. CUNNINGHAM's research focuses on ethics, corporate
social responsibility, social enterprises and stakeholder engagement. Her research is published in a number of journals including
the *Journal of the Academy of Marketing Science*, the *California
Management Review*, the *Journal of Business Ethics* and the *Journal
of International Marketing*. She has also written over forty cases,
and she is the co-author of three marketing textbooks. She joined
Dalhousie University in January 2009, and is currently the Acting
Dean, Faculty of Management. Before joining Dalhousie, she was a
professor at Queen's School of Business. Professor Cunningham is also
an acclaimed teacher. Her awards include the PricewaterhouseCoopers'
Leaders in Management Education award, and the Academy of
Marketing Science's Outstanding Teacher. She has a PhD in business
administration from Texas A&M University.

TIMOTHY M. DEVINNEY is University Chaired Professor of Strategy
at the University of Technology, Sydney. He was previously on the faculties of the Australian Graduate School of Management, UCLA and
Vanderbilt University. His current research projects examine ethical
decision-making by consumers, employees, investors and managers.
His recent publications appear in the *Journal of Marketing, Journal of
International Business Studies, Journal of Business Ethics, California
Management Review, Journal of Management, Long Range Planning*
and *Academy of Management Perspectives.* He is an Associate Editor
of *AOM Perspectives*, a director of the Management Research Network
of SSRN, and on the editorial board of ten other leading journals.

MINETTE E. DRUMWRIGHT's research interests are in the areas of
corporate social responsibility, business ethics and marketing for nonprofit organizations. She is an associate professor in the Department
of Advertising and Public Relations in the College of Communication
at the University of Texas at Austin. She previously has been on the

marketing faculties of the University of Texas Business School and the Harvard Business School. She is currently faculty chair of U.T.'s Bridging Disciplines Program in Ethics and Leadership. Her articles and cases have been published in a variety of books and journals, including the *Journal of Marketing, Journal of Advertising, Journal of Public Policy and Marketing* and *California Management Review.* She has a PhD in business administration from the University of North Carolina at Chapel Hill.

ASSÂAD EL AKREMI is an Associate Professor of Management at the University of Toulouse, where he also is a researcher at the Management Research Center (CRM – CNRS). In addition to CSR, his current interests include social exchange, organizational justice, social identity, workplace deviance and research methods.

JEAN-PASCAL GOND is Assistant Professor at the International Centre for Corporate Social Responsibility (ICCSR) at the Nottingham University Business School. He is also Research Fellow at Audencia, Nantes Ecole de Management. His research builds on organization theory and economic sociology and investigates the social construction of Corporate Social Responsibility (CSR), CSR across cultures, and the role of social rating agencies in the development of Socially Responsible Investment. His research has appeared in journals such as *Human Relations, Journal of Business Ethics, Business Ethics Quarterly, Business and Society, Finance Contrôle Stratégie* and *Revue Française de Gestion.* He has recently co-written with Jacques Igalens a French book on CSR: *La Responsabilité Sociale des Entreprises.*

JACQUES IGALENS is Professor at the Toulouse Business School (IAE) at the Toulouse Capitole University. He is also Research Fellow at the Management Research Center (CRM), a CNRS laboratory. His research builds on organization theory and human resources management and investigates corporate social responsibility (CSR). His research has appeared in journals such as the *Journal of Organizational Behavior, Journal of Business Ethics, Revue de gestion des ressources humaines, Finance Contrôle Stratégie* and *Revue Française de Gestion.* He has recently co-written, with Jean-Pascal Gond, a French book on CSR: *La Responsabilité Sociale des Entreprises.* He is editor of the *Responsible Organization Review.*

PAUL T.M. INGENBLEEK is Assistant Professor of Marketing at Wageningen University. He has a PhD from Tilburg University (2002). His research interests focus on the domain of marketing strategy and include, among others, the interactions between marketing and corporate social responsibility, sustainable development, pro-poor development, and standards and institutions in international agro-food chains. His work is published or forthcoming in journals such as the *Journal of Business Research, Journal of Product Innovation Management, Marketing Letters* and *Journal of Macromarketing*. He is leading several policy-oriented projects for the Agricultural Economics Research Institute (LEI-WUR) in the domains of sustainable development, pro-poor development and animal welfare in food and agricultural industries.

EMMA V. KAMBEWA is a marketing economist for the WorldFish Center, East and Southern Africa regional office in Malawi. Her research interests include the coordination of marketing channels, value chain analyses, smallholder market access, poverty reduction strategies and sustainable natural resource management. She has published a book, *Contracting for Sustainability*, an analysis of the Lake Victoria–EU Nile perch chain, and a paper in the *Journal of Macro-marketing*. She has chapters in *Governance Regimes for Quality Management in Tropical Food Chains, Integrated Agrifood Chains and Networks, Management and Organization, Agrofood Chains* and *Networks for Development*. Her main focus at WorldFish Center is value chain analysis, marketing and trade in relation to fisheries and aquaculture. She is also an African Women in Agriculture Research and Development (AWARD) Fellow from which she wants to fast-track the building of her carrier as a female scientist and leader in the agriculture and natural resource sector in developing economies.

DAVID I. LEVINE is the Eugene E. and Catherine M. Trefethen Professor of Business Administration at the Haas School of Business at the University of California, Berkeley. He is also Chair of the University's Center for Health Research and Chair of the Advisory Board of the Center on Evaluation for Global Action (CEGA). Dr Levine's work has emphasized organizational learning (and failures to learn). Several of his books examine causes and effects of public and private policies to promote organizational learning in large organizations: *Reinventing the Workplace* (1995) and *The American*

Workplace: Skills, Pay and Employee Involvement (Cambridge University Press, 1999). His other work has examined means to promote continuous improvement in public policies (see *Working in the Twenty-First Century: Government Policies to Promote Opportunity, Learning and Productivity in the New Economy,* 1998).

ADAM LINDGREEN is Professor of Strategic Marketing at Hull University Business School. He was previously on the faculties of the Catholic University of Louvain and Eindhoven University of Technology. Dr Lindgreen received his PhD from Cranfield University. He has published in *Business Horizons, Industrial Marketing Management,* the *Journal of Advertising,* the *Journal of Business Ethics,* the *Journal of Business and Industrial Marketing,* the *Journal of Marketing Management,* the *Journal of Product and Innovation Management,* the *Journal of the Academy of Marketing Science* and *Psychology & Marketing,* among others. His most recent books are *Managing Market Relationships, Market Orientation, Memorable Consumer Experiences, The Crisis of Food Brands* and *The New Cultures of Food.* His research interests include business and industrial marketing, consumer behaviour, experiential marketing, relationship and value management, and corporate social responsibility. He serves on the boards of many journals and is editor of the *Journal of Business Ethics'* section on corporate responsibility and sustainability. Dr Lindgreen's awards include the 'Outstanding Article 2005' from *Industrial Marketing Management.* In 2006, he was made an honorary Visiting Professor at Harper Adams University College.

JORDAN J. LOUVIERE is Professor of Marketing and Executive Director of the Centre for the Study of Choice (CenSoC) at the University of Technology, Sydney. He was previously on the faculties of Sydney University, University of Utah, University of Alberta, University of Iowa, University of Wyoming and Florida State University. His current research projects include integration of structural equation and choice models, choice models for single persons, integration of basic science with choice models, the behavior of the error variance in latent dependent variable models, measurement models based on best–worst choices and theory and methods for valuing the equity of brands. His recent papers have appeared the *International Journal of Research in Marketing,* the *Journal of Consumer Research, Marketing Science, Journal of Mathematical Psychology, Social Science and*

Medicine, Journal of Health Services Research & Policy, Population Health Metrics, The Journal of Choice Modeling, International Journal of Nonprofit and Voluntary Sector Marketing, Agricultural Economics and *Health Economics, Policy and Law*. He works with Australian, US and other firms on choice modelling applications. He is on the editorial boards of the *Journal of Choice Modeling* and the *International Journal of Research in Marketing*. He is an OZ Reader for the Australian Research Council, and has received numerous research grants from the ARC and other funding sources.

JULIE MANGA PhD, is an organization development consultant, executive coach, facilitator and researcher helping executives and managers be more resourceful, grounded and wise as they navigate the ever-changing, fast-moving, uncertain and demanding circumstances of their work. Dr Manga was a Senior Research Associate at the Boston College Center for Corporate Citizenship for five and a half years, supporting executives and managers in effectively catalysing change towards more responsible and sustainable business practice through applied research, consultation, coaching and facilitating a peer-to-peer learning network of corporate responsibility executives from Fortune 500 companies.

PHILIP MIRVIS is an organizational psychologist whose research and private practice concerns large-scale organizational change, corporate citizenship and the character of the workforce and workplace. He is currently a senior research fellow of the Center for Corporate Citizenship, Boston College. A regular contributor to academic and professional journals, he has authored or edited ten books, including the highly acclaimed study of national attitudes, *The Cynical Americans*, a US national survey of corporate human resource investments, *Building the Competitive Workforce* and, covering twenty years of experience with mergers, *Joining Forces*. His latest works are about developing a leadership community, *To the Desert and Back*, and business in society, *Beyond Good Company: Next Generation Corporate Citizenship*.

FRANÇOIS MAON holds an MSc in management and is currently undertaking PhD studies at Louvain School of Management, Université catholique de Louvain, examining strategies for corporate social responsibility (CSR) implementation and stakeholder dialogue development. François has conducted research in Europe and the United States and has presented papers at numerous marketing, management, and business and society conferences. His publications include articles in *2008 Academy of Management Best Papers Proceedings* as well as in *Supply Chain Management: An International Journal* and *Journal of Business Ethics*. He has co-edited special issues on CSR-related topics in leading international journals.

NICOLA MISANI is Assistant Professor of Management at Università Bocconi and a research fellow at the SPACE Research Centre, Università Bocconi. His current research interests revolve around the strategic implications of corporate social responsibility, its effects on consumers, and the financing of sustainable ventures. His academic work has appeared on national and international refereed journals, including the *Journal of Business Ethics, Business Strategy and the Environment* and *Business Ethics: A European Review.*

FRANCESCO PERRINI is Full Professor of Management and Bocconi SIF Chair of Social Entrepreneurship at the Institute of Strategy, Department of Management, Università Bocconi, Milan, Italy. He is head of Bocconi CSR Unit and director of Bachelor of Business Administration and Management (CLEAM) at Università Bocconi. He is also senior professor of Corporate Finance and Real Estate Finance at SDA Bocconi School of Management. He is director of CSR Activities Group at SDA Bocconi. His research areas comprise management of corporate development processes, from strategy implementation (acquisitions and strategic alliances) to financial strategies and valuation; small- and medium-sized enterprises; and social issues in management: corporate governance, corporate social responsibility, sustainability, social entrepreneurship, social innovation and socially responsible investing. His recent articles have been published in *Academy of Management Perspectives, California Management Review, Corporate Governance: An International Review, Journal of Business Ethics, Business Strategy and the Environment* and *Business Ethics: A European Review.*

V. KASTURI RANGAN is the Malcolm P. McNair Professor of Marketing at the Harvard Business School. Until recently the chairman of the Marketing Department (1998–2002) and a faculty director of the School's Research Division (2004–9), he is now the co-chairman of the School's Social Enterprise Initiative. His current research is focused on understanding the needs and wants of the global poor, those living on less than $5/day. His second stream of research focuses on how to improve the practice of CSR. Kash Rangan has engaged in a variety of executive education programmes, consultancies and advisory activities for numerous commercial and nonprofit enterprises. He has been on the faculty of the Harvard Business School since 1983.

N. CRAIG SMITH is the INSEAD Chaired Professor of Ethics and Social Responsibility at INSEAD, France, and the Academic Director of the Corporate Social Responsibility and Ethics Research Group in the INSEAD Social Innovation Centre. He was previously on the faculties of London Business School, Georgetown University and Harvard Business School. His current research examines ethical consumerism/consumer activism, marketing ethics, deception in marketing, mainstreaming corporate responsibility, and strategic drivers of corporate responsibility/sustainability. His recent publications appear in *Business Ethics Quarterly*, *California Management Review*, *Journal of the Academy of Marketing Science*, *Journal of Consumer Psychology*, *Journal of Marketing* and *Journal of Public Policy & Marketing*. He has another recent book (with Lenssen) on *Mainstreaming Corporate Responsibility* (2009). He consults with various organizations on business/marketing ethics and corporate responsibility/sustainability, and serves on the Scientific Committee of Vigeo (a social responsibility rating agency), the Advisory Board of Carbon Clear (a carbon management consultancy), and the Ethics Advisory Board of SNS Asset Management.

VALÉRIE SWAEN is Associate Professor of Marketing and of Corporate Social Responsibility at the Louvain School of Management, Université catholique de Louvain in Belgium, as well as at the IESEG School of Management in France. She is an active member of the CCMS (Center of Excellence on Consumers, Markets and Society) and of the LOUVAIN CSR NETWORK. Her current research projects examine brand management, relationship marketing, consumer and employee perceptions about corporate social responsibility. Her recent publications appear in *Journal of Business Ethics*, *Recherche et Applications en Marketing*, *Revue Française du Marketing*, *Systems Research and Behavioral Science* and *Corporate Reputation Review*.

ANTONIO TENCATI is Assistant Professor of Management and CSR at Università Bocconi. He is Senior Researcher at SPACE Bocconi and a member of the CSR Unit, Department of Management, Università Bocconi. He is also a member of the Business Ethics Faculty Group of the CEMS-MIM (Community of European Management Schools – Master in International Management) Programme. His research interests include business management, management of sustainability and corporate social responsibility, environmental management, innovation and operations management. His recent articles have been published in *Journal of Business Ethics, Business Strategy and the Environment, Business Ethics: A European Review* and *Corporate Governance: The International Journal of Business in Society.*

AAD VAN TILBURG is Associate Professor of Marketing at Wageningen University. His research interests include the functioning and performance of market actors, markets, marketing channels and supply chains. He has published in *Agribusiness, Agricultural Economics, European Review of Agricultural Economics, Journal of Business Venturing, Journal of Development Economics, Journal of Regional Science, Journal of African Economies, Journal on Chain and Network Science* and *Netherlands Journal of Agricultural Science.* He was co-editor of *Agricultural Marketing and Consumer Behavior in a Changing World* (1997), *Agricultural Marketing in Tropical Africa* (1999), *Agricultural Markets beyond Liberalization* (2000) and *Tropical Food Chains* (2007). He is a visiting professor in the European Microfinance Master of Science programme in Brussels, a joint activity of the Université Libre de Bruxelles (Solvay Business School), Université Paris Dauphine and Wageningen University. His focus there is on the relations between trade transactions and microfinance, especially with respect to rural areas.

SUSHIL VACHANI is Professor of Strategy and Innovation at Boston University. He received his education at Harvard Business School, Indian Institute of Management, Ahmedabad and Indian Institute of Technology, Kanpur. He previously worked with the Boston Consulting Group, where he designed business strategies for American, Japanese and European multinationals. He also worked with Philips India and the Tata Group in India. His research interests include strategy and innovation at the bottom of the pyramid, multinational–government relations, impact of NGOs on international business and management of diversified multinationals. His research has been published in *Journal of International Business Studies, International Business Review, Harvard Business Review, California Management Review* and other publications. He is editor of *Transformations in Global Governance: Implications for Multinationals and other Stakeholders* (2006), co-editor of *The Role of MNCs in Global Poverty Reduction* (2006) and author of *Multinationals in India: Strategic Product Choices* (1991).

DAVID VOGEL holds the Solomon P. Lee Chair in Business Ethics at the Haas School of Business and is Professor in the Department of Political Science at the University of California, Berkeley. He is the author of seven books on business–government relations and corporate social responsibility. His most recent book, *The Market for Virtue: The Potential and Limits of Corporate Social Responsibility*, received the 2008 best book award from the Social Issues Division of the Academy of Management. Vogel lectures frequently to academic and professional audiences in the United States and Europe and is the editor of the *California Management Review*.

Foreword

With the political and media spotlight falling on climate change, sustainability, the ethics of business leaders (and those in the financial services preceding the recession) as well as the other global problems in the under-developed world of poverty, HIV, etc., the business world is beginning to see the necessity of being more socially and ecologically responsible. This is not just about being 'green', but about exploring the full range of socially responsible behaviours. As Theodore Zeldin suggested in his book *An Intimate History of Humanity*: 'The Green Movement could not become a major political force so long as it concerned itself primarily with natural resources rather than with the full range of human desires. Its setbacks are yet another example of idealism being unable to get off the ground because it has not looked broadly enough at human aspirations in their entirety'.[1] This book, edited by Craig Smith and his colleagues, provides the research base to this growing and increasingly important field. They focus on three key issues of corporate responsibility: embedding corporate responsibility, marketing and corporate responsibility and corporate responsibility and developing countries. Their contributors are comprised of some of the leading international scholars in the field from eight different countries: Australia, Belgium, Canada, France, Italy, the Netherlands, UK and the United States. This volume is based on state of the art research, which illustrates the importance of corporate responsibility, not only in terms of the ethical and environmental challenges but also because of their business imperative. More and more research is indicating that organizations who behave more responsibly, positively impact their bottom line.[2]

This book also supports Malcolm Gladwell's contention, in his book *The Tipping Point*, that change can make a difference: 'look at the world around you. It may seem like an immovable, implacable place. It is not. With the slightest push –in the right place- it can be tipped'.[3] This is the challenge that confronts all businesses, big and small, and this book provides the evidence of what is possible and achieveable. We hope that you will find this book useful in your scholarship, as well as in any change programmes you are considering in your organization, as we all move into a post-recession period of greater social and environmental responsibility.

Cary Cooper, Lancaster University Management School
Jone L. Pearce, University of California, Irvine
Series editors

Notes

[1] T. Zeldin, An Intimate History of Humanity (London: Vintage, 1998).
[2] E. Bichard and C.L. Cooper, Positively Responsible: How Business Can Save the Planet (Oxford: Butterworth Heinemann, 2008).
[3] M. Gladwell, The Tipping Point (London: Abacus, 2000).

Introduction: Corporate responsibility and global business

N. CRAIG SMITH, C.B. BHATTACHARYA,
DAVID VOGEL AND DAVID I. LEVINE

Corporate responsibility has gone global. Business leaders, as well as leaders from government and civil society, increasingly argue that business must play a constructive role in addressing massive global challenges.[1] Business is not responsible for causing most of the problems associated with, for example, extreme poverty and hunger, child mortality and HIV/AIDS – and, arguably, it is only indirectly responsible for most of the problems of climate change. However, it is often claimed that business has a responsibility to help ameliorate many of these problems and, indeed, it may be the *only* institution capable of effectively addressing some of them. As a result, corporate responsibility has secured the attention of business leaders, governments and NGOs to an unprecedented extent. Thus this book, *Global Challenges in Responsible Business* – which originated in an international conference on corporate responsibility organized at London Business School – addresses the implications for business of corporate responsibility in the context of globalization and the social and environmental problems faced by global business today.[2]

The book offers a rich set of articles reflective of research on corporate responsibility, many of which are informed by empirical studies. It focuses on three key corporate responsibility issues for global business: embedding corporate responsibility within the organization, the relationship between corporate responsibility and marketing, and implementing corporate responsibility in developing countries. As well as contributing to our understanding of corporate responsibility and global business and identifying implications for further research, the articles here also provide insight for practitioners, who find increasingly that they must address these issues.

Embedding corporate responsibility: engaged employees

The first four chapters of the book examine the challenges of embedding corporate responsibility. All four chapters illustrate the critical role of employee engagement in embedding corporate responsibility and suggest a need for further research on the dynamics of how employees both initiate and respond to corporate responsibility policies and programmes.

In Chapter 1, Gond *et al.* examine the role of employees in explaining the relationship between corporate social responsibility and corporate financial performance. They suggest that corporate social responsibility (CSR) can lead to employees identifying with responsible companies. In addition, norms of reciprocity suggest employees reciprocate responsible behaviour exhibited by their employer. This identification and reciprocity, in turn, can increase work quality, lower employee turnover, and improve organizational efficiency, all of which can improve financial performance. The authors identify implications for human resource policies and practices, such as involving employees in the design of CSR strategy.

Berger *et al.*, in Chapter 2, draw upon elite interviews with multiple informants in twenty-six companies, nonprofits and consulting firms involved in eleven social alliances. Social alliances – defined by Berger *et al.* as 'long-term, strategic relationships between companies and nonprofits that have at least one noneconomic (i.e. social) and one economic goal' – are poorly understood, yet proponents claim they offer great potential to embed corporate responsibility. In keeping with the model in Chapter 1 by Gond *et al.*, Berger and her colleagues suggest that social alliances provide a means for employees to achieve professional goals while finding personal meaning in the workplace by doing good. These outcomes are likely to benefit the firm financially while the alliance also results in benefits to the firm's partners.

Chapter 3, by Mirvis and Manga, explores the role of middle managers as change agents attempting to embed corporate responsibility in their organizations. It is based on research with eight North American multinational corporations. The practices of these organizations illustrate how corporate responsibility can be embedded – and not least as a result of the passion of the practitioners involved. Passionate and inspiring business leaders are not found only at the top of organizations. As Mirvis and Manga show, committed mid-level executives also may effect change and they do so by employing tactics such as building on small wins and reusing or 'piggy-backing' on existing structures and schemes.

The concluding chapter of Part I, Chapter 4, sounds a cautionary note. Drawing on a detailed case study of a CSR initiative in a European energy company, Acquier shows how the initiative became marginalized because of the failure by 'Energy Co.' to adopt a coherent CSR management model. The author defines a management model as a combination of a definition of performance, a set of management objectives, and organizational devices, processes and skills. This is one way of thinking about what embedding corporate responsibility in a firm should involve. The Acquier study shows how the company's CSR activities, not just its statements of good intent, affect how employees respond.

Marketing and corporate responsibility: communication as a key component

Consumer concerns about CSR issues drive many companies' attention to corporate responsibility. All three chapters in Part II focus on this relationship and suggest that further research is required on how companies can more effectively communicate with consumers about CSR practices.

In Chapter 5, Auger *et al.* present the findings of experimental research on ethical consumerism conducted in six countries (the United States, Germany, Spain, Turkey, India and Korea). Their experiments forced consumers to make trade-offs between functional product features (e.g. brand and price) and social product features (e.g. whether or not the product was manufactured by children). This provided a basis for identifying segments of consumers who placed a greater value on socially acceptable products than other consumers. They used AA batteries and athletic shoes as the focal products. While 'ethical segments' were identified for both batteries and shoes, only a small proportion of consumers belonged to both, suggesting ethical consumerism may vary across product categories and social issues. Cultural differences were less of a factor in predicting segment membership than previous research would suggest. Perhaps most importantly, Auger *et al.* report that many consumers in their sample were unaware of the social features of the products they purchase, suggesting the need for greater communication about and public understanding of the social and environmental dimensions of consumer purchasing decisions.

Chapter 6, by Maon *et al.*, examines how different stakeholders respond to CSR, using home-furnishing retailer IKEA as a case study. The authors interviewed twenty external stakeholders, including human rights NGOs, environmental NGOs, trades unions, an SME interest group, city councils, CSR consultants and an international research foundation. They also spoke with senior IKEA managers, and surveyed IKEA consumers. At IKEA, multiple stakeholders are important audiences for communication about CSR initiatives. At the same time, two-way communication with stakeholders also influences IKEA's CSR policies. Stakeholders' perceptions of CSR at IKEA varied along several important dimensions. Thus the authors suggest that appropriately tailored messages and communication tools need to be employed for each of the firm's stakeholders.

In Chapter 7, Perrini *et al.* note the difficulties presented in research of the aggregate relationship between corporate social performance and corporate financial performance and instead test a more specific component within the relationship. Using data from 400 telephone interviews with consumers of retail chains in two Italian cities, they examined the role of consumer trust and found that consumers who viewed retailers as more socially oriented (as a result of Fair Trade policies) demonstrated more trust in the retailer. This trust, in turn, translated into greater brand loyalty, with improved economic performance as the likely consequence. A key caveat again, however, is that the CSR policy must be effectively communicated to consumers.

Corporate responsibility and developing countries: understanding the context

Globalization has dramatically increased the presence of multinational corporations in developing countries. Many of the global challenges we noted at the outset of this chapter – challenges posed for business as well as for broader society – are identified within the UN Millennium Development Goals and are specific to developing countries.[3] In the three chapters in Part III, we consider the social and environmental impacts of developing country sourcing and the distribution obstacles in serving the 'bottom of the pyramid' (BOP).

Taken together, they demonstrate the need for more research on the characteristics of developing country contexts and their implications for corporate responsibility in multinational corporations.

In Chapter 8, Kambewa *et al.* present a case study on the sourcing of Nile perch from Lake Victoria. Nile perch production was intended to bring economic and social benefits to the region. While it did so initially, after a decade or so it also brought ecological degradation and increased poverty because of the misuse of the lake's resources. Kambewa *et al.* show how these upstream problems become the responsibility of the downstream participants in the supply chain. They highlight how such companies need to become aware of the sustainability implications of their sourcing and become involved with their channel partners to develop solutions, the complex developing country context notwithstanding.

Chapter 9, by Rangan and Barton, also looks at the complexities of developing country contexts, focusing on the case study of the Tintaya copper mine in Peru, owned at the time by BHP Billiton, the world's largest mining company. The case illustrates how corporate responsibility – especially in regard to environmental performance and resettlement of affected people – is the key to maintaining a social license to operate in extractive industries. From a business case perspective alone, it seems, an embedded approach to corporate responsibility is imperative in this sector – without public permission to operate, mining companies can find their operations shut down. In light of the Tintaya case, Rangan and Barton offer a framework for analysis of the three main levels of the social and environmental impact of the extractive industry, and the associated implications for stakeholder engagement and company control.

Finally, Chapter 10, by Vachani and Smith, highlights the potential societal and economic benefits of companies serving the BOP – the 2.7 billion people in the world who live on less than $2 a day – and the obstacles to be overcome in reaching the rural poor specifically. The authors provide five case studies of 'socially responsible distribution' drawn from across the corporate, government and NGO sectors. The case studies are used to identify initiatives that can provide poor producers and consumers with increased market access for goods and services that they can benefit from buying or selling. These initiatives help neutralize the disadvantages suffered by poor producers and consumers; specifically, inadequate physical links to markets, information asymmetries and weak bargaining power. As in Chapters 8 and 9, particular attention is given to the specific requirements of the developing country context. They recommend strategies for bridging the infrastructure gap, the provision of producer-empowering information, leveraging technology, and promoting cross-sectoral collaboration.

The world has changed

The global financial crisis and recession that dominate the news as we write this introduction (in March 2009) have left many predicting a sharp downturn in attention to corporate responsibility. But this would be precisely the wrong response. The financial crisis is in substantial part due to a failure of corporate responsibility and avoiding its reoccurrence requires more attention to corporate responsibility, not less.

It is likely that we will see budgets cut for certain corporate responsibility projects. But commentators who suggest that this points to a diminished need for corporate responsibility misunderstand the concept. Quite possibly, we will see banks and other institutions engaging in fewer employee-volunteering schemes, or less microfinance lending or cutting donations to charity, for example, but this is not where their primary responsibilities lie. Fundamentally, corporate responsibility has to do with corporations fulfilling their obligations to society in ways that reflect a social contract between business and society.[4] Many banks and other parts of the financial services sector certainly have failed to do this.

Arguably, the billions of euros, dollars and pounds governments around the world have spent bailing out banks is testimony to the failure of corporate responsibility by these institutions. It is all the more evident when we look at the lack of responsibility evident in specific practices, from the lax due diligence in securitization of subprime mortgages, to the mispricing of risk associated with complex financial products such as derivatives, to compensation schemes that rewarded financial executives with huge bonuses based on short-term performance that was reversed in the long term.[5] Certainly, other parties bear some responsibility for the financial crisis, such as regulators, the credit rating agencies, and shareholders who failed to demand evidence of rigorous risk assessments and failed to address the moral hazard of executive compensation and bonus schemes, but the primary blame must lie with the banks themselves. Mismanagement and incompetence are evident, but so too is a lack of social responsibility.

Surprisingly, perhaps, Milton Friedman, the late Nobel Prize-winning economist and long-time critic of corporate responsibility, likely would have agreed with us. As he famously observed: 'There is one and only one social responsibility of business – to use its resources and engage in activities designed to increase its profits so long as it stays within the rules of the game, which is to say, engages in open and free competition without deception or fraud.'[6] While we would argue that corporate responsibility amounts to much more than aiming to increase the firm's profits within the 'rules of the game', many financial institutions have failed to meet even this basic standard.

Former US Federal Reserve Chairman Alan Greenspan, asked by US lawmakers to offer his explanation for the causes of the financial crisis, commented: 'Those of us who have looked to the self-interest of lending institutions to protect shareholders' equity (myself especially) are in a state of shocked disbelief.'[7] The demise of the investment banks and the large-scale destruction of shareholder value of 2008 have called into question the view that market discipline will ensure the best economic outcomes. Something more than attention to their own self-interest is required of managers and the institutions they manage – and in all businesses, not just banks. They need to act consistent with their social responsibilities.

Early responses to the financial crisis already include calls for more attention to corporate responsibility. Following the election of President Barack Obama, Howard Schultz, CEO of Starbucks Coffee Company, wrote a widely-cited opinion piece advocating 'responsible capitalism'. He observed that the challenging economic climate had caused many business leaders to become fixated on the short term and put corporate social responsibility on the back-burner. But Schultz wrote that this was the wrong response, saying: 'Now is a time to invest, truly and authentically, in our people, in our corporate responsibility and in our communities. The argument – and opportunity – for companies to do this has never been more compelling.'[8]

Undoubtedly, some corporate responsibility projects will fall by the wayside with the justification that short-term economic interests must prevail. However, these projects are likely to be in companies that were not truly committed to corporate responsibility to begin with. The crisis is likely to reduce the amount of hype often associated with corporate responsibility and reveal who is serious. It is also likely to lead to more focused initiatives and to more attention to responsibility fundamentals – meeting the basic obligations of the company to society, be it in the financial services sector or in manufacturing.

The immediate consequences of the crisis also call for responsible approaches to cost reductions and lay-offs. Already, some business leaders have shown leadership by cutting their own compensation as they lay off workers and seek employee wage cuts. The same line of thinking might even be followed by consumers who, as concerned citizens, could come to question their role and responsibility in the financial crisis and in building a sustainable society. For example, there would be no sub-prime crisis without consumers who took on mortgages they could not afford in the hope of refinancing on the back of seemingly ever-increasing property values, mortgage mis-selling notwithstanding. Equally, responsible production is more likely to follow from responsible consumption, when it comes to issues like climate change or sweatshop labour in supply chains.

Thus, despite arguments to the contrary, we foresee more attention to corporate responsibility in these troubled economic times, not less, and especially more attention to responsibility fundamentals. We might even see greater attention to consumer responsibility. The global challenges of responsible business today are unlikely to disappear anytime soon, financial crises and recession notwithstanding. If anything, these economic difficulties heighten the case for greater attention to corporate responsibility, if not a fundamental rethinking of the role of business.

Notes

1 See, for example, reports of the annual meetings of the World Economic Forum at Davos: www.weforum.org/en/events/AnnualMeeting/index.htm (accessed 6 March 2009).
2 The conference, entitled 'Corporate Responsibility and Global Business: Implications for Corporate and Marketing Strategy', was held at London Business School in July 2006. The book editors were the conference co-chairs.

3 See: www.un.org/millenniumgoals (accessed 6 March 2009).

4 See, for example: Thomas Donaldson, *Corporations and Morality* (Englewood Cliffs, NJ: Prentice Hall, 1982); Ian Davis, 'The Biggest Contract: Ian Davis on Business and Society', *The Economist*, 26 May.

5 Warren Buffet's February 2009 letter to investors in Berkshire Hathaway provides an accessible account of some of the major underlying problems of the 2008 financial crisis. See: www.berkshirehathaway.com/letters/2008ltr.pdf (accessed 6 March 2009).

6 Milton Friedman, 'The Social Responsibility of Business is to Increase its Profits', *New York Times Magazine*, 13 September 1970.

7 'Greenspan Shocked at Credit System Breakdown', *Reuters*, 23 October 2008. See: www.reuters.com/article/GCA-CreditCrisis/idUS-TRE49M58W20081023 (accessed 6 March 2009).

8 See Howard Schultz, 'Yes Business Can', in *The Huffington Post*, 6 November 2008, at: www.huffingtonpost.com/howard-schultz/yes-business-can_b_141969.html (accessed 19 February 2009).

PART I

Embedding corporate responsibility

1 | A corporate social responsibility– corporate financial performance behavioural model for employees

JEAN-PASCAL GOND, ASSÂAD EL AKREMI,
JACQUES IGALENS AND VALÉRIE SWAEN

Introduction

Today's CEOs are under pressure to address pervasive environmental, social and ethical issues. Companies are held accountable for the direct and indirect consequences of their actions and face a plethora of issues such as ensuring environmental sustainability and sound labour practices, sourcing skilled employees in areas with limited educational systems, ensuring the respect of workers' rights and meeting the needs of the world's poor. A vast range of activities now comes under the corporate social responsibility umbrella: 'from volunteering in the local community to looking after employees properly, from helping the poor to saving the planet'.[1] According to a 2007 McKinsey global survey, managers consider that society has greater expectations for business to take on public responsibilities than it had five years ago.[2]

The existence of a positive relationship between corporate social responsibility (CSR) and corporate financial performance (CFP), however, remains considered by many as a necessary condition to justify the managerial relevance of the CSR concept. As Michael Porter observed:

Although there is a lot of feeling that 'we ought to do it' amongst analyst executives and a lot of corporate statements about companies' social ambition and efforts, there are also a lot of uncomfortable sentiments about why companies should be doing it. Corporate leaders are now giving lip service to this area [corporate social responsibility], but they do not ultimately understand it. No matter what they say in public, when you get behind the scenes with executives and directors, they will ask you 'why should we invest in social initiatives?' We may all care deeply about saving the world but if we cannot answer this question properly, we have a problem.[3]

The business case for CSR has always been a matter of concern for both academics and executives, and the question of the financial impact of CSR is as old as the very idea of social responsibility itself. The emergence of corporate philanthropy and paternalism in the late nineteenth century, prefiguring the contemporary CSR turn, was based on the mixed motives of owners whose actions were driven by religious motives as well as the will to attract a workforce of quality.[4] As early as 1953, Howard Bowen, an institutional economist recognized by many scholars as the father of CSR,[5] dedicated a full chapter of his seminal book to the economic viability of the 'social responsibility doctrine', anticipating many of the further critics and controversies about the business appropriateness of socially responsible behaviours.[6] The relationship between CSR and CFP, as a research topic, maintained its attractiveness in the academic arena for over fifty years, generating a corpus of more than 120 empirical studies building on various theoretical explanations to investigate the nature of a global relationship between CSR and CFP.

To date, most empirical studies have reported conflicting and obscure linkages between CSR and CFP.[7] Besides empirical and methodological shortcomings, the study of the CSR–CFP relationship is impoverished by a strong theoretical weakness: the search for a universal and general answer to a question that is by its very nature contingent on numerous factors and strongly dependent on the features of the institutional contexts in which corporations operate.[8] To quote David Vogel: 'Asking if Corporate Social Responsibility does pay is a too simplistic question because the answer will never be "yes" or "no" but always: "it depends".'[9] Following parallel insights, numerous authors have recently call for a move beyond the search of a global relationship between CSR and CFP, and the development of models explaining the underlying mechanisms of CSR impacts on stakeholders' attitudes and behaviours.[10] Such a research orientation is congruent with a more global shift in the contemporary CSR debate from the analysis of the 'whether to make substantial commitments to CSR' to the explanation of 'how' CSR programmes and actions should be designed to improve performance.[11]

However, while numerous authors have already investigated the influence of CSR on consumer behaviour, little is known about the influence of CSR on employees' behaviours or about the impact of these CSR-related employees' behaviours on CFP.[12] The purpose of this chapter is to fill this gap by providing an integrative behavioural model to investigate the mechanisms underlying the 'CSR–CFP' relationship in the case of employees – a stakeholder relatively neglected in the existing CSR literature.

Building on stakeholder and organizational behaviour theories, we consider employees as a group conceptually distinct from the management of the corporation, who perceive, evaluate and react to actions undertaken by their corporations in the CSR domain.[13] We suggest that socially responsible (or irresponsible) practices of the corporation might indeed influence employees' perceptions of justice and attitudes such as commitment, satisfaction and trust that motivate them to engage in organizational citizenship behaviours (or in counter-productive and deviant behaviours) that ultimately determine the firm's performance. More specifically, the integrative model of CSR–CFP for employees we provide hereafter draws on insights from social identity theory and social exchange theory.[14] According to social identity theory, individuals are predisposed to reinforce their self-esteem and bolster their self-images by identifying themselves with groups and organizations recognized for their social engagement and responsibility. In spite of the importance of the impact that this identification could have on employees' attitudes and behaviours, social identity theory does not integrate the notions of reciprocity, expectations and mutual obligations which are needed to understand the contribution of these behaviours to the performance of the company. Building on social exchange theory, we suggest that employees can develop a sense of obligation, according to the norm of reciprocity and might engage in organizational citizenship behaviours or counter-productive work behaviours as a mutual action rewarding or punishing corporate social responsible (or, in contrast, irresponsible) practices, especially those directed at employees and work conditions.

The chapter is organized as follows. We briefly review the existing evidence concerning the CSR–CFP interaction and outline the minor role dedicated to employees in the strategic approaches of CSR. Then, we present the three stages of our behavioural model of CSR–CFP for employees by distinguishing inputs (CSR perceived by employees), processes (employees' attitudes and behaviours linked to these perceptions) and outputs (ultimate impacts on human resources performance and CFP). We also show what moderators can affect CSR influence on employees and outline how our model can account for the dynamics of interaction between the corporation and its employees around CSR policies. In the final section, we assess the managerial relevance of the model.

Opening the CSR–CFP black box: employee behaviour as a missing link

The quest for an elusive link

The search for a global relationship between CSR and CFP in academia generated the publication of more than 120 empirical studies. Two recent meta-analyses have investigated the statistical validities of these works, suggesting a small – but positive – statistical relationship between CSR and CFP.[15] However, Margolis and Walsh, among many other authors, have pointed out numerous methodological shortcomings of these studies, such as missing control variables in research designs.[16] Vogel recently criticized the whole managerial relevance of that stream of research.[17] Indeed, producing actionable knowledge for managers about CSR requires moving beyond the search for an (elusive) general link between CSR and CFP, in order to better understand 'how' and 'why' CSR can actually affect corporate financial performance under specific circumstances. General frameworks such as stakeholder theory suggest that CSR and CFP are positively linked, but they do not provide in-depth analysis of the underlying mechanisms through which stakeholders' behaviours related to CSR can affect financial performance.[18] The business case for CSR can be established only if scholars can provide managers with a set of mid-range theories explaining how specific stakeholders will react to CSR. And such a perspective implies a move towards a strategic perspective on CSR.

The move towards strategic CSR

Even traditionally sceptical observers of corporate practices recently acknowledged the economic and social potential of this concept and have come to recognize that CSR is maybe simply 'good business'.[19] The call for an in-depth understanding of the underlying mechanisms explaining the CSR–CFP relationship reflects the upsurge of a market-driven approach to CSR in practice – a tendency coined by Vogel as the construction of 'markets for virtue' – and also in emerging theoretical perspectives.[20] In recent years, research efforts on CSR have moved towards a more strategic (or economic) perspective, focused on the conditions under which CSR could contribute to profit maximization. Baron defines strategic CSR as the use of CSR to capture market value.[21] Such a value capture can occur through the minimization of threats in non-market environments or through the direct contribution of CSR strategy to the construction of competitive advantage.[22] In a 2006 special issue of the *Journal of Management Studies*, McWilliams *et al.* promoted a strategic perspective on CSR by offering a set of contributions clarifying the economic foundations of CSR, taking Friedman's perspective on CSR seriously, or looking at the influence of CSR on corporations' dynamic capabilities.[23]

In line with that stream of research, the stakeholder perspective on the CSR–CFP relationship aims at highlighting the role played by stakeholders in the processes of CSR–CFP interaction.[24] Building on previous empirical findings, two complementary integrative models have already been proposed to account for the central role of consumer behaviours in the influence of CSR on corporate performance.[25] These models show the contingent nature of CSR's influence on consumer behaviour and suggest that many variables and moderators could affect the processes of CSR's influence on profitability. Research on socially responsible investment has also suggested that shareholders' and investors' attitudes towards CSR could affect corporate behaviours and financial performances.[26] Extending that new line of theory development, we suggest focusing research on the explanations of the impacts of CSR on employees' attitudes and behaviours, and on the moderating and mediating roles of these variables on the construction of the CSR–CFP relationship.

A key (but neglected) stakeholder for strategic CSR

Corporations and governmental institutions have already recognized the central role of employees in CSR deployment inside and across organizations. According to a report of the European Commission, CSR is directly related to dimensions such as 'quality employment, lifelong learning, information, consultation and participation of workers, equal opportunities, integration of people with disabilities and anticipation of industrial change and restructuring'.[27] The European

Commission is indeed promoting initiatives building on CSR to help prevent the social and societal consequences of restructuring, a practice directly related to employee management.

In some European countries, such as France, employees are considered as the main stakeholder towards whom the CSR policy should be oriented. A poll conducted by the Sofres in 2001 among French people revealed that 'employees' (71%) are considered together with 'customers' (78%) as the two most important stakeholders to keep satisfied in order to be seen as socially responsible, far ahead of shareholders (6%).[28] In the 2007 McKinsey global survey of 391 UN Global Compact participant CEOs, CEOs ranked employees as the stakeholder group that has the greatest impact on the way a firm manages societal expectations, with consumers a close second. Moreover, employees and consumers are joining NGOs and activists in making increasing demands on companies.[29]

In the UK, the Department of Trade and Industry (DTI) created the CSR Academy, an organization who launched a 'CSR competency framework'. This framework aims at helping human resource managers to put CSR into practice and its ultimate goal is to embed CSR into day-to-day activities for employees: 'It aims to make CSR an integral part of business practice, regardless of the organization's size or its type of markets.' It draws on case studies of 'best practices' of UK corporations and demonstrates how CSR imperatives and human resource management can be integrated to improve corporate performance. Among the many examples provided, the framework reports the case of Perfecta, a supplier of ingredients for the food industry, who have attracted and retained a more qualified workforce by designing a package of work–life balance initiatives. The large UK retailer Tesco has also developed a programme to actively offer employment opportunities to staff that have been out of work for several years, lone parents, older people who have been made redundant or young unemployed people. EDS, a British corporation employing 117,000 people in fifty-three countries and providing information technology, applications and business process services, have already used that framework to embed CSR and stimulate socially responsible forms of behaviours from its employees.[30] A report from the CSR Academy, based on twelve case studies, concluded that: 'CSR became an instrument for change in an organization's behaviours, attitudes and performance … HR will often be the function best able to contribute to the effective implementation of the behaviours and attitudes that successful business contributing initiatives need.'[31]

Numerous US firms such as Hewlett Packard, FedEx or Timberland have already deployed community volunteering programmes, directly involving employees in the process of CSR deployment. According to Kotler and Lee, these actions can indirectly contribute to business goals, by constructing new markets through the economic development of the assisted communities – as in the case of Hewlett Packard's 'i-community' programme – or by enhancing corporate image. These authors also suggest that volunteering programmes can directly increase employees' satisfaction and motivation at work.[32] In 1996, KPMG allowed its staff in Britain to spend two hours per month of their paid-for time on work for the community. After a while it came to be seen as a business benefit. The plan has expanded to half a day per month and now adds up to 40,000 donated hours per year.

Overall, this real-world evidence suggests that employees are perceived as central to the development of strategic CSR in many countries and that CSR has a special and important significance for human resource management. This acknowledgement of the central role played by employees contrasts with the role dedicated to this stakeholder in the majority of CSR. Corporate employees do paradoxically appear as a relatively neglected stakeholder in a recent upsurge of research exploring the potential impact of CSR from a business point of view. Table 1.1 summarizes the findings of previous empirical studies.[33]

Mainly based on signalling theory and social identity theory, these works suggest that the socially responsible practices of corporations send a positive signal to potential workers, who are likely to identify with a more responsible organization, especially if their values fit with the promoted practices. That body of research has shown the influence of a socially responsible reputation on corporate attractiveness for prospective employees such as MBA students. A SustainAbility study found that a positive reputation in the areas of environment and human rights management increases a company's ability to attract and retain staff, and that a negative reputation in those fields decreases it.[34] A recent survey even shows that those with MBAs were willing to forgo financial benefits in order to work for a corporation with a better reputation for CSR.[35] In the same vein, the 2007 Global Business Barometer conducted by the Economist Intelligence

Table 1.1 *Empirical studies on the influence of CSR on employees*

Study	Focus*	Key theory/mechanism	Method	Main results
Turban and Greening (1997)	External	Social identity theory Signalling theory	Survey of MBA students	Corporate social performance (CSP) is positively related to corporations reputation and attractiveness as employers
Maignan et al. (1999)	Internal	Resource-based view of competitive advantage	Survey of marketing executives	Market-oriented and humanistic corporate cultures lead to proactive corporate citizenship, which in turn has a positive influence on employees commitment, customer loyalty and business performance as perceived by marketing executives
Greening and Turban (2000)	External	Social identity theory Signalling theory	Experiment on MBA students	Prospective job applicants are more likely to pursue jobs from socially responsible firms than from firms with poor social performance reputation
Albinger and Freeman (2000)	External	Signal theory Recruitment theory	MBA and graduate students, and low-income job seekers	Organizational CSP is positively related to employer attractiveness only for job seekers with high levels of job choice. CSP appears consequently as a lever to capture the most qualified employees
Maignan and Ferrell (2001)	Internal	Resource-based view of competitive advantage	Survey of employees	A market-oriented culture is conducive of corporate citizenship, which in turn influence employee commitment and business performance
Backhaus et al. (2002)	External	Social identity theory Signalling theory	Survey and experiment on under graduate business students	Environment, community relations and diversity dimensions of CSP have a largest influence on organizational attractiveness than other CSP facets

	Focus*	Theory	Method	Findings
Peterson (2004)	Internal	Social identity theory	Survey of business professionals	Perceptions of corporate citizenship is positively related to organizational commitment and the link is stronger among employees who believe in the importance of CSR
Smith et al. (2004)	External	Fit individual/organizational values	Graduate and undergraduate students	Affirmative action programs are perceived more favourably than diversity management programmes and have a stronger influence on organizational attractiveness for prospective students
Ng and Burke (2005)	External	Fit individual/organizational values	MBA students	Diversity management programmes influence positively job choice decisions from women and ethnic minorities
Aguilera et al. (2006)	Internal	Organizational Justice theory/Social exchange theory	Survey of employees	Strong support for the influence of CSR on social exchange and subsequently on job performance and organizational commitment
Carmeli et al. (2007)	Internal	Organizational identification	Survey of employees and supervisors	Positive influence of perceptions of external social performance on identification, then adjustment and then job performance
Brammer et al. (2007)	Internal	Social identity theory	Survey of employees	Positive influence of external forms of CSR on employees' commitment subject to important gender variations

Note: * An 'external' focus means that the study assesses the influence of CSR on prospective employees building on external mechanisms (e.g. reputation); an 'internal' focus means that the study is focused on CSR influence on actual employees relaying on internal mechanisms (e.g. identification).

Unit further indicates the positive impact of corporate responsibility policy on potential and existing employees for 37.5 per cent of the 1,122 respondents.[36] These studies confirm the business appropriateness of communicating CSR actions to prospective employees such as graduates, a practice already undertaken by corporations such as the consultancy Accenture, or the UK-based semiconductor corporation ARM Holding plc.[37] Other empirical studies established that diversity programmes can influence the employment choices of women and/or people from ethnic minorities.[38] Moreover, it has been demonstrated that the adoption of 'family friendly' practices by corporations could be perceived as a signal of good management by investors and has a positive influence on the market appreciation of corporate stocks.[39] Therefore, this body of research confirms the managerial insight that CSR can play a key role in employee selection by attracting the most skilled workers.

This previous research has mainly investigated external levers of CSR influence on employees' behaviours. However, CSR reports largely cover issues related to internal management, principally companies' policies and actions with respect to employees' training, considering that those policies create a feeling of belonging to the organization and impact the level of employees' involvement and loyalty to the organization.[40] Furthermore, a 2007 pilot study from the Society for Human Resource Management suggests that managers perceive CSR as having a positive impact on employee loyalty and employee recruitment.[41] The 431 HR professionals surveyed in the United States believed that CSR practices can really improve employees' morale (3.32 on average on a scale from 1 (no degree at all) to 4 (to a large degree)), employee loyalty (3.26 on average), position as an employer of choice (3.15 on average) and recruitment of top employees (2.95 on average). In recent years, an emerging stream of research started investigating the influence of CSR on incumbent employees (see Table 1.1). These empirical studies have focused on the analysis of the influence of CSR policies on employee (or organizational) commitment and they provide strong empirical support for that relationship.[42] However, if we except Aguilera *et al.*'s (2006) study that also assessed CSR influence on job performance, none of these works has explored CSR influence on other employees' attitudes and behaviours in the workplace.[43] Furthermore, most of these studies rely primarily on social identification as a mechanism explaining CSR influence on employees.[44] However recent research suggests that CSR may influence employees through other mechanisms than identification (e.g. social exchange) and CSR may influence other employee attitudes, needs and behaviours besides commitment.[45] For instance, CSR can directly influence employees' adoption of socially responsible behaviours within the corporation.

Moreover, conceptual research investigating socially responsible behaviours at the corporate level and at the employee level has followed parallel paths.[46] Consequently, 'Employee Citizenship' and 'Organizational Citizenship' as concepts and streams of research did not cross-fertilize and, to date, no integrative model has been provided to explain how these two perspectives could be linked to each other. The purpose of the following section is to fill that gap by providing such a model in order to move forward the research agenda on CSR influence on employees' behaviours.

A CSR–CFP behavioural model for employees

The aim of the integrative model is to shed light on why, how and when employees respond to CSR actions. First, why do employees care about CSR initiatives developed by their company? By understanding employees' motives, the company can improve its communication strategy and enhance employees' awareness about CSR actions. Second, how and when does perceived CSR affect employees' attitudes and behaviours? Recent research has shown that stakeholders' reactions to CSR initiatives are not straightforward, nor are they homogeneous.[47] In order to understand employees' reactions to CSR initiatives, we develop an integrative framework drawing on social identity theory and social exchange theory.

Identification with socially responsible companies: respect and pride

Organizational identification can be defined as the degree to which organizational members perceive themselves and the organization as sharing the same defining attributes.[48] Thus, people tend to identify with organizations when they perceive an overlap between salient organizational attributes and individual attributes. According to social identity theory,[49] people are more likely to identify with an organization under the following conditions: when they perceive that (a) this organization is highly prestigious and has an attractive image; and (b) the organizational identity can enhance their self-esteem as members. In order to develop and maintain a favourable sense of self-worth and self-esteem, people seek to join and stay with high-status organizations. Moreover, when people identify with an organization, they also look for a status within it; so their sense of identity is determined by the treatment they receive from the organization and its agents. 'Two judgements are important: the judgement that one belongs to a high-status organization (pride) and the judgement that one has high status within that organization (respect).'[50]

Social identity theory provides a sound theoretical background to understanding why employees care about CSR initiatives developed by the company to which they belong. First, an organization's character as revealed by its CSR activities is 'not only fundamental and relatively enduring but also often more distinctive' than other facets of corporate activities.[51] Therefore, employees are likely to identify with socially responsible companies, especially when values enacted by these companies match employees' self-identity. Second, socially responsible firms are likely to gain a positive reputation in the public eye. Employees feel proud to belong and work for a company that is acknowledged for its positive contribution to society.[52] Employees would rather be known to be working for a good citizen that contributes to the welfare of society than for a poor citizen that cares only for its own interest. The results of a survey administered to 781 employees in six European companies (Zurich, BT, Centrica, KPMG, the Littlewoods Organization and PricewaterhouseCoopers) show that seven in ten staff say that the company's ethical stance affects their pride a great deal.[53] Third, good human resource practices generally make a great contribution to embedding CSR values and initiatives. By reflecting the respect that employees derive from their organization, HR practices can be a strong driver of organizational identification. For example, in its Sustainable Development Report (2003), Casino, a French retailer, highlights this vision, asserting that 'in line with its values of mutual respect and dialogue, Casino is committed to providing employees with high-quality jobs and is taking every possible measure to ensure long-term employment'. Moreover, by being active in CSR, companies can improve the employment relationship and enhance employees' commitment and organization-relevant citizenship behaviours. Employees who feel greater pride in their company and receive greater respect from it are more likely to engage in citizenship behaviours.[54]

Social exchange and CSR: norms of reciprocity

Besides organizational identification, employees' reactions to CSR initiatives may be governed by the norm of reciprocity, defined broadly as a pattern of mutually contingent exchange of gratifications.[55] This norm is the basis of social exchange relationships. 'By discharging their obligations for services, individuals demonstrate their trustworthiness and the gradual expansion of mutual service is accompanied by a parallel growth of mutual trust.'[56] Drawing on social exchange theory, we postulate that employees' reactions to CSR actions depend on their cognitive evaluation of the favourability of the exchange of effort and resources between them and the company. The sense of obligation, as a moral norm, assumes that employees should help those who have helped them. Thus, employees tend, under certain circumstances, to reciprocate the positive treatment they receive from the organization. In fact, the obligation of repayment depends on the value imputed by employees to CSR actions, the motives and resources of the organization. For example, research has shown that employees perform pro-social behaviours when 'organizational practices that engender favourable justice perceptions incur a sense of obligation to recompense the organization in a manner befitting a social exchange relationship'.[57] Many empirical studies have also demonstrated that employees tend to steal company property when they feel underpaid in order to reciprocate the unfair behaviour of the company.[58]

Overview of the model

Our model articulates three building blocks to account for the mediating role of employees' attitudes and behaviours between CSR initiatives as perceived by employees and CSR outcomes in terms of HR and financial performance, as shown in Figure 1.1. The input block of the model describes the ways through which social initiatives can influence and frame employees' perceptions of CSR. Then, according to social identification mechanism, the model shows how these perceptions can affect employees' attitude at work and the social exchange

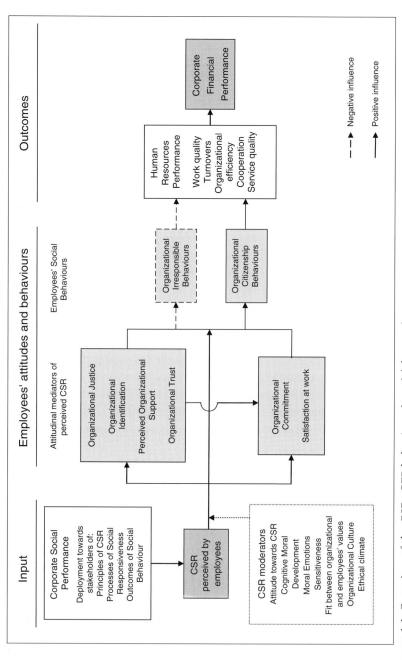

Figure 1.1 Overview of the CSR–CFP behavioural model for employees

mechanism explains how these attitudes can affect employees' behaviours. Finally, the model traces how these behaviours generate outcomes in term of human and, ultimately, financial performance.

Input: CSR as perceived by employees

The deployment of CSR initiatives

Previous research suggests that the CSR of a given firm can be captured through two complementary perspectives: the Corporate Social Performance (CSP) model and the Stakeholder concept. The former addresses the question of the nature of CSR, while the latter clarifies the groups towards whom these behaviours are deployed.

The CSP model suggests that social responsibility is deployed across multiple levels of the business organization through *principles* guiding organizational behaviours, *processes* aimed at identifying and managing social and environmental issues and the *outcomes* of these processes, taking the form of policies, programmes and impacts of organizational behaviours on its environment.[59] That model is useful to capture the 'what' of CSR, i.e. its meaning and its practices in organizations, moreover it has been usefully used to analyse the links between CSR and human resource management. In a given corporation, CSR can be captured at the three levels of the CSP model: *principles* that could be formalized in documents such as codes of conduct, or expressed by managers when interviewed; *processes* of stakeholder management, such as an ISO 14 001 management system; and *outcomes* such as the effective reduction of pollution or a community involvement programme.

The stakeholder concept addresses the question of 'to whom is the corporation responsible?'. Freeman provides an answer by considering that the responsibility of the corporation has to be assumed towards 'groups or individuals that could affect or be affected by the pursuit of corporate objectives'. These groups could be employees, managers or suppliers, but also the neighbours of a plant or NGOs. According to that perspective, CSR reflects the capacity to manage stakeholders in order to obtain their adhesion to corporate objectives.[60]

Ideally, an exhaustive portrait of the social responsibility of a given corporation can be described through a matrix crossing the three levels of principles, processes and outcomes with the whole range of corporate stakeholders. Practically, the three levels can be used as a managerial heuristic to classify the various facets of CSR and these dimensions can be assessed for the main stakeholders of the corporations, such as customers, employees, shareholders, the natural environment and the community.

Employees' perceptions of CSR

As a stakeholder group, employees are likely to perceive CSR principles, processes and outcomes, evaluate and judge these three dimensions and react according to these prior judgements and evaluations. Employees may react positively or negatively to corporate actions in the CSR domain, due to their specific psychological needs, or due to the alignment or misalignment of those actions with their own values and beliefs. However, we can not assume that employees will systematically evaluate and react to all the facets of the actual CSR actions of their corporation: why should we expect employees from the company headquarters to be influenced by CSR programmes conducted in offshore subsidiaries if there is no internal communication about these programmes? It appears obvious that employees will only evaluate and react to what they perceive of their corporations' socially responsible or irresponsible behaviours. Therefore, the first step of our model captures the influence of the multiple dimensions of corporate social performance on employees' perceptions of CSR.

One of the important questions, as far as stakeholder management is concerned, is the problem of stakeholders' representation. Companies such as Lafarge or Total France used to set up stakeholder panels in order to gather information about their stakeholders' needs and satisfaction. As far as employees are concerned, labour unions could be seen as the natural representatives. However, the place and role of unions are different according to the institutional and cultural context; it may be difficult to generally consider unions as 'the employees' voice' or 'the eye of employees' for CSR issues. Thus, we choose not to integrate unions in the analysis, assuming that their role has to be considered when the model will be tested in a specific context.

In our model, we assume that *only CSR as perceived by employees is likely to influence employees' attitudes and behaviours.* Such perceived CSR can differ from the actual level of CSR or CSP as assessed by corporate management or external organizations and can also vary across employees and across categories of employees. According to the concepts of CSR we presented, we can expect that these perceptions will be structured either around the different corporate stakeholders and/or the three channels of principles, processes and outcomes. We can also expect that employees will react more favourably to a proactive CSR programme designed for them as a stakeholder rather than to actions oriented towards other stakeholder groups. Previous research has already developed tools to assess socially responsible orientations of managers and/or consumers that can be adapted to assess employee perceptions.[61] However, further research is needed to design a CSR scale appropriate for the employment context.

Social identification: how perceived CSR affects employee attitudes

Building on previous research on social identity theory in organizational behaviour, it can be expected that perceived CSR will influence five central employee attitudes: organizational justice; perceived organizational support; organizational trust; organizational commitment; and job satisfaction.

Organizational justice

According to social exchange theory, 'fairness is a social norm that prescribes just treatment as a moral principle'.[62] Thus, justice could be an end in itself in the sense that people think it is the 'right way to treat human beings' and are upset when they realize that their company is accountable for the violation of justice principles. CSR initiatives can influence employees' perceptions of justice in two ways. First, CSR can impact perceived fairness directly. A company dedicated to displaying CSR actions is much more able to create a friendly and fair climate in the organization and to induce perceptions of fair treatment among employees (especially if CSR initiatives include employee-related issues such as improving working conditions, establishing fair wages and non-discrimination policies). In France, an institutional label, 'Egalitée', is given to companies such as PSA Peugeot

Citroën that have initiated specific policies for promoting fair career practices and breaking glass-ceiling barriers to the advancement of women. Likewise, in the Danone approach to CSR ('Danone Way'), one of the main levers is to 'refuse all forms of discrimination based on race, gender, religion, nationality and age and encourage diversity whilst ensuring equal opportunities in terms of access to jobs, remuneration, and promotion to positions of responsibility'. Second, CSR actions can have an indirect effect on perceived fairness. As a socially contagious process, perceptions of organizational justice can disseminate inside and outside the company. Recent research has shown that employees can, as third parties, form justice judgements and react to the way other people are treated by the company.[63] For example, there is evidence that in lay-off situations, survivors' reactions can be stronger than the victims' response as they can withhold productivity, or engage in sabotage.[64] In this regard, many companies have developed employment alternatives in downsizing situations. Since 2001, Danone constituted Employment and Mobility Teams, committed to helping to find alternative roles for employees affected by a multi-year restructuring process in its biscuits line. By the end of 2004, 94 per cent of those who had lost their jobs had found alternatives.

Perceived organizational support

Perceived organizational support is defined as global beliefs developed by employees about the extent to which the company appreciates their contributions and cares about their well-being.[65] CSR initiatives tend generally to signal a company's efforts to improve employees' welfare, as a relevant stakeholder group and develop positive relationships with them; the way these efforts are experienced by employees determines the perceived organizational support. Thus, employees can use CSR actions as criteria to assess the extent to which their company values them and cares about their well-being, even outside work. For example, among its People Development Principles, Nestlé asserts its willingness to support employees by encouraging flexible working conditions and inciting its employees to have interests outside work. Another CSR programme, named 'Competence sponsorship', is developed in France by Admical; this programme has been adopted by companies such as France Télécom and Sodexho in order to support their employees engaged in humanitarian relief.

Organizational trust

As social exchange relationships require trusting others to reciprocate, the primary problem is to prove oneself as trustworthy.[66] By
initiating CSR actions, a company shows its commitment to 'do
the right thing' and to respect the human dignity of its employees.
Therefore, CSR initiatives can be perceived as sincere care and concern for employees. This is expected to lead to greater trust in the
company and its top management. For example, the Danone business
model asserts that the critical value is mutual trust with stakeholders. Companies such as Total and Accor have developed opinion polls
among their employees in order to understand their expectations and
to improve organizational practices accordingly; the principal purpose of these practices is to improve mutual trust with employees.

Organizational commitment

'Corporate ethical values may be a strong predictor of commitment',[67]
as companies that possess strong values and cultures may enjoy a different bond with their employees than organizations using market-
based approaches to binding employees. Organizational commitment
is defined as the relative strength of an employee's identification with
the company, hence increasing the desire to maintain membership. By
means of managerial surveys, research has shown that 'the more proactive the corporate citizenship, the greater the employee commitment
to the organization'.[68] CSR initiatives are likely to generate stronger
bonds between the organization and its employees and induce increased
employee commitment. Drawing upon social identity theory, employees'
reactions to CSR are contingent on the amount of congruence or overlap they perceive between the company's character (its CSR activities)
and their own values. Moreover, recent empirical research has found a
positive relationship between external CSR and organizational commitment.[69] Thus, it seems that employees' involvement in the company can
also be indirectly influenced by external stakeholder management.

Job satisfaction

Employee-related CSR actions focus on the improvement of HR
practices by providing better rewards and incentive schemes, by

developing career opportunities for all employees, by increasing training and competence development and by improving communication
and feedback systems. Managerial academic literature has shown
that employee satisfaction is generally linked to rewards (e.g. pay,
promotion and recognition), job attributes (e.g. autonomy, feedback
and responsibility), relationship with the supervisor (e.g. support and
respect) and organizational characteristics (e.g. working conditions,
policies and procedures).[70]

Moreover, CSR initiatives can be perceived by employees as a means
by which the company top management supports ethical behaviour.
Employees should experience higher job satisfaction if they are aware
that the legitimate authority of the company respects ethical values
because this can reduce cognitive dissonance and stress resulting from
a conflict between their ethical values and orders of top management.[71] In addition, research has shown that the ethical climate in the
organization can influence the level of job satisfaction. 'Employees,
who find themselves in an organization that promotes the company's
interest at the expense of other considerations including employees'
interests and ethical values, will feel that fundamental values and
their personal rights have been violated. This is expected to lead to a
lower level of job satisfaction.'[72]

Social exchange: how employees' attitudes affect their social behaviours

Organizational citizenship behaviours

Consistent with norms of reciprocity, CSR practices that create perceptions of fairness, support, trust and commitment incur a sense
of obligation among employees to reciprocate and recompense the
company by displaying organizational citizenship behaviours (OCB).
OCB are discretionary behaviours that are not specified by role prescription and not explicitly rewarded, but which facilitate the accom-
plishment of organizational goals.[73] Such behaviours include acts
such as having active involvement in organizational affairs, helping
co-workers with a job-related problem, accepting orders and organizational rules without fuss, or tolerating temporary unsatisfying
work conditions without complaining. When a company shows its
dedication to act as a responsible citizen, employees may commit

themselves to act as exemplary organizational members. There exists an implicit agreement of reciprocity between the company and its workers: employees exhibit citizenship because of the development of covenants with organizations based on mutual trust and shared values. Employees for whom an organization guarantees greater socio-economic benefits are most likely to return the favour and to engage in behaviours that protect the organization and serves its various goals such as OCB.[74] Moreover, the social exchange perspective suggests that perceptions of job and pay equity (which are likely to exist in good citizen companies) are positively related to extra-role behaviours. High levels of perceived organizational support, engendered by CSR initiatives, create obligations within employees to repay the company. For instance, employees of the New Belgium Brewery agreed unanimously to sacrifice their bonuses in order to permit to the company to invest in a sustainable energy source necessary for its manufacturing operations.[75]

Organizational irresponsible behaviours

According to social exchange theory, employees can have a tendency to punish a company if they attribute responsibility for wrongdoing to this organization. When they perceive unfairness, employees make assessments concerning attributions of responsibility. If they believe that their company violated social norms of 'doing good', then they feel exploited. Therefore, they may have the desire to retaliate and to punish the company by engaging in irresponsible and antisocial behaviours that harm the allegedly irresponsible company. These behaviours can be defined as acts that are volitional and have the intention to harm the organization and/or its agents or to break its rules. By contrast with OCB, research has found that the promotion and the development of ethical climates, perceived as fair and supportive for employees, reduce levels of engagement in irresponsible misbehaviours at work.[76] From the perspective of organizational justice, if CSR principles assert that a company has a moral responsibility vis-à-vis the welfare of its stakeholders such as employees, then a company responsible for mistreatment of its employees becomes potentially subject to reciprocation, revenge and negative social sanctions.[77]

Moreover, this perspective can clarify why and how irresponsible behaviours evolve and spread in organizations. Besides socialization and identification processes, the vicious dynamics of reciprocity norms can have spillover effects in terms of the expansion of an unethical climate and the normalization of irresponsible behaviours. For instance, an empirical study has demonstrated that members of a corrupt organization have a tendency to induce newcomers to engage in small acts of corruption that are relatively harmless but are at the same time overt and binding.[78]

Outcomes: impact on HR and financial performance

Impact of behaviours on HR performance

Both citizenship and irresponsible employee behaviours are likely to affect human resource performance. The influence of organizational citizenship behaviours on numerous dimensions of human resource performance is well established in previous research.[79] Indeed, it has been demonstrated that these behaviours can influence positively the quality of work, diminish employee turnover, improve organizational efficiency and the quality of the service delivered to customers, and increase cooperation between employees. Finally, this previous research also showed that employees adopting these behaviours are more likely to be perceived as performing better. In contrast, the adoption of irresponsible behaviours by employees is likely to negatively affect organizational efficiency and HR performance.

A direct consequence of these outcomes is that CSR, through the processes of social exchange and identification, can increase employee productivity and ensure employee retention. Therefore, our model provides a strong theoretical case for the managerial claim that CSR contributes to employee retention.[80]

Impact on corporate financial performance

The positive outcomes in terms of human resources performance due to the diffusion of employees' pro-social behaviours – and the corollary prevention of antisocial behaviours – will ultimately influence the bottom line. That link is more likely to appear in intensive knowledge industries where talents are rare and in sectors where employees' commitment to organizational goals is a necessary condition for success. Such an impact on financial performance is congruent with previous empirical research that has already established that a bundle of proactive HRM practices can contribute indirectly to the bottom line, and demonstrates that HR performance can influence consumer behaviours and consequently corporate performance in the marketplace.[81]

Moderators of CSR influence on employees

The extent to which perceived CSR will affect employees' attitude and behaviours will depend on many individual and organizational factors. At the individual level, personal characteristics such as global attitude towards CSR, emotional sensitiveness or cognitive moral development can affect the likelihood of a positive impact of perceived CSR on their work attitudes and behaviours. Employees already supporting the idea of CSR are more likely to attribute corporate engagement in CSR to 'favourable' motivations (e.g. genuine interest in the cause) and hence to get identified through the attitudinal processes we highlighted.[82] Previous research has also suggested that emotional sensitiveness and cognitive moral development can influence individual tendency to undertake socially responsible behaviours in organizations.[83] Organizational features such as the ethical climate or the organizational culture can also influence the effect of CSR initiatives on employees, as demonstrated by Maignan and colleagues in a prior empirical study.[84] Finally, the fit between individual and organizational value is also likely to determine the influence of perceived CSR on employees' attitudes and behaviours.

Dynamics of exchanges: virtuous versus vicious circle

The model presented in Figure 1.1 appears simplistic and bi-directional: CSR influences employees' perceptions which in turn influences employees' attitudes; then these attitudes impact employees' behaviours towards their organization, generating positive or negative outcomes for the corporation. Social exchange theory invites us to move forward and to integrate into the framework the consequences of organizational citizenship or irresponsible behaviours in the long run. It could indeed be expected that employees' responsible or irresponsible behaviours will influence others employees' perception and evaluation of CSR, reinforcing their positive and/or negative attitudes. As a consequence a norm of positive versus negative social exchange

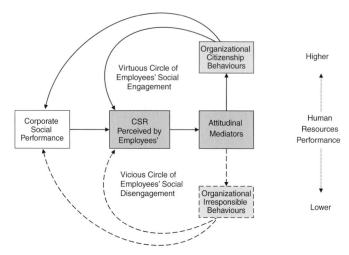

Figure 1.2 CSR influence on the dynamics of corporations–employees social exchanges

could be progressively distilled inside the organization, generating a dynamics of interaction between employers and employees. Figure 1.2 presents two possible opposing lifecycles for employee–corporation interactions: the vicious circle of employees' social disengagement and the virtuous circle of employees' social engagement.

The vicious circle

The bottom of Figure 1.2 describes the vicious circle of employee disengagement, corresponding to a low norm of reciprocity or the development of negative social exchanges between employees and their corporations. According to this process, the diffusion of socially irresponsible behaviours inside the organization will reinforce negative perceptions of CSR by employees. In an organization where employees frequently observe irresponsible behaviours, CSR will be at best interpreted through a cynical lens as window dressing. Attempts to reconstruct CSR reputation inside the corporation can be hampered by employees' negative attributions motivated by their observation of the behaviour of others.[85] An organization mismanaging the congruency of its CSR strategy, by favouring some stakeholders very strongly and managing others irresponsibly, could experience such cynical attribution of its CSR actions. In such organizations, deviant behaviours from both employees and the corporations can become a norm: the collapse of Enron and Andersen provided an illustration of the potential institutionalization and maintenance of irresponsible behaviours inside and between organizations.

The virtuous circle

An opposing mechanism can also take place, as suggested by the top part of Figure 1.2. Here, the logic of corporate and employees' extra-role exchange around socially responsible actions is functioning as a real amplifier, following the logic of reciprocal gift and counter-gift. Employees' perception of CSR will be reinforced by the observation of their peers' behaviour, reinforcing the credibility of corporate engagement and the congruency of CSR actions. Such a virtuous circle is particularly likely to develop if CSR programmes are congruently managed in order to balance the benefits of the different stakeholders.

In this second case, the equilibrium of social exchange between corporation and employees will be high and get reinforced across time. A higher level of human resources performance, and ultimately of corporate financial performance, can be expected from such a positive spiral of employee engagement. Numerous corporations have demonstrated that such a virtuous circle can be constructed. For instance, Lafarge, the cement and aggregate giant, developed a huge Human Resource Management programme to fight efficiently the diffusion of HIV in its African subsidiaries. That programme included a partnership with Care France, an NGO part of Care International and contributed to positively affect employee morale and ultimately their turnover and their commitment.[86]

Managerial implications of the model

The objective of this chapter was to propose a model explaining how employees' perceptions about the socially responsible posture of their company can affect corporate financial performance by influencing employees' attitudes and behaviours inside the company. Our model suggests that CSR influences not only prospective employees but also current employees. CSR programmes and policies may help organizations to market themselves towards their 'internal customers' – employees. Moreover, by mapping the various attitudinal and behavioural channels through which CSR actions can influence employees, our model delivers precious insights for the design of strategic CSR.

CSR as an internal marketing tool

If the proposed relationships between CSR and employees' attitudes and behaviours can be supported empirically, then CSR could be considered as a way to promote the organization to its members, in order to stimulate the adoption of citizenship behaviours (OCB) through the mechanism described earlier. In addition, CSR programmes could lead to increased organizational effectiveness, performance and success. CSR may further reduce voluntary turnover rate among employees because of the group attractiveness and cohesiveness. These benefits are far from being insignificant in the present context of intensive competition and they illustrate the value of communicating CSR goals to employees and other stakeholders (customers, media and government) at the same time.

Including employees in the design of the CSR strategy

The model suggests that organizations should canvass employees' opinions on different issues related to CSR and to involve them as a central stakeholder in the design of CSR strategy. As reported in the case studies conducted in Accenture or British Telecom, the capacity to link people management and CSR is essential in order to 'make CSR happen'.[87] Employee support can be obtained through the involvement of the human resource management function in the design of the CSR strategy. Such a perspective invites firms to investigate CSR issues that are of interest for employees. Those issues could be related to employees themselves (working conditions, level of wages etc.) but not only this: our model suggests that corporate social initiatives targeting other stakeholders can also have a positive impact on employees' attitudes and behaviours (e.g. impact of the company on the natural environment, company's behaviour with respect to child labour in developing countries).

However, more data collection inside companies is needed to assess employees' interests in terms of CSR, as well as the way they want companies to act with respect to those issues. Further research will have to investigate employees' perceptions of their organization's CSR. Those future studies will help business to design constructive social involvement programmes and internal communication channels taking into account CSR issues of interest to employees.

Strategic implications for CSR

As a whole, our model suggests considering investment in employees through CSR as a key strategic resource in the construction of CFP. Such a perspective invites firms to see CSR as an investment that could contribute to develop human resources and ultimately CFP rather than a cost. A carefully designed CSR strategy can help to activate the virtuous circles of corporate and employee social engagement and to reap the associated benefits in term of human resource performance, while preventing the development of irresponsible behaviours from employees.

The design of strategic CSR remains a difficult exercise, due to the multiplicity of contradictory claims from corporate stakeholders. Our approach, by clarifying the mechanisms underlying the influence of CSR on CFP through employees' attitudes and behaviours, provides a crucial complement to models solely focused on customers in order to balance those claims and to design the CSR strategy appropriately. A next step will be to integrate these models in order to provide managers with ways to develop fully the strategic potential of CSR for their business.

Conclusion

Past research has shown that CSR can play an important role in external communication for attracting highly skilled prospective employees but has little to say about the influence of CSR on existing employees. Building on social identification and social exchange theory, this chapter offers a new model mapping the various mechanisms whereby CSR influences employee behaviours, attitudes and performance in the workplace.

This research suggests that CSR influences employees not only by increasing their identification with the corporation but also by altering the dynamics of social exchange that takes place within the corporation. In particular, our model shows how CSR can stimulate organizational citizenship behaviours and prevent irresponsible behaviours. The model also makes explicit the various outcomes that could be expected from a CSR policy effectively communicated to employees, such as increased productivity, decreased staff turnover (retention), improved service quality and/or improved organizational effectiveness.

In so doing we develop the business case for CSR from the employee perspective and highlight the conditions under which a virtuous circle of mutually rewarding behaviours from corporation and employees can be triggered.

Notes

1 See 'Corporate Social Responsibility, Just Good Business', *The Economist*, 17 January 2008, p. 3.

2 See 'Shaping the New Rules of Competition: UN Global Compact Participant Mirror', McKinsey & Company report, July 2007, www. mckinsey.com/clientservice/ccsi/pdf/Shaping_the_new_rules.pdf.

3 Interview of Michael Porter, 'CSR: A Religion with too many Priests?', *European Business Forum*, www.ebf.online, interview realized by Mette Morsing at the Copenhagen Business School, 2003.

4 See N. Craig Smith, 'Corporate Social Responsibility: Whether or How?', *California Management Review*, 45/4 (summer 2003): 52–76. For an historical investigation of the emergence of corporate philanthropy and corporate social responsibility in US, see Morrell Heald, *The Social Responsibilities of Business. Company and the Community, 1900–1960* (Cleveland, OH: The Press of Case Western Reserve University, 1970).

5 Acknowledgements of the pioneer role of Bowen can be found in Archie B. Carroll, 'A Three-Dimensional Conceptual Model of Corporate Performance', *Academy of Management Review*, 4/4 (1979): 497–505; or Donna Wood, 'Corporate Social Performance Revisited', *Academy of Management Review*, 16/4 (1991): 691–718. For an evaluation of classical economics argument against the social responsibility doctrine, see Chapter 10, entitled 'The Doctrine of Social Responsibility: Some Criticisms', in Howard Bowen, *Social Responsibilities of the Businessman* (New York: Harper and Brothers, 1953), pp. 107–26. Bowen reviewed and criticized arguments against social responsibility such as the increased costs related to investments in social responsibility, the competition biases that could be introduced through these corporate behaviours or the

instrumental use of the social responsibility doctrine by businessmen to increase their power.

6 See the famous controversies generated by the publications of Theodor Levitt, 'The Dangers of Social Responsibility', *Harvard Business Review* (September–October, 1958): 41–50; and Milton Friedman, 'The Responsibility of Business is to Increase its Profits', *New York Times Magazine*, 33 (1970): 122–6.

7 For critical and broad reviews of the CSR-CFP literature, see Jennifer J. Griffin and John F. Mahon, 'The Corporate Social Performance and Corporate Financial Performance Debate. Twenty-five Years of Incomparable Research', *Business and Society*, 36/1 (1997): 5–31; Joshua D. Margolis and James P. Walsh, *People and Profits? The Search for a Link between a Company's Social and Financial Performance* (Mahwah, NJ: Erlbaum, 2001); Joshua D. Margolis and James P. Walsh, 'Misery Loves Companies: Whither Social Initiatives by Business?', *Administrative Science Quarterly*, 48 (2003): 268–305.

8 Timothy Rowley and Shawn Berman, 'A Brand New Brand of Corporate Social Performance', *Business and Society*, 39/4 (2000): 397–418. See also Margolis and Walsh (2001).

9 David Vogel, 'Is there a Market for Virtue? The Potential and Limits of CSR', paper presented at Third Annual ICCSR Research Symposium, Nottingham University Business School on Business and Government, 16 September 2005.

10 For example, Donna J. Wood and Raymond E. Jones, 'Stakeholder Mismatching: A Theoretical Problem in Empirical Research in Corporate Social Performance', *International Journal of Organizational Analysis*, 3/3 (1995): 229–67; David Vogel, *The Market for Virtue. The Potential and Limits of Corporate Social Responsibility* (Washington, DC: Brookings Institution Press, 2005). C.B. Bhattacharya and Sankar Sen, 'Doing Better at Doing Good: When, Why and How Consumers Respond to Corporate Social Initiatives', *California Management Review*, 47/1 (fall 2004): 9–24.

11 Smith (2003).

12 Bhattacharya and Sen (2004); Michael J. Barone, Anthony D. Miyazaki and Kimberly A. Taylor, 'The Influence of Cause-Related Marketing on Consumer Choice: Does One Good Turn Deserve Another', *Journal of the Academy of Marketing Science*, 28/2 (spring 2000): 248–62; Tom J. Brown and Peter A. Dacin, 'The Company and the Product: Corporate Associations and Consumer Product Responses', *Journal of Marketing*, 61 (January 1997): 68–84.

13 Such a perspective is consistent with the perspectives on employees provided by Deborah E. Rupp, Jyoti Ganapathi, Ruth V. Aguilera and Cynthia A.

Williams, 'Employees' Reactions to Corporate Social Responsibility: An Organizational Justice Framework', *Journal of Organizational Behaviour*, 27 (2006): 537–43; Wood and Jones (1995); and Harry J. Van Burren III, 'An Employee Centred Model of Corporate Social Performance', *Business Ethics Quarterly*, 15/4 (2005): 687–709.

14 For the former theory, see Blake Ashforth and Fred Mael, 'Social Identity Theory and the Organization', *Academy of Management Review*, 14/1 (1989): 20–40; and H. Tajfel and J.-C. Turner, 'The Social Identity Theory of Intergroup Behaviour', in S. Worchel and W.G. Austin (eds.), *Psychology of Intergroup Relations* (Chicago: Nelson Hall, 1985), pp. 7–24. For the latter theory, see Peter Blau, *Exchange and Power in Social Life* (New York: Wiley, 1964); and Russell Cropanzano and Marie S. Mitchell, 'Social Exchange Theory: An Interdisciplinary Review', *Journal of Management*, 31/6 (2005): 874–900, for the latter theoretical framework.

15 José Allouche and Patrick Laroche, 'A Meta-analytical Examination of the Link between Corporate Social and Financial Performance', *Revue Française de Gestion des Ressources Humaines*, 57 (2005): 18–41. See also Marc Orlitzky, Franck L. Schmidt and Sarah L. Rynes, 'Corporate Social and Financial Performance: A Meta-analysis', *Organization Studies*, 24/3 (2003): 103–441.

16 See Abagail McWilliams and Donald Siegel, 'Corporate Social Responsibility and Financial Performance: Correlation or Misspecification?', *Strategic Management Journal*, 21/5 (2000): 603–9, about the previous study of Sandra A. Waddock and Samuel B. Graves, 'The Corporate Social Performance-Financial Performance Link', *Strategic Management Journal*, 18/4 (1997): 303–19.

17 Margolis and Walsh (2001 and 2003) and Vogel (2005).

18 Rowley and Berman (2000).

19 Contrast *The Economist* (2008), with *The Economist*, 'The Good Company. Survey on CSR', 20 January 2005.

20 Vogel (2005).

21 David P. Baron, *Business and its Environment*, 5th edn (Upper Saddle River, NJ: Prentice Hall, 2005).

22 See Lee Burke and Jeanne M. Logsdon, 'How Corporate Social Responsibility Pays Off', *Long Range Planning*, 29/4 (1996): 495–502.

23 Abagail McWilliams, Donald S. Siegel and Patrick M. Wright, 'Corporate Social Responsibility: Strategic Implications', *Journal of Management Studies*, 43/1 (2006): 1–18; Brian W. Husted and José De Jesus, 'Taking Friedman Seriously: Maximizing Profits and Social Performance', *Journal of Management Studies*, 43/1 (2006): 75–91; Alfred A. Marcus and Marc H. Anderson, 'A General Dynamic Capability: Does it Propagate

Business and Social Competencies in the Retail Food Industry?', *Journal of Management Studies*, 43/1 (2006): 19–46.

24 Wood and Jones (1995).

25 Douglas A. Schuler and Margaret Cording, 'A Corporate Social Performance – Corporate Financial Performance Behavioral Model for Consumers', *Academy of Management Review*, 31/3 (July 2006): 540–58. See also Bhattacharya and Sen (2004).

26 See Pietra Rivoli, 'Making a Difference or Making a Statement? Finance Research and Socially Responsible Investment', *Business Ethics Quarterly*, 13/3 (2003): 271–87.

27 Quoted for the report *Corporate Social Responsibility: A Business Contribution to Sustainable Development*, Communication from the Commission, COM(2002)347 final of 02/07/02 (Brussels, July 2002), p. 19.

28 The results of this poll are reported in Patrick d'Humières and Alain Chauveau, *Les pionniers de l'entreprise responsable* (Paris: Edition d'Organisation, 2001), pp. 183–93.

29 See 'Shaping the New Rules of Competition: UN Global Compact Participant Mirror', McKinsey and Company report, July 2007, www.mckinsey.com/clientservice/ccsi/pdf/Shaping_the_new_rules.pdf.

30 See the report of the CSR Academy by Ian Redington, *Making CSR Happen: The Contribution to People Management*, edited by the Chartered Institute of Personnel and Development, 2005. Available online through the CSR Academy website: www.csracademy.org.uk.

31 Redington (2005), p. ix.

32 Philip Kotler and Nancy Lee, *Corporate Social Responsibility. Doing the most Good for your Company and your Cause* (New York: John Wiley and Sons, 2004). See especially Chapter 7, pp. 175–206.

33 References of the studies listed in the table are, respectively: Daniel B. Turban and Daniel W. Greening, 'Corporate Social Performance and Organizational Attractiveness to Prospective Employees', *Academy of Management Journal*, 40/3 (January 1997): 658–73; Isabelle Maignan, O.C. Ferrell and G.T.M. Hult, 'Corporate Citizenship: Cultural Antecedents and Business Benefits', *Journal of the Academy of Marketing Science*, 27 (1999): 455–9; Daniel W. Greening and Daniel B. Turban, 'Corporate Social Performance as a Competitive Advantage in Attracting a Quality Workforce', *Business and Society*, 39/3 (September 2000): 254–303; Heather S. Albinger and Sarah J. Freeman, 'Corporate Social Performance and Attractiveness as an Employer to Different Job Seeking Populations', *Journal of Business Ethics*, 28/3 (December 2000): 243–53; Isabelle Maignan and O.C. Ferrell, 'Antecedents and Benefits of Corporate Citizenship: An Investigation of French Businesses', *Journal of Business Research*, 51 (2001): 1–15; Kristin Backhaus,

Brett A. Stone and Karl Heiner, 'Exploring the Relationship Between Corporate Social Performance and Employer Attractiveness', *Business and Society*, 41/3 (September 2002): 292–318; Dane K. Peterson, 'The Relationship between Perceptions of Corporate Citizenship and Organizational Commitment', *Business and Society*, 43/3 (September 2004): 269–319; Wanda J. Smith, Richard B. Wokutch, Vernard K. Harrington and Bryan S. Dennis, 'Organizational Attractiveness and Corporate Social Orientation: Do Our Values Influence Our Preference for Affirmative Action or Managing Diversity?', *Business and Society*, 43/1 (March 2004): 69–96; Eddy S.W. Ng and Ronald J. Burke, 'Person-organization Fit and the War for Talent: Does Diversity Management make a Difference?', *International Journal of Human Resource Management*, 16/7 (July 2005): 1195–210; Ruth Aguilera, Deborah E. Rupp, Joyti Ganaphati and Cynthia A. Williams, 'Justice and Social Responsibility: A Social Exchange Model', paper presented at the Society for Industrial/Organizational Psychology Annual Meeting, Berlin, 2006; Abraham Carmeli, Gershon Gillat and David A. Waldman, 'The Role of Perceived Organizational Performance in Organizational Identification, Adjustment and Job Performance', *Journal of Management Studies*, 44/6 (September 2007): 972–92; Stephen Brammer, Andrew Millington and Bruce Rayton, 'The Contribution of Corporate Social Responsibility to Organizational Commitment', *International Journal of Human Resource Management*, 18/10 (2007): 1701–1719.

34 SustainAbility (2001), 'Buried Treasure: Uncovering the Business Case for Corporate Sustainability', pp. 26–7.

35 Result reported in David B. Montgmery and Catherine A. Ramus, 'Corporate Social Responsibility Reputation Effects on MBA Job Choice', *Working Paper 1805 Stanford Graduate School of Business*, 2003.

36 The 2007 Global Business Barometer, a survey conducted by the Economist Intelligence Unit on behalf of *The Economist*, conducted in November–December 2007, on 1,122 respondents in Europe, Asia and North America.

37 See Redington (2005), for detailed cases studies reporting these practices and their outcomes for the concerned organizations.

38 See Smith *et al.* (2004) and Ng and Burke (2005).

39 See Ray Jones and Audrey J. Murrel, 'Signaling Positive Corporate Social Performance. An Event Study of Family-Friendly Firms', *Business and Society*, 40/1 (March 2001): 59–79.

40 Jean-Yves Saulquin and Guillaume Schier, 'Le développement durable et la notion de performance organisationnelle : une application à la GRH', in Michel Dion, Dominique Wolff *et al.* (eds.), *Le développement durable: Théories et applications au management* (Paris: DUNOD, 2008).

41 Society for Human Resource Management Research (2007), *2007 Corporate Social Responsibility: United States, Australia, India, China, Canada, Mexico and Brazil, a Pilot Study*, www.hranb.org/pdf/ CorpSocRespSuvey2007.pdf.

42 See Aguilera *et al.* (2006); Brammer *et al.* (2007); Maignan and Ferrell (2001); Maignan *et al.* (1999) and Peterson (2004).

43 See Aguilera *et al.* (2006).

44 See, for example, Carmeli *et al.* (2007).

45 See, for example, Rupp *et al.* (2006) and Aguilera *et al.* (2006).

46 For a comparison of both fields of research, see Valérie Swaen and Isabelle Maignan, 'Organizational Citizenship and Corporate Citizenship: Two Constructs, One Research Theme?', in Sheb L. True, Pelton Lou and O.C. Ferrell (eds.), *Business Rites, Writs and Responsibilities: Readings on Ethics and Social Impact Management*, Michael J. Coles College of Business, USA, 1 (2003): 107–34. See also: D. Swanson and P. Niehoff, 'Business Citizenship Outside and Inside Organizations', in Jörg Andriof and Malcom McIntosh (eds.), *Perspective on Corporate Citizenship* (Sheffield, UK: Greenleaf Publishing, 2001).

47 Bhattacharya and Sen (2004).

48 Ashforth and Mael (1989).

49 Tajfel and Turner (1985); Ashforth and Mael (1989: 24); Michael G. Pratt, 'Social Identity Dynamics in Modern Organizations: An Organizational Psychology/Organizational Behavior Perspective', in Michael A Hogg and Deborah Terry (eds.), *Social Identity Processes in Organizational Contexts* (Philadelphia: Psychology Press, 2001), pp. 13–30.

50 Tom R. Tyler, 'Cooperation in Organizations', in Michael A Hogg and Deborah Terry (eds.), *Social Identity Processes in Organizational Contexts* (Philadelphia: Psychology Press, 2001), p. 159.

51 Bhattacharya and Sen (2004).

52 Turban and Greening (1997); Brown and Dacin (1997).

53 M. Tuffrey, *Good Companies, Better Employees, The Corporate Citizenship Company* (London: The Good Company, 2003), www. corporate-citizenship.co.uk.

54 Tom R. Tyler and Steven Blader, *Cooperation in Groups: Procedural Justice, Social Identity and Behavioural Engagement* (New York: Psychology Press, 2000).

55 Alvin W. Gouldner, 'The Norm of Reciprocity: A Preliminary Statement', *American Sociological Review*, 25 (1960): 161–78, p. 161.

56 Blau (1964: 94).

57 Kelly L. Zellars and Bennett J. Tepper, 'Beyond Social Exchange: New Directions for Organizational Citizenship Behavior Theory and Research',

in J. Martocchio (ed.), *Research in Personnel and Human Resource Management* (Greenwich, CT: JAI Press, 2003), pp. 395–424, at p. 397.

58 Jerald Greenberg, 'Employee Theft as a Reaction to Underpayment Inequity: The Hidden Cost of Pay Cuts', *Journal of Applied Psychology*, 75/5 (1990): 561–8. See also Jerald Greenberg, 'Who Stole the Money, and when? Individual and Situational Determinants of Employee Theft', *Organizational Behavior and Human Decision Processes*, 89 (2002): 985–1003.

59 Wood (1991).

60 Robert. E. Freeman, *Strategic Management: A Stakeholder Approach* (Boston: Pitman, 1984). For an approach of CSR consistent with that view see also Clarkson, 'A Stakeholder Framework for Analysing and Evaluating Corporate Social Performance', *Academy of Management Review*, 20/1 (1995): 92–117.

61 See Kenneth E. Aupperle, Archie B. Carroll and John D. Hatfield, 'An Empirical Examination of the Relationship between Corporate Social Responsibility and Profitability', *Academy of Management Journal*, 28/2 (1985): 446–63; Isabelle Maignan and O. C. Ferrell, 'Measuring Corporate Citizenship in Two Countries: The Case of United States and France', *Journal of Business Ethics*, 23 (1999): 283–97; Isabelle Maignan and O.C. Ferrell, 'Nature of Corporate Responsibilities: Perspectives from American, French and German Consumers', *Journal of Business Research*, 56 (2003): 55–67.

62 Blau (1964: 157).

63 Daniel P. Skarlicki and Carol T. Kulik, 'Third-party Reactions to Employee (Mis)Treatment: A Justice Perspective', *Research in Organizational Behavior*, 26 (2005): 185–231. See also Peter Degoey, 'Contagious Justice: Exploring the Social Construction of Justice Organizations', in Barry M. Staw and Robert I. Sutton (eds.), *Research in Organizational Behavior* (New York: JAI Press 2000), pp. 51–102.

64 Joel Brockner and Jerald Greenberg, 'The Impact of Layoffs on Survivors: An Organizational Justice Perspective', in J. Carroll (ed.), *Advances in Applied Social Psychology: Business Settings* (New York: Lawrence Erlbaum Associates, 1990), pp. 45–75.

65 Robert Eisenberger, Florence Stinglhamber, Christian Vandenberghe, Ivan Sucharski and Linda Rhoades, 'Perceived Supervisor Support: Contributions to Perceived Organizational Support and Employee Retention', *Journal of Applied Psychology*, 87 (2002): 365–73.

66 Blau (1964: 98).

67 Shelby D. Hunt, Van R. Wood and Lawrence B. Chonko, 'Corporate Ethical Values and Organizational Commitment in Marketing', *Journal of Marketing*, 53 (July 1989): 79–90, p. 85.

68 Maignan *et al.* (1999: 10); see also Peterson (2004).

69 Brammer *et al.* (2007).

70 Paul E. Spector, *Job Satisfaction: Application, Assessment, Cause, and Consequence* (Thousand Oaks, CA: Sage Publications, 1997).

71 Chockalingam Viswesvaran, Satish P. Deshpande and Jacob Joseph, 'Job Satisfaction as a Function of Top Management Support for Ethical Behavior. A Study of Indian Managers', *Journal of Business Ethics*, 17 (1998): 365–71.

72 Hian Chye Koh and El'fred H.Y. Boo, 'The Link between Organizational Ethics and Job Satisfaction: A Study of Managers in Singapore', *Journal of Business Ethics*, 29 (2001): 309–24, p. 313.

73 Thomas S. Bateman and Dennis. W. Organ, 'Job Satisfaction and the Good Soldier: The Relationship between Affect and Employee Citizenship', *Academy of Management Journal*, 26 (1983): 587–95.

74 John W. Graham, 'An Essay on Organizational Citizenship Behavior', *Employee Responsibilities and Rights Journal*, 4 (1991): 249–70.

75 Rupp *et al.* (2006).

76 Yoav Vardi, 'The Effects of Organisational and Ethical Climates on Misconduct at Work', *Journal of Business Ethics*, 29/4 (2001): 325–37. See also James C. Wimbush and Jon Shepard, 'Toward an Understanding of Ethical Climate: Its Relationship to Ethical Behavior and Supervisory Influence', *Journal of Business Ethics*, 13 (1994): 637–47.

77 Robert Folger, 'Fairness as Deonance', in Stephen Gilliland, Dirk Steiner and Daniel Skarlicki, *Theoretical and Cultural Perspectives on Organizational Justice* (Greenwich: IAP, 2001), pp. 3–33. See also Robert Folger, Russell Cropanzano and Barry Goldman, 'What is the Relationship between Justice and Morality', in Jerald Greenberg and Jason Colquitt (eds.), *Handbook of Organizational Justice* (Mahwah, NJ: Erlbaum, 2005), pp. 215–45.

78 Blake E. Ashforth and Vikas Anand, 'The Normalization of Corruption in Organizations', in Roderick M. Kramer and Barry M. Staw (eds.), *Research in Organizational Behavior*, 25 (2003): 1–52.

79 J.M. George and Kenneth Bettenhausen, 'Understanding Prosocial Behavior, Sales Performance, and Turnover: A Group-Level Analysis in a Service Context', *Journal of Applied Psychology*, 75/6 (1990): 698–709; P.M. Podsakoff, M. Ahearne and S.B. MacKenzie, 'Organizational Citizenship Behavior and the Quantity and Quality of Work Group Performance', *Journal of Applied Psychology*, 82/2 (1997): 262–70; P.M. Podsakoff and S.B. MacKenzie, 'Organizational Citizenship Behaviors and Sales Unit Effectiveness', *Journal of Marketing Research*, 31 (1994): 351–63; P.M. Podsakoff and S.B. MacKenzie, 'The Impact of Organizational Citizenship Behavior on Organizational Performance: A

Review and Suggestions for Future Research', *Human Performance*, 10 (1997): 133–51; Sarah M. Walz and Brian P. Niehoff, 'Organizational Citizenship Behaviors and Their Effects on Organizational Effectiveness in Limited-Menu Restaurants', in J.B. Keys and L.N. Dosier (eds.), *Academy of Management Best Papers Proceedings* (Statesboro, GA: George Southern University 1996), pp. 307–11.

80 See Tuffrey (2003).

81 See Brian Becker, Marc Huselid and Dave Ulrich, *The HR Scorecard – Linking People, Strategy and Performance* (Harvard: Harvard Business School Press, 2001).

82 Bhattacharya and Sen (2004).

83 See Susan C. Schneider, Karin Oppegaard, Maurizio Zollo and Quy Huy, 'Managers as Agents of Social Change: Psychological Antecedents to Socially Responsible Behavior', paper presented at the Academy of Management, New Orleans, 2004.

84 Maignan *et al.* (1999).

85 For analysis of the reasons why the search of legitimacy by an organization through actions like CSR can in fact decrease its legitimacy, see Blake Ashforth and Barrie W. Gibbs, 'The Double Edge of Organizational Legitimacy', *Organization Science*, 1/2 (1991): 177–94.

86 For a detailed analysis of this case, see Franck Aggeri, Eric Pezet, Christophe Abrassart and Aurélien Acquier, *Organiser le développement durable. Expériences des entreprises pionnières et formation de règles d'action collective* (Paris: Vuibert, 2005).

87 See Redington (2005).

2 | *The integrative benefits of social alliances: balancing, building and bridging*

IDA E. BERGER, PEGGY H. CUNNINGHAM
AND MINETTE E. DRUMWRIGHT

Introduction

There is no shortage of societal problems: a global AIDS epidemic, a global climate crisis, a widening gap between rich and poor, abject poverty, inaccessible healthcare, to name a few. Historically, problems such as these have fallen almost exclusively within the purview of governments and nonprofit organizations, but in recent years, corporations have been called upon to span sector boundaries and become involved with social problems that plague the globe. As such, corporate social responsibility has never been more prominent on the corporate agenda, but key questions beg for further investigation. How can companies most effectively contribute to solving social problems? How can corporate social responsibility be embedded in companies? Despite their immense resources and capabilities, companies typically have little history or expertise in dealing directly with social problems. Many argue that collaboration across sector boundaries is at least part of the solution. That is, companies must collaborate in meaningful and enduring ways with nonprofit organizations and governments as they respond to the world's ills. One way for them to do so is to form what we call 'social alliances', which are collaborative partnerships that span sector boundaries. Social alliances are long-term, strategic relationships between companies and nonprofits that have at least one non-economic (i.e. social) and one economic goal.

The authors thank the Marketing Science Institute and the Social Sciences and Humanities Research Council of Canada for their support of this work. They also thank Craig Smith and H.W. Perry, Jr., for their helpful comments on earlier versions of the manuscript.

Social alliances have great potential to embed corporate social responsibility within a company in effective and enduring ways, yet these organizational forms are complex and poorly understood. The purpose of this research is to understand the forces that give rise to social alliances, the processes that enable them to become embedded in companies and the outcomes that provide motivation to continue them.

Background

Three ongoing discourses are germane to our study. Each represents a set of forces or factors at a distinct level of analysis, supportive of and contributing to the growth of social alliances. At the macro level are the socioeconomic forces underpinning the rise of cross-sectoral, inter-organizational alliances. At the micro level are the challenges faced by individual workers, who are trying to construct an integrated, meaningful personal identity. These macro and micro forces intersect at the meso or intermediate level driven, in part, by the new relational focus in marketing strategy. We will explore these themes in the context of social alliances.

Scholars have drawn on three theoretical explanations for alliance formation among companies: transaction-cost theory, institutional theory and resource dependency theory.[1] We consider the usefulness of these theories in understanding and explaining social alliances and conclude that none fully explains this phenomenon.

Methods

Since our research objective was to understand complex interactions, diffuse processes, perceptions, beliefs and values that are often tacit, we used a field-based approach called elite interviews. The term 'elite interviews' is commonly used to refer to long interviews of decision-makers as opposed to consumers, an electorate, or a mass population.[2] Unlike highly structured interviews, elite interviews are designed to ascertain the decision-makers' understanding of the phenomenon, its meaning to them and what they consider relevant.[3] Elite interviews are especially useful when one cannot be sure what interpretation, code, norm, affect or rule is guiding the actors.[4] Elite interviewing is a particularly valuable tool when one wants to understand the meaning of events and actions to the actors. It stresses the informant's definition of the situation, encourages the informant to structure the account of the situation and allows the informant to reveal his or her notions of what is relevant.[5]

To qualify as a research site, a partnership had to meet the criteria specified by our definition of social alliances. Specifically, both the company and the nonprofit had to have strategic goals for the partnership, and both had to embrace a non-economic objective focused on improving social welfare. In addition, the relationships had to involve a long-term commitment that had evolved well beyond the initial phases of strategic philanthropy or cause-related marketing. We required that the partnerships be at least four years old. Eleven social alliances involving twenty-six organizations were examined: ten companies (one company had two social alliances, both of which were included in the sample), eleven nonprofits and five consulting firms. The consulting firms were identified by informants at our research sites as playing important roles in their social alliances. The social alliances ranged in age from four to fourteen years. The companies ranged in revenues from $800 million to more than $100 billion and represented a variety of industries. The nonprofits ranged from $6 million to more than $900 million in income and they represented a variety of causes.

At each site, we interviewed multiple informants in an attempt to get as complete an understanding of the social alliance as possible. Interviews ranged in length from one and a half hours to two hours. Sixty-nine in-depth personal interviews were conducted with representatives of the companies, nonprofit organizations and consulting firms involved in the eleven social alliances. We sought to enrich our data with accounts of partnerships that either had failed or had not succeeded to the degree that would enable them to meet our criteria as social alliances. As a result, we conducted twenty-one additional interviews with people involved in company–nonprofit relationships that did not qualify as social alliances. Anonymity was provided to all informants and organizations to increase frankness and to mitigate against biases related to social desirability and posturing. The interviews were recorded and transcribed, except in a few situations in which recording was infeasible. In these cases, extensive notes were taken.

An interview protocol was utilized to guide the interviews. It was developed based on preliminary interviews with fifteen experts, including professors with expertise in marketing, advertising, management or qualitative methods and practitioners experienced in company–nonprofit collaborative efforts. It was pre-tested with a manager from a company, the head of a foundation and a manager from a nonprofit organization, all of whom had been involved in social alliances. It should be noted, however, that informants were given control of the interviews so that they could discuss issues of importance to them. In this way, we allowed themes to emerge from the data, which we may not have foreseen at the beginning of the research project.

Data were also collected from eight other sources to enable triangulation:

(1) participant observation at meetings or other forums in which we had an opportunity to watch the partners interact;
(2) internal documents (e.g. reports, memos, briefing papers);
(3) communications between the partners (e.g. memos, proposals);
(4) internal publications (e.g. employee magazines, newsletters);
(5) documents for external distribution (e.g. print advertisements, press releases, brochures);
(6) articles from newspapers and magazines;
(7) videos of commercials and broadcast news stories; and
(8) videos of presentations by executives (e.g. press conferences, speeches, presentations at sales meetings).

Not all sources were available for all research sites, but we were able to obtain material from at least four types of sources at each site in addition to the interviews.

The data were analysed systematically and intensively using standard qualitative data analytic methods.[6] Specifically, the coding approach recommended by Strauss was followed.

Limitations

The methodological limitations of qualitative fieldwork are well known and judicious attempts were made to mitigate their effects. Considerable judgement is inevitably required by the qualitative analyst and consequently subjectivity of interpretation is often a concern.[7] To establish the reliability of our findings, initial data analysis was undertaken by all three authors working independently. Commonality of themes and perspectives were subsequently identified, debated and iteratively agreed upon. Further, in reporting the findings, we made extensive use of direct quotations from the key informants. We quote as liberally as space permits and, unless otherwise noted, include only quotations that are representative of the comments of several informants. As acknowledged above, anonymity was granted to all informants and organizations to help mitigate biases and demand effects related to social desirability and posturing. Having the viewpoints of multiple organizational members and organizational partners (e.g. companies, nonprofits and consultants) provided a check on the reports of individual informants, further increasing our confidence in the veracity and reliability of our data. Using multiple sources of data in addition to the interviews (e.g. external and internal documents) also enabled us to check for convergence. While the majority of our data focus on partnerships that qualified as social alliances and thus had succeeded to at least some degree, we augmented our data by conducting interviews with informants who had been involved in partnerships that had failed or had not achieved social alliance status. Although the companies and nonprofits chosen may not be representative of the total population, they do vary on many dimensions, including size, geographical location, industry or type of cause, thereby portraying the range and depth of the phenomena of interest.

Findings

Our interviews were dominated by three overriding themes: allying across sector boundaries, integrating personal identities and relating across organizational boundaries. These themes emerged as macro, micro and meso-level topics and issues. We report and then discuss each in turn.

Theme 1: allying across sector boundaries

In narrating the emergence and development of social alliances, our informants identified sector specific, macro-level forces that motivated the partners to ally across sector boundaries. In particular, company managers pointed to the growth and evolution of company marketing initiatives with a social dimension.[8] These initiatives typically were prompted by consumer expectations that companies should contribute to their communities. Nonprofit managers recounted pressures to apply marketing and business techniques to the management of their endeavours to demonstrate greater effectiveness and efficiency. Our interviews revealed, however, that the primary driver of social alliance formation was the recognition that critical organizational goals could not be achieved without the complementary capabilities and skills obtained through a full cross-sector partnership.

While a social alliance need only encompass one non-economic goal and one economic goal to fit our definition, in actuality, it was the full adoption of the cross-sector partner's goals that gave rise to and sustained the alliance form. That is, the social alliance only fully emerged once the company embraced the non-economic or social objective and the nonprofit embraced the economic objective. Both partners had to move beyond traditional roles of philanthropic relationships. A company manager described the company's expanded role and how fully the company became involved in accomplishing the goals of its non-profit partner as follows:

We really want to be involved in the nuts and bolts of the delivery of this [cause] programme rather than being the company that writes out the big cheque, and then someone else worries about the details ... it was a risk for us to take [this] on as a company.

This cross-sector goal congruence bridged, and in the best cases dissolved, the sector boundaries, linking the partners' work and success. Another company manager described the partnership as follows:

Their [the partners] work is integrally related to our work; their success is integrally related to our success ... [It's like a] circle with links that are welded together.

Sometimes the understanding and adoption of the partner's goals was immediate and integral to the partnership from the beginning but, more typically, it involved a process of interaction, dialogue, compromise and learning that transformed the partners into each other's advocates, enabling them to bring their skills to bear on behalf of the partner. A nonprofit manager described such a situation:

Over a period of us working with them over a couple of months, they [the company] became strong advocates with a much more comprehensive approach because they are very smart, they are business people, they think about how you leverage and get the most out of the dollar.

For many nonprofits, the first step in the goal-sharing process was the recognition that they possessed and could offer economic value to their company partners, as one nonprofit manager explained:

And that was really, to me, the turnkey in our relationship ... It was putting a value on what we have that they need ... because we realized we have value, they knew we knew we had value, and then you have a partnership.

Nonprofits also had to come to a deep understanding of the company's business, as one nonprofit manager explained:

[You need to spend a lot of time] understanding what are the marketing objectives of those companies. What are their new products? What market share they're hoping for. What demographics they're trying to penetrate. What are their employee morale issues? What are their public relations challenges?

Given the push that companies feel to be more socially responsible, one thing they want from a relationship with a nonprofit is to generate a feeling of goodwill towards the company. Social alliances typically encompassed strategic company objectives, however, that extended beyond simply acquiring goodwill. One informant put it this way:

Most nonprofits have kind of a simplistic notion that a company is interested in the goodwill – kind of a good corporate image – that they can get by affiliating with a nonprofit. Companies can buy that goodwill ... Usually they need something more than that if you want to build a long-term, sustainable relationship.

Furthermore, goal sharing had to be genuine and authentic. One nonprofit manager referred to this as the 'sniff test':

Well, the sniff test is about their sincerity. How real are you in wanting to do something about [the cause]? Is it just like a sexy cause that looks good and is going to sell bars of soap? Or is this real? In [company's] case, it is just so very real.

Interestingly, we heard of a 'sniff test' on the other side as well. Nonprofits, we were told, need to be genuine in their desire to work with and contribute value to the company's economic 'cause'. They had to be willing to give as well as to get and benefits had to be reciprocal:

I mean you really have to want them to be your partner, period ... one thing that the corporations sniff out really fast is that disingenuous, you-owe-us-because-you're-a-big-corporation [attitude].

Finally, many viewed social alliances as more difficult than traditional philanthropic relationships and, therefore, both partners had to be willing to work hard:

It's [the social alliance approach] a way of looking at social issues and taking on new challenges – beyond government, beyond philanthropy. It's the hardest work of all. It's really, really hard. It's much easier to fund a research programme.

In sum, the key to initiating and developing social alliances was the adoption of multi-sector goals and criteria. Partners had to be able to view problems and issues from the perspective of the other. Once shared goals were adopted and internalized, it became clear to each organization that it alone did not have the skills, expertise or resources to accomplish the multi-faceted, cross-sector goals.

I think that it's given us access and opportunity to accomplish the objectives that we set out to achieve that we knew organizationally we didn't have the expertise to accomplish.

Once begun, these alliances initiated an evolutionary process in which a new organizational form developed. Evolution included adaptations (1) to better match structures and timelines, (2) to innovate processes, (3) to expand performance measures and (4) to integrate managements. When structures and timelines were not well matched, one or both partners needed to make changes to facilitate engagement. For example, in an alliance in which a company had national and regional headquarters, the nonprofit needed to develop a structure for interacting at both levels. Similarly, when working with a nonprofit composed of largely autonomous units, a highly centralized company needed to accommodate a more decentralized structure to interact fully with the key nonprofit units.[9] In another case, the nonprofit had to change its yearly cycle (particularly its vacation periods) to accommodate the media-planning cycle of its corporate partner. In a final example, a company manager talked about successfully changing the nonprofit's granting cycle:

We found out that [keeping the programme stable from year to year in terms of doing two funding cycles a year] ... enables us to really service the organizations far better; that there wasn't such a long time between grant cycles. We learned that both partners needed to evolve processes to accommodate the other.

Evolution was not always easy. Decision-making styles, risk perceptions, timeframes, planning horizons and approval processes often differed. For example, decision-making in companies was often more hierarchical, while decision-making in nonprofits was often more consensual and participative. What was considered expeditious and action-oriented in a company was sometimes perceived as impetuous and authoritarian in a nonprofit. What was considered prudent by a nonprofit was sometimes perceived as slow and bureaucratic by a company. Unless both partners were flexible in adapting processes and understanding the constraints and needs of the other, the social alliance was likely to be a source of continual frustration.

Each partner also needed to expand its set of performance measures to encompass measures that mattered to the other partner. This adaptation typically required each partner to embrace multiple bottom lines. For example, the publicity and recognition that a company partner received became an important measure for the nonprofit partner to track and report. Similarly, the company partner needed to look beyond the amount of money raised to appreciate indicators of real impact on the social cause. One company even began to consider the amount of government funding that the cause received as an important indicator of alliance success. An informant who advised a number of companies described the measurement challenge this way:

Every year, we have a mutual understanding of what the relationship is, what outcomes it needs to meet, to satisfy ... I guess the other piece of what we urge organizations to do is to understand how your partner is going to measure it ... understand more than just how it's good for you. So at the end of the year, there shouldn't be a lot of guessing as to whether you're going to have a relationship again next year.

In the best social alliances, company managers distinguished the partnership as different from other business-oriented collaborations because its effectiveness is measured 'with an eye to improvement'. Implicit in this notion of 'improvement' is a perspective that goes beyond the individual partners to society as a whole.

It's different because we know ... that what we're doing is benefiting this country in many ways ... So the motivation is different ... In [the alliance], we're measuring effectiveness but not with an eye to terminate the relationship. We're measuring effectiveness with an eye to improvement.

We saw that in the most established partnerships, the management of the alliance became so integrated that the core competency of each organization was drawn upon and utilized. For example, a company redesigned a nonprofit's information systems, inventory management and distribution systems. A nonprofit created a volunteer service programme for a company. In some cases, this integration was not limited to the social alliance. It extended into other areas of both partners' operations as they drew more generally on each other's strengths and expertise. One company redesigned and simplified the nonprofit partner's grant-making process, while in another instance, a nonprofit led team-building workshops and leadership training for its company partner.

In sum, macro-level forces drove organizations to the social alliance form. Full acceptance of both economic and non-economic goals by both parties permitted the social alliance to evolve and realize its objectives, creating economic and social benefits. These relationships are captured in the top layer of Figure 2.1.

Discussion

Theorists have focused on one of three explanations for the rise of strategic alliances.[10] Following transaction-cost theory, alliances are seen as a breakdown in either markets (when transaction costs become too high) or hierarchies (when control or knowledge costs become too high). Following institutional theory, alliances are seen

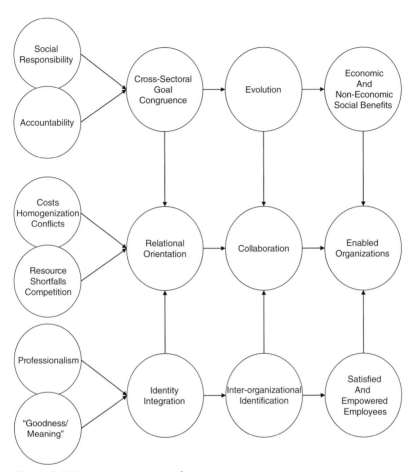

Figure 2.1 Drivers, processes and outcomes

as a mechanism for gaining institutional legitimacy among a diverse set of stakeholders. Following resource-dependence theory, alliances are seen as mechanisms for gaining control of critical assets, skills or resources. All three of these theories have some relevance to the formation of social alliances; however, none is able to explain the complete story. While the company partner may enter the alliance to gain access to customers or channel members (implying a market failure hypothesis), the nonprofit partner was never 'in a market' in the classic sense. In fact, the nonprofit partners are seeking to behave 'as if they were in a market' – looking for a 'marketing perspective', a 'marketing orientation' or a 'marketing method' to apply to social problems.

The nonprofit perceives no 'market failure' situation; rather, it seeks to achieve success through market-based activities. Similarly, while the company partner may be seeking institutional legitimacy,[11] the nonprofit risks legitimacy by 'getting into bed' with business. Finally, both partners may seek resources or assets (in terms of skills, recognition or reputation) from an alliance; however, most would agree that there are easier, less risky methods of resource acquisition. Instructive as the extant theories may be, none fully explains social alliance formation, evolution or longevity. The impetus for alliances is more than market failure (i.e. the inability to achieve goals through a market mechanism), it is more than institutional illegitimacy and it is more than resource deficiency. The impetus may be all these things, but it is also much more. The impetus to ally was driven by the acceptance of emergent, new, previously unknown or unrecognized goals and by an expanding perception of what duty and social responsibility entail. For example, by adopting the goal of educating underserved women or providing hunger relief or increasing healthcare accessibility, a company's role in society changes. 'You have to give back to the community', said one informant, 'and as corporate citizens, we do. It's important'. The company is then evaluated not only in terms of wealth generation for a limited set of stakeholders, but also in terms of 'social citizenship', taking into account a broad and diverse set of stakeholders. Similarly, by adopting the goal of providing consumer value, moving more product, or signing up more customers, a nonprofit changes the traditional role of a social institution. As one nonprofit informant put it, 'It's not good enough anymore to just do something for the good of the cause'. Another spoke of how he advises other nonprofits:

[I give nonprofits advice] around the broader concept of how to position themselves to create wealth. We don't just like to go out and find a corporate partner for them. It's how to think about their assets in ways not thought about before. Most nonprofits think about them in terms of their mission, but not in terms of leveraging and marketing purposes and so forth.

Social alliances blur traditional sector boundaries as organizations reach beyond their traditional domains, visions and roles. As an organizational form, social alliances bridge socio-political sectors, creating a new context for tackling social problems. Because they cross traditional boundaries, they make possible expanded channels of communication with more stakeholders, they allow for the development of trust and they facilitate norms of reciprocity and cooperation. As a result, social alliances generate economic and social benefits.

Theme 2: integrating personal identities

Our data revealed that micro-level forces were also at play as many of our informants described their struggles to integrate diverse personal identities.[12] For example, one company informant, who had a strong personal social agenda, lamented that as a businessman it was not his role to make the world a better place despite his personal conviction to do so. This predicament presented a significant conflict for him and he expressed a strong desire to integrate his business and personal values and make a difference in the world through his work. As another example, a nonprofit informant, who had a strong desire to achieve, lamented that as a nonprofit employee, a 'do-gooder', she often felt that she was perceived as unaccomplished and less savvy from a business perspective. This perception presented a significant conflict for her and she expressed a strong desire to be recognized for professionalism within her nonprofit role. As more and more nonprofits recruit 'business types', such concerns are likely to become even more of an issue.

Social alliances provided a venue through which both company and nonprofit workers could integrate their professional and personal identities. Company workers could integrate their work-related professional identities with the personal meaning and purpose of nonprofit missions and causes. The alliances provided an opportunity for individuals to achieve success for themselves, contribute to their employer's goals and have a positive impact on their community and society. As one company informant said, 'You can be great at what you do in your job. But if you're not giving back to the community, it's not enough'. Likewise, social alliances provided an opportunity for nonprofit workers to integrate the meaning that they derived from their work on behalf of the cause with a professional identity, which they derived from engagement with the company.

Workers involved directly with *social alliances* became deeply and emotionally engaged with their partners and identified with their partners:

What I found in them [partners] was a level of commitment and dedication and passion for what they're involved with that I immediately responded to ... and you begin to feel things happening and ideas building upon one another that is really exciting – a very dynamic process.

They worked actively to prompt their co-workers to identify with the partner organization as well. As one nonprofit worker asserted, 'You try to turn every [nonprofit] employee into as deep as possible an integrator of understanding of the company'. Likewise, a company employee explained, 'I try to get people to believe in this [the cause] more than they believe in anything else'.

Social alliances not only helped participants integrate their own personal and professional identities, they also served as a catalyst for inter-organizational identification.[13] That is, alliance participation helped the company employees identify with their own organization and with the nonprofit organization and its mission. Similarly, it helped the nonprofit employees identify with their organization and with the partner company. Sometimes the integration resulted in individuals literally crossing the 'sector divide' and moving from the company to a nonprofit or vice versa.

Social alliances enhanced employee satisfaction, helping to attract and retain employees. For example, a company employee, who had been a summer intern, reported that she accepted a full-time position because the company 'has a culture of giving something back to people' through its social alliance. She also expressed her 'excitement' as she joined the team working on the social alliance, calling it a 'fun but complex task'. Another company informant described the satisfaction that the social alliance provided him:

You felt like you were part of something that was alive, and that was a great thing. I have never in my business life been involved with something on a business level with a business associate that involved quite the same level of personal commitment and passion.

Another informant stressed that the partnership 'satisfied an employee satisfaction need as well as a customer satisfaction need'.

Yet another noted, 'Moreover, people who work at [company] just feel good about the extra effort they put into the [nonprofit] programme. It helps them feel good about themselves'. A company manager attributed increased employee empowerment and morale to the social alliance:

I think that the empowerment that we give our employees [through the social alliance] is terrific. Maybe it's making employees feel better about working for [company] to the extent that their morale is boosted and they feel better about the company.

In sum, the drive of an individual worker to 'achieve' at a professional level while also 'doing good' and finding 'personal meaning' in an integrated way prompted involvement in social alliances. Through identity integration and inter-organizational identification, employee satisfaction was increased. These relationships are illustrated in the bottom layer of Figure 2.1.

Discussion

The drive to integrate one's personal identity represents a shift in societal values. Capitalist societies have benefited from a managerial worldview favouring differentiation between public and private realms. However, recent ethical scandals as well as recognition of the physical (cardiac, cancer, obesity), psychological (stress disorders, depression, drug abuse) and societal (family dysfunction, hunger, delinquency) costs of this orientation have led many to question this 'weltanschauung', or comprehensive view of the world and human life.[14] The idea that 'I am one person at home and another at the office', or that 'I must park my morals with my car', is being challenged by those accepting greater responsibility for the social consequences of market actions and those seeking greater integration of their multiple 'selves'.

Marketing scholars have become accustomed to thinking about consumption and spending behaviours as both composite elements of and expressions of personal identity. Historically, the gender, social class, culture and cohort to which one was born defined one's identity. Today's society, however, provides for considerable fluidity in identity definition.[15] Social actors are free to create identities of their choice on a minute-by-minute basis, using props available in the marketplace.[16] Employer and type of employment are at least as indicative of 'who one is' as what one buys. The greater the discrepancy between the 'professional–productive-self', the 'personal–consumptive-self' and the 'social–other-oriented-self' the greater the psychological stress and consequent health and productivity risk. Therapists, clergy and business leaders counsel individuals to seek greater balance between the cognitive and emotional being, between work and family, between ethics and economics, and between the personal and the professional.

In our interviews, we saw and heard evidence of these shifting values. We found company managers who felt it was time to 'give back' and who wanted to leave a mark beyond shareholder price and earnings. Similarly, we found nonprofit managers who wanted to play in the big leagues and had ambitions to achieve in the economic marketplace. For such individuals, social alliances represented a vehicle that effectively supported identity integration, entrepreneurship, passion and engagement. As a result, involvement with the alliance enriched the lives, skills and knowledge of these individuals, leading to increased satisfaction.

Theories of organizational identification have long focused on how individuals define and maintain their self-concept based on the cognitive connection they make with their referent organization.[17] The experiences of our informants suggested that connections to social alliances represent a vehicle not only for identification but also for identity integration. Identifying with these cross-sector organizations offered workers the opportunity to integrate the professional and the personal, the ethical and the economic, the company identity and the nonprofit identity. We saw this integrated identity in particular among informants who valued elements of both organizations, leading to a more balanced, holistic and satisfying identity.

Theme 3: relating across organizational boundaries

The macro and micro drivers and processes interacted with, and were reinforced by, factors operating at the organizational level. For example, a given company's need to create a differential advantage, attract and retain customers, attract and retain qualified employees, or acquire access to channels could drive it towards a social alliance. Likewise, a given nonprofit's need to expand and retain its funding sources, respond to new competitors and attract and retain volunteers, could drive it towards a social alliance. Such meso forces created an openness to a relational orientation and a willingness to develop and maintain relationships.

Traditionally, marketing's role has been characterized in transactional terms as 'the creation of value for buyers and [the] capture of a significant part of that created value'.[18] 'Relationship marketing' goes well beyond this definition by positioning marketing as the initiator, creator and maintainer of relationships. In this view, marketing plays a critical role in spanning organizational boundaries. We saw this boundary-spanning role repeatedly in social alliance relationships. The boundary spanning served as a catalyst for collaboration, reinforcing the macro and micro forces.

The individuals who initiated, championed and shepherded these social alliances were the initial boundary spanners and the prime catalysts for collaboration. They had to represent their own organizations to their partners and they had to advocate on behalf of their partners within their own organizations. One company manager described it this way:

We are [the nonprofit] voice internally. If there are spokespeople for nonprofits, I guess we are they to some extent ... Some of us have been in nonprofits and talked to people in their organization, and every one of us is convinced that nonprofits have a role to play in our society, which no one else can play or is equipped to play. They do certain things very well.

Another company manager described how a nonprofit manager had successfully spanned the organizational boundaries and engendered collaboration:

She was right there; she came in and made visits to the home office to talk to executives, to talk to the buying organization, and all the support staff, to make herself known to the CEO. She attended our store managers' meeting twice a year, and that is being in touch with maybe 1,000 people at a time. She even made herself known with the executives in the US. And just the personal touch, the personal relationship, was really important. I don't think that she left anything unturned.

Because they had many of the characteristics of new business entrepreneurs, we called these boundary spanners 'social alliance entrepreneurs'. They were innovative, resourceful and well connected to others in their organizations. They were viewed as people with high integrity whom others trusted and respected. They had a high energy level and brought an engaging, infectious passion to their work.[19] Company employees who champion corporate social initiatives have previously been referred to as 'enviropreneurs' and 'policy entrepreneurs' and share many characteristics with social alliance entrepreneurs. However, our data demonstrated that social alliance entrepreneurs can be employees of companies, nonprofits or consulting firms. Some of our informants were serial social alliance entrepreneurs, such as the senior brand manager who noted that she had used or designed a partnership effort for every brand she had ever managed.

Importantly, the alliance did not represent just another assignment for these individuals. For example, one informant represented the view of many when she asserted, 'I brought as much of my personal commitment and dedication to this as I possibly could'. The collaborative effort typically involved a sense of moral commitment, as one social alliance entrepreneur explained:

There is a common objective where we come together, yet the two groups will have different needs. And from time to time that results in issues, but ... there was a strong belief from both sides that what's being done is right.

The same informant went on to describe how the nonprofit partner acted as a moral compass for the brand, ensuring that everything brand managers did was on the 'up and up'.

[Nonprofit partner] watches closely, not just the programmes we are involved in but the brand in general. At least, I assume that they are watching. It certainly felt that way. And it ensures that everything the brand does is in line.

Social alliance entrepreneurs had dual roles in which they operated both as boundary spanners and boundary protectors. They entered the partner organization as immigrants who willingly embraced the host culture and encouraged their co-workers to do so as well. They became catalysts for relationships between people in two different cultures and worlds. However, social alliance entrepreneurs also needed to play another more protective role that at times seemed contradictory to their boundary-spanning role. They needed to be boundary protectors or 'buffers'.[20] In other words, they needed to operate as emigrants who recognized and were willing to guard what was valuable in their own culture. For example, one company manager told of how she had to be vigilant in making sure that the social alliance did not work at cross purposes with the company's other objectives and priorities. Another company manager described this boundary protection task as managing compromises: 'I think it's to learn the art of compromise, and learn the art of picking the right battles, or you can fight all day long.' Clearly, social alliance entrepreneurs needed to discern when to facilitate and when to buffer. In other words, they could neither assimilate to, nor segregate from, either culture.

For both partners, a successful relationship meant identifying, creating and appropriating – or extracting value – from highly complex relationships, not just transactions or contracts. The complexity of the relationship was rooted in dyads that were not accustomed to working together. Furthermore, they worked on activities without established procedures, in structures that were still evolving.[21] To succeed, social alliances had to engender learning, diffusion and mobilization. A nonprofit manager described what he had learned from his company partner:

I've learned a lot about perseverance. And they're professional. I've learned a lot of professionalism from them – to be really prepared for meetings and to have value added.

We found that the best social alliances involved intensive educational efforts and demanded considerable learning on the part of both partners. Nonprofits had opportunities to learn business skills from companies and companies had opportunities to learn how to motivate and energize people, manage volunteer efforts and allocate charitable donations more effectively. These skills largely represent 'explicit knowledge', knowledge that can be 'transmitted in formal language, including grammatical statements, mathematical expressions, specifications, manuals and so forth'.[22]

Less obvious, but particularly compelling, was the degree to which both companies and nonprofits had the opportunity to acquire 'tacit knowledge'. Tacit knowledge is deeply rooted in actions and experience as well as in ideals, values or emotions; it is experiential learning.

One company informant referred to the social alliance as a 'learning laboratory'. Nonprofits had opportunities to learn the skills that embody the best of the free enterprise system – e.g. resourcefulness, innovation and the ability to 'think outside the box'– from their corporate partners. For example, one nonprofit developed and pilot-tested two new revenue-generating services and a new product line with its company partner. The nonprofit's chief executive characterized the company as 'a creative partner that we constantly get to take new risks with'.

In the most successful cases, awareness and commitment to the social alliance were diffused through both organizations in a manner that was mobilizing. Typically, diffusion was the result of building networks of engagement. One informant referred to this as 'stratified engagement', that is, engagement between the organizations at multiple levels, often between counterparts (such as directors of management information services). A company manager explained:

They [the nonprofit] knew that they couldn't just have contact with me. They had contact with my staff; they had contact with my boss, my boss's boss. I mean all that was done incredibly well ... They basically managed the relationship. I think that is a very key portion of ... competency that nonprofits need to develop ... the ability to, you know, do account development, the same way a corporation would in their sales division.

Diffusion and networking were particularly important during times of staff rotation or turnover. A nonprofit informant explained:

Everybody that we worked with on that campaign is gone from the company ... It's up to us to make lateral relationships.

The network of engagement sometimes extended to encompass third parties, suppliers or business-to-business customers of the company, who could provide additional sources of funding. In other cases, engagement involved non-economic stakeholders such as government officials or professionals such as doctors or lawyers. No matter which party provided the entrée, it was incumbent on the other to cultivate these relationships. In critiquing her organization's performance, a nonprofit informant admitted, 'There were third party connections that we could have solidified more.'

Learning, diffusion and mobilization processes represented commitment to and institutionalization of both the multi-sector perspective and the alliance activity itself. Maintaining the alliances was not without difficulty and commitment to the alliance, and even to the partner's goal, was periodically challenged. The true test of institutionalization was what happened during trying situations, when trade-offs had to be made. One company informant recounted a situation in which her company experienced a severe financial downturn, yet the investment in the social alliance continued. Expenditures clearly needed to be prioritized, but in this case, there was no automatic deferral to classic 'business' priorities.

Both companies and nonprofits were enriched and enabled through the collaborative efforts. Companies were able to inject their cultures and their workforces with the sense of higher meaning and purpose that they observed in their nonprofit partners, which transcended the day-to-day business of commerce. They were able to instill a sense of idealism, of making a difference that matters. One company manager spoke of how 'humbling' it was for him to work with dedicated nonprofit people:

This is more personal than professional. But it's amazing to see – I don't think the staff at [nonprofit] is paid that much. And here I am in a corporate job, and I have a nice job; it's a good job … It's extremely humbling for me to see them living life and living life to the fullest and being extremely happy and dedicated.

In a similar vein, nonprofits were able to inject their organizations with agility, drive, ambition, competition, an appreciation for excellence and a sense of accountability for outcomes. In short, both partners were better enabled to realize their potential.

In sum, organizational or meso-level needs on the part of both companies and nonprofits drove both partners towards a relational orientation. The relational orientation prompted the development of a social alliance. Through the social alliance, the partners collaborated in such a way that both organizations were more effectively enabled to reach their potential. These relationships are illustrated in the middle layer of Figure 2.1. As portrayed in Figure 2.1, note that macro and micro level processes and outcomes converge at the meso level and reinforce social alliance development.

Discussion

The relational context and invoked processes can either contribute to or impede alliance success. We saw from our interviews that a strong relational thrust supported by processes of learning, mobilization and diffusion undergirded social alliance activity and success. What made these issues particularly critical was the 'distance' in perspective, form and function between organizations from different sectors. This distance served to magnify the challenge, volatility and instability identified as common to all alliances.

Das and Teng (2000) suggested that alliances between organizations are particularly unstable, volatile and often disappointing because of three inherent and predictable tensions.[23] Psychologically, alliances must balance tendencies towards short-term orientations with tendencies towards long-term orientations. Structurally, alliances must balance motivations towards rigidity with motivations towards flexibility. Behaviourally, they must balance tendencies towards competition with tendencies towards cooperation. For an understanding of social alliances, this relational-tensions framework is particularly powerful. Cognitively, structurally and behaviourally, companies certainly tend towards hierarchy, a short-term orientation and competition, while nonprofits tend towards participation, a long-term orientation and cooperation. Balancing these tendencies may be the key challenge in social alliance management. It is what makes the alliance management task and the alliance relationship so complex. However, achieving and maintaining this balance are key sources of benefits, resource transfer, innovation, trust, identification and, ultimately, alliance success. Strong drives to ally (implying shared cross-sector goals) and integrate (implying inter-organizational identification), coupled with market forces favouring relationships, serve to facilitate the balancing of these tendencies through integrated, stratified, diffused collaboration. Successful collaborations result in increased flexibility and mutually beneficial collective action.

Balancing, building and bridging

More broadly, building these cross-sector social alliances, managing these complex relationships and constructing more integrated identities create bonds and bridges between individuals (within and between organizations), between organizations (within and between sectors) and between social processes. By so doing, social alliances contribute to the blurring of distinctions between socio-cultural categories, including for-profit–nonprofit boundaries, private–public sector boundaries and market–social domain boundaries. Social alliances make more tangible the dual facts that market actions have societal implications, meanings, responsibilities and consequences, and that social causes can be marketed, bought and sold, acquired, possessed, consumed and discarded.

In the best case, what can a social alliance achieve? How can we integrate or understand the multi-level outcomes of these partnerships? One approach to these questions is to consider the ability of social alliances to contribute to society's stock of human, financial and/or social capital. Through the integration of disparate organizations and the mobilization of support for social causes, social alliances have the potential to create all three kinds of capital.

We saw in our data that the individuals involved in these alliances are themselves often transformed by the activity. Their lives are enriched through their engagement with new people and from the challenge of solving 'out-of-the-ordinary' problems. It is not a coincidence that many informants were lively, engaged, engaging, creative, motivated people. They spoke of being involved in thinking 'outside the box', of learning new ways of dealing with people, of developing new skills and of having a different perspective on their lives. Nonprofit workers developed a greater understanding of the methods, processes and issues that drive the for-profit world. Company employees learned ways of motivating colleagues and market partners, such as customers and suppliers, beyond rational, economic factors. They learned skills (such as inspiration, persuasion and moral suasion) that went beyond the 'stick-and-carrot' method they had previously relied on to achieve cooperation and compliance. We found participants on both sides of social alliances who had crossed or were considering crossing to the other side. It appeared that those who became deeply involved in social alliance activities could improve their problem-solving skills, people management skills, personal confidence, feelings of empowerment, with personal and job satisfaction. These attitudes, skills and perceptions represent additions to the stock of human capital available to the organizations directly involved in the alliance as well as to the communities in which they operate.

The organizations involved in these social alliances were also altered. Both the companies and the nonprofit organizations were enabled in terms of their ability to move, generate or use resources. For the social alliance to succeed, the organizations needed to develop flexibility; they needed to learn new ways of mobilizing employees and partners. They needed to develop bases of trust and commitment other than contracts. Because these activities needed to be closely tied to organizational mission, they forced organizations to re-evaluate the values that underpin their missions and to integrate their missions into everyday activities. Not only do social alliances highlight the core values of organizations, they also provide ways and models of affirming and living those values on a daily basis. Social alliance activities provide models of behaviour that focus on reciprocity, trust and collective concern. The social alliance experience changes organizational norms from ones that focus on the self or the individual to ones that focus more on the 'other' and the collective.

These observations suggest that over time, organizations involved in social alliances will be more flexible, their missions and values will be more transparent and diffuse, they will demonstrate norms of reciprocity and collective care, they will depend less on hierarchical networks of relationships between employees and they will experience less turnover and easier recruitment. These organizational changes should serve to increase the financial capital of the social alliance partners. Social alliance activities may increase memberships and donations for the nonprofit. Similarly, as a result of the differential advantage created by the social alliance or through the increased productivity of a more motivated workforce, sales (and therefore financial resources) of the corporate partner should increase.

In the best of cases, yet another type of capital can be created – social capital. Social capital is that set of features of social organization that facilitate cooperation and collaboration for mutual benefit.[24] Social capital exists in networks of relationships characterized by extensive obligations, expectations and trustworthiness; rich, multiplexed, information channels; and norms of reciprocity and collective interest.[25]

The concept of social capital has received substantial attention in the media and in academic circles through the work of Robert Putnam.[26] Using the metaphor of 'Bowling Alone', Putnam argues that there has been a precipitous decline in civic engagement in America since the

Second World War. As participation in civic organizations has declined, so has the resource that enables social actors to work together to pursue shared goals and objectives.[27] While controversy exists over various aspects of Putnam's work, most experts agree that social capital is a highly desirable asset. Some experts assert that the patterns of civic engagement are not so much declining as shifting away from neighbourhoods and into work organizations.[28] Thus, the workplace may be a very fertile venue for the cultivation and growth of social capital.

Our data suggest that social alliances can provide compelling benefits for both companies and nonprofits. For companies, they provide a workplace mechanism for creating social capital, as workers and customers become engaged at a grassroots level with a nonprofit organization, its cause and the community that it serves. Corporate volunteerism programmes focused on the social alliance cause are one means of achieving this engagement. Such engagement creates important by-products for both organizations. It provides the company with new attitudes and ways to interact with economic stakeholders like customers, suppliers or channel members, as well as non-economic stakeholders like government, activists, community groups and professional communities. In essence, social alliances create the learning, attitudes, skills and competencies that form the underpinnings for an increasing number of 'extra-market' relations. Likewise, 'extra-workplace' relations are created between a company and its workers. For nonprofits, social alliances provide a new arena in which to interact with constituents; 'extra-philanthropic' relations are established. Thus, a social alliance can create enhanced opportunities for the development of multiplexed relationships that can enhance trust, relational norms and information flow.

At a societal level, the existence of social alliances and the creation of social capital enhance society's ability to solve more macro social problems. Through these alliances between sectors, society develops the resources to deal with issues that affect all sectors but are beyond the capability of any one sector to solve. The trust that is developed between the company and the nonprofit organization allows each to break down previously held stereotypes of the other. Each better recognizes the potential contribution that the other sector can make. The relationships set up systems of obligations and expectations that can be relied upon. Furthermore, the activities can enhance social norms of collective action.

What we find in the best case is that the social alliance can result in the creation of a new entity that represents the integration of formerly separate sectors – commercial and nonprofit. This entity has characteristics of both participating partners, but it is a clone of neither. It is vibrant and entrepreneurial. It is a catalyst and a laboratory for learning. It empowers and mobilizes both organizations. Most importantly, it has multiple bottom lines – bottom lines for individuals, organizations and society at large. In short, a social alliance can result in enriched lives, enabled organizations and an enhanced capacity for productive problem-solving within the larger society.

Social alliances appear to be a very effective way to embed corporate social responsibility in a company in an enduring way. Through the cross-sector sharing of goals, a new cross-sector organizational form is created and, as it evolves, social purposes and behaviours become embedded in the company. As both economic and non-economic benefits are realized, there is motivation to continue the social alliance and further embed social responsibility behaviours in the company. Our data suggest that a social alliance is an organizational form that can achieve both economic and non-economic benefits over the long term. Obviously, not all social alliance outcomes are positive or beneficial to society, and not all social alliances develop or evolve smoothly and without challenges. In this chapter, we have highlighted the forces, processes and positive outcomes. Some of the problems and challenges are well described elsewhere.[29] Nonetheless, social alliances clearly demonstrate tremendous potential for providing powerful, positive benefits and for embedding corporate social responsibility initiatives in companies.

Notes

1 Rajan Varadarajan and Margaret H. Cunningham, 'Strategic Alliances: A Synthesis of Conceptual Foundations', *Journal of the Academy of Marketing Science*, 23/4 (1995): 282–96; reprinted in J. Sheth and A. Parvatiyar (eds.), *Handbook of Relationship Marketing* (Thousand Oaks, CA: Sage Publications, 1999), pp. 271–302.

2 Lewis Anthony Dexter, *Elite and Specialized Interviewing* (Evanston, IL: Northwestern University Press, 1970).

3 Dexter (1970); Grant McCracken, 'Culture and Consumption: A Theoretical Account of the Structure and Movement of the Cultural Meaning of Consumer Goods', *Journal of Consumer Behavior*, 13/1 (1986): 71–85.

4 Dexter (1970); Nigel G. Fielding and Jane L. Fielding, *Linking Data* (Newbury Park, CA: Sage Publications, 1986); Catherine Marshall and Gretchen B. Rossman, *Designing Qualitative Research* (Newbury Park, CA: Sage Publications, 1989); Matthew S. Miles and A. Michael Huberman, *Qualitative Data Analysis*, 2nd edn (Newbury Park, CA: Sage Publications, 1994); Anselm L. Strauss, *Qualitative Analysis for Social Scientists* (Cambridge: Cambridge University Press, 1990).

5 Dexter (1970); Nigel King, 'The Qualitative Research Interview', in Catherine Cassell and Gillian Symon (eds.), *Qualitative Methods in Organizational Research: A Practical Guide* (Thousand Oaks, CA: Sage Publications, 1994); McCracken (1986); Helen B. Schwartzman, *Ethnography in Organizations* (Newbury Park, CA: Sage Publications, 1993).

6 Strauss (1990); Susan Spiggle, 'Analysis and Interpretation of Qualitative Data in Consumer Research', *Journal of Consumer Research*, 21 (December 1994): 491–503; Minette E. Drumwright, 'Socially Responsible Organizational Buying: Environmental Concern as a Noneconomic Buying Criterion', *Journal of Marketing*, 58 (July 1994): 1–19; Minette E. Drumwright, 'Company Advertising with a Social Dimension: The Role of Noneconomic Criteria', *Journal of Marketing*, 60 (October 1996): 71–88.

7 Dexter (1970).

8 For an examination of the forms that corporate societal marketing initiatives take, see Minette E. Drumwright and Patrick Murphy, 'Corporate Societal Marketing', in Paul N. Bloom and Gregory Gundlach (eds.), *The Handbook of Marketing and Society* (Thousand Oaks, CA: Sage Publications, 2001).

9 Also refer to Ida E. Berger, Peggy H. Cunningham and Minette E. Drumwright, 'Social Alliances: Company/ Nonprofit Collaboration', *California Management Review*, 47 (fall, 2004): 58–90.

10 Ranjay Gulati, 'Social Structure and Alliance Formation Patterns: A Longitudinal Analysis', *Administrative Science Quarterly*, 40/1 (1995): 614–53.

11 Jay M. Handleman and Stephen J. Arnold, 'The Role of Marketing Actions with a Social Dimension: Appeals to the Institutional Environment', *Journal of Marketing*, 63 (July 1999): 33–48.

12 For a comprehensive overview of the linkage between personal and organizational identities, see Ida E. Berger, Peggy H. Cunningham and Minette Drumwright, 'Identity, Identification and Relationship through Social Alliances', *Journal of the Academy of Marketing Science*, 34/2 (2006): 128–37.

13 Jane E. Dutton, Janet M. Dukerich and Celia V. Harquail, 'Organizational Images and Member Identification', *Administrative Science Quarterly*,

39 (June 1994): 239–63. Note: our findings here are in contrast to those of John Peloza, 'The Marketing of Employee Volunteerism', *Journal of Business Ethics*, 85 (April): 371–86. Peloza's study of corporate volunteerism showed that while employees increased their identification with their organization and saw their volunteerism as good corporate citizenship, their identification with the cause did not increase.

14 Linda Duxbury, Christopher Higgins and Catherine Lee, *Balancing Work and Family Roles: An Evaluation of Alternative Work Arrangements* (Ottawa: Health and Welfare, 1993).

15 McCracken (1986).

16 Susan Fournier, 'Consumers and their Brands: Developing Relationship Theory in Consumer Research', *Journal of Consumer Research*, 24/4 (1998): 343–72.

17 Kimberly D. Elsbach, 'An Expanded Model of Organizational Identification', *Research in Organizational Behavior*, 21 (1999): 163–200.

18 John U. Farley, 'Looking Ahead at the Marketplace; It's Global and it's Changing', in Donald R. Lehmann and Katherine E. Jocz (eds.), *Reflections on the Futures of Marketing: Practice and Education* (Cambridge, MA: Marketing Science Institute, 1996), p. 17.

19 These individuals are similar to the ones Varadarajan P. Rajan, 'Marketing's Contribution to Strategy: The View from a Different Looking Glass', *Journal of the Academy of Marketing Science*, 20/4 (1992): 335–44, referred to as 'enviropreneurs' and Drumwright (1994 and 1996) referred to as 'policy entrepreneurs'.

20 J. Meyer and B. Rowan, 'Institutional Organizations: Formal Structure as Myth and Ceremony', *The American Journal of Sociology* (1977): 340–63.

21 Carol Beatty and Brenda Barker, *Building Smart Teams: A Road Map to High Performance* (Thousand Oaks, CA: Sage Publications, 2004).

22 Ikujiro Nonaka and Hirotaka Takeuchi, *The Knowledge-Creating Company* (New York: Oxford University Press, 1995), p. viii.

23 T.K. Das and Bing-Sheng Teng, 'Instabilities of Strategic Alliances: An Internal Tensions Perspective', *Organizational Science*, 11/1 (2000): 77–102.

24 Robert D. Putnam, 'Tuning In, Tuning Out: The Strange Disappearance of Social Capital in America', *PS: Political Science and Politics*, 27 (December 1995a): 664–83.

25 James Coleman, 'Social Capital in the Creation of Human Capital', *American Journal of Sociology*, 94 (supplement) (1988): S95–120.

26 Robert D. Putnam, *Making Democracy Work* (Princeton: Princeton University Press, 1994); Robert D. Putnam, 'Bowling Alone: America's

Declining Social Capital', *Current*, 373 (June 1995b): 3–7; Putnam (1995a).

27 James Coleman, *Foundations of Social Theory* (Cambridge, MA: Harvard University Press, 1990); Putman (1995b).

28 For an illustrative example see Maria T. Poarch, 'Civic Life and Work: A Qualitative Study of Changing Patterns of Sociability and Civic Engagement in Everyday Life', Doctoral dissertation, Boston University, 1997.

29 Berger *et al.* (2004).

3 | *Integrating corporate citizenship: leading from the middle*

PHILIP MIRVIS AND JULIE MANGA

In scaling a wall of rock, a climber must find and make effective use of the meager or substantial handholds on the wall. Some handholds that seem promising may ultimately lead a climber to a dead end, while others allow a person to reach the desired destination. Different climbers, presented with the same rock face, may choose a different set of handholds and, therefore, follow a slightly different path.

Using this rock-climbing metaphor, Laurie Regelbrugge, then a manager of corporate responsibility at the oil and gas operator Unocal, described how she found 'handholds' to establish traction and create opportunities to align and integrate citizenship throughout her company. This is an account of how she and other middle managers led change in their companies, not from the typical planned, top-down model but rather through what some term an 'emergent-pragmatic' or catalytic approach.[1]

Here we first look at the problems these practitioners faced, some of the tactics employed and their rationale for adopting the catalytic versus top-down model of change. The chapter then examines several key components of this model in action and what insights emerged about leading change from the middle. The data were gathered in the Executive Forum – a multi-year business/university learning group that brought these practitioners together to swap knowledge and offer one another advice and that provided the basis for this research on integrating corporate citizenship into firms.

Challenges for integration

Case 1: from silos to cooperation

At Petro-Canada, the northern nation's largest oil company, managers seeking to develop a more holistic approach to citizenship recognized that many social and environmental issues were being addressed within the company, but in functional silos. Hazel Gillespie, a community relations manager and David Stuart, in the Environment, Health, Safety and Security function, recalled that their many activities were 'contributing to the company's internal and external reputation', but observed, 'We weren't doing it in a coordinated, concentrated, focused, strategic way.' Even when efforts were aligned, Stuart noted, 'It was largely because of personal relationships, rather than any kind of systematic management system.'

In search of demonstration projects that would promote coordination and show the value of citizenship in the company, Gillespie and Stuart 'piggy-backed' on three initiatives already underway aimed at strengthening the corporate reputation, updating a total loss management system and devising a framework for dealing with aboriginal rights in regions where their firm operates. These three initiatives brought them into contact with groups concerned with communication and company values, business performance and control, and external relations with stakeholders. Work in these separate projects helped Gillespie and Stuart to gain the credibility and allies to move forward with a proposal to the company's executive team to establish a corporate-level citizenship governance structure and director-level position that would underpin a more integrated approach to citizenship at Petro-Canada.

Case 2: from issues management to corporate responsibility

As one of the big pharmaceutical companies, Abbott faced heightened public scrutiny about issues such as access to medicine and product affordability. Yet, the company's senior management was focused on its therapy pipeline, competition and ever-present pressures for profit. Reeta Roy described her challenges as follows: 'I was hired for a job in "issues management," in the public affairs department, and different elements of citizenship were handled by different parts of the group … When I took on the position, I did some internal research with senior executives, interviewing them about the issues confronting our business and our industry, and did some external benchmarking.' Roy recognized that what Abbott really needed was not a stronger issues management unit but a unified policy function. Kevin Callahan, who would later become Director of Global Citizenship and Policy, described their strategy of bringing diverse interests together to move this agenda forward, 'You have to pull together a group of people, externally and internally, whom you can use as a sounding board to start testing some of your initial strategies and thinking about action.'

Case 3: from corporate policies to business practices

In the mid 1990s Unocal underwent a significant restructuring that shifted it away from downstream activities – retail and refining – to focus on exploration and production. This led the company into developing countries, especially in Southeast Asia. Many of the other oil companies had, in their global operations in developing markets, encountered costly boycotts, work shutdowns and damage to their reputation. Unocal's 'license to operate' was therefore increasingly at risk.

This situation required Unocal to deepen its competence in dealing with an increased number and variety of communities and stakeholders. 'It made sense to begin by focusing on business operations where these issues are large and there is a lot to be gained or lost', reported Greg Huger, who oversaw Corporate Responsibility at Unocal. Huger and his team's approach was to talk with business unit managers about their strategies and the social and environmental issues associated with them. Eventually, conversation led to the issue of community stakeholders and their effects on business operations. In this context Huger and his team would present their ideas on proactive stakeholder engagement as a means for understanding and responding to risks facing the business. Huger noted, 'In all situations, there's something to build on. It gives us a basis for considering new action.'

The Executive Forum

The Executive Forum, hosted by the Boston College Center for Corporate Citizenship, is one of an increasing number of business/ university learning consortia that focus on new developments facing industry, where there is no common understanding of, or agreement about, the situation among business executives and academics have neither sufficient theory nor evidence to recommend 'best practice'.[2] Participants in the forum included: Abbott, Advanced Micro Devices (AMD), Agilent Technologies, JPMorgan Chase, Levi Strauss & Co.,

Petro-Canada, Unocal Corporation and Verizon.[3] The Center's research team engaged regularly with project contacts from each company, individuals who despite their variety of titles and functions had taken a high degree of ownership of their company's corporate citizenship activities (hence they are termed corporate citizenship practitioners here). The bulk of the information reported here comes from conversations with and observations of the practitioners and their colleagues.

At the outset of the project, the research team conducted baseline interviews in each company among a range of individuals relevant to their company's citizenship efforts. The team also completed a similar set of interviews as the project was ending. These interviews addressed the pre- and post-distribution of roles and responsibilities for citizenship activities, perceptions of top- and peer-level executive attitudes towards and involvement in these roles, accounts of strategies deployed and so on. The Center hosted five two-day plenary sessions and ten conference calls in which the participants were able to interact with each other while the project team gathered data on their progress. The team also made site visits and reviewed documents and analytic tools covering practitioners' influence networks, social issues maps, etc. as part of data collection.

Paths to corporate citizenship

Definitions of corporate citizenship are many and varied. Perhaps this shouldn't surprise – not too long ago, corporate citizenship was equated with philanthropy and handled mainly by the community affairs function in companies. The field is still in what scholars call a 'pre-paradigmatic' phase, where there is scant agreement on definitions and terms and no consensus has been reached about what it includes and does not include in its boundaries.[4] Our Center's concept of citizenship encompasses the total actions of a corporation (commercial and philanthropic) and considers to what extent these actions minimize harm, maximize benefit, make the company accountable and responsive to stakeholders and support responsible financial results. Bettignies makes the point that terms such as citizenship and sustainability incorporate notions of ethics, philanthropy, stakeholder management and social and environmental responsibilities into an integrative framework that guides corporate action.[5] Our interest here is not so much in what a company calls its citizenship

> **Alignment:** to connect corporate citizenship to business objectives through a cohesive, company-wide framework and strategy that is commonly understood in different parts of the business and that leads to consistent attitudes, interests and understandings. This means creating a coherent context for corporate citizenship in a firm.
>
> **Integration:** to embed shared corporate citizenship principles and responsibilities in business units and functional areas including corporate staff units, human resources, and supply chain. This often means creating cross-unit systems, processes and structures
>
> **Institutionalization:** to ensure the sustainability of corporate citizenship by formalizing it in standard business practices and infusing into the mindsets of company personnel. This translates into statements of mission and values and efforts to make citizenship an integral part of a company's culture.

Figure 3.1 Aligning, integrating and institutionalizing citizenship

efforts (nomenclature varied across the sample) but rather how comprehensive and inclusive a company regards its role in society.

There are a number of models and some research on the development of corporate citizenship in organizations.[6] Broadly, Mirvis and Googins find that conceptions of company responsibilities become more complex at successive stages of development, and that organizational structures, processes and systems used to manage citizenship are more elaborate and comprehensive.[7] Expressed more formally, the Center has found that companies with the most advance citizenship profiles and practices have *aligned* their citizenship efforts with their business strategies, *integrated* citizenship into their organization structure and processes and *institutionalized* it into the mindsets, values and culture of their organization (see Figure 3.1).[8]

The companies studied here sought to move citizenship from a position of relative marginality to its management as a mainstream business activity. And many progressed from managing citizenship from functional 'silos' to cross-functional and corporate committees and a few began to achieve more formal integration through a combination of structures, processes and systems. How did these companies move forward towards these objectives?

There are three common approaches to developing citizenship in a company.[9] A small and select set of firms, for one, seem to be 'born' to this philosophy. Studies of Ben & Jerry's through the 1980s, along with the Body Shop, Esprit, Smith & Hawken, Patagonia and so on, suggest that firms founded on principles of citizenship make it central to their business models and integral to their organization and culture from the get-go. A second route to citizenship stems from crisis. The Shell Group's response to socio-environmental calamities in the mid-1990s illustrates movement from crisis management to a complete makeover of policies and practices and ultimately of company values and culture. Complementary studies of Nike and Chiquita show a similar progression.

The third trajectory, the most common one, involves a process of planned change. In generic form, this typically involves some form of diagnosis or fact-finding of the situation at hand, identification of performance gaps or problems and possible solutions, and development of action strategies and their attendant goals, followed by the implementation of proposed changes in an organization. There are, however, different ways to activate, sequence, navigate and lead this process, as exemplified by the companies studied here.

Top-down approach

Many models for advancing corporate citizenship advocate a planned approach that addresses simultaneously and systematically a company's risks and opportunities on the social, ethical and environmental fronts.[10] In this approach, practitioners develop a comprehensive, strategic and long-term plan for citizenship. It is typically executed from the top down in a formal change programme.

There is much to recommend this counsel. First, leadership and ongoing support from the top of the organization can focus attention on and lessen resistance to needed changes in priorities, structures and behaviour. Second, a comprehensive and planned approach builds momentum for change and promotes coordinated movement on multiple fronts. Third, a strategic perspective adds seeming relevance and urgency to change for line managers who might otherwise not see the importance of moving forward on citizenship in light of other competing, short-term concerns.

What are the problems with this model? First, in many companies, absent a crisis, top management may not initially regard corporate citizenship as a strategic requirement or have the time, energy or political capital to invest in leading system-wide change in this arena. Second, corporate staff units, who would be called upon to integrate their efforts, often don't see the necessity or value of working together, particularly as they are often stretched by their own

Traditional Top-Down   Catalytic

   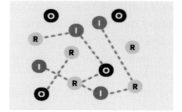

- ❏ Fixed plan   ❏ Adaptive and responsive
- ❏ Top-down, change from one source   ❏ Multidirectional, multisource change
- ❏ Managers as implementers   ❏ Managers as strategists and catalysts
- ❏ Directive   ❏ Emergent
- ❏ Predictable outcomes assumed   ❏ Lack of predictability recognized as part
                                              of process

Figure 3.2 Models of organizational change

agendas and competing for scarce resources. Third, many line managers, likely suffering from chronic 'change fatigue', are not apt to give even a top-down model their full support.

More broadly there are questions as to whether, even in the best of circumstances, a makeover of corporate citizenship in a company can be effectively managed through a strategic programme led from the top down. In many respects, citizenship fits into the class of situations that Emery and Trist call 'meta-problems' where understandings of risks, cause-effects and benefits are not agreed upon and even validity of information and how best to interpret it are open to question.[11] In such cases, practitioners have been advised to adopt what Weick has described as a less expansive, more gradual 'meta-strategy' where, for example, actions conceived of as 'small wins' limit the disruption and hence resistance to change in an organization, and the modest actions taken, help to clarify the situation and open possibilities for further movement.[12]

Leading change from the middle: a catalytic approach

In the three vignettes presented, and indeed in all the Executive Forum companies, change was activated and led from the middle of the organization in a non-programmatic, more or less organic pattern. In some cases, the middle-managers-cum-change-agents had tacit senior executive support behind them; in others scarcely any high level support at all. Interestingly, in a few of the cases, the managers made substantial progress in the face of daunting business downturns. What characterized their gradualist strategy?

Opportunism

One factor is opportunism – capitalizing on a seemingly unrelated event or chance occurrence. In Unocal's case, for example, a May 2002 shareholder proxy proposed that the company adopt the International Labour Organization (ILO) principles, including the right to free association. When the resolution garnered over 30 per cent of shareholder votes, it caught the attention of Unocal's CEO. The company was already revising its code of conduct and the shareholder resolution was transformed into an opportunity to engage both external and internal stakeholders in extensive dialogue. The CEO pledged that the team revising the code of conduct would take the concerns raised by stakeholders into consideration. This lent legitimacy and gave a high-level imprimatur to developing a stakeholder consultation process in the company.

This is an example of what Isenberg terms 'strategic opportunism'.[13] It had a multiplier effect as the consultations helped to move citizenship forward more broadly. Regelbrugge reported: 'It was another good step in our continued dialogue with people who want to see a lot of change within the company.' After the revised code was officially released, a similar shareholder resolution filed in late 2002 was withdrawn based on the content of the new code. And Unocal continued to meet with stakeholder groups to discuss how the code should be implemented. Greg Huger noted, 'The withdrawal of a shareholder proposal after release of the new code was a very obvious plus to the senior management of the company as well as to a lot of people who followed the company externally.' Unocal then expanded its stakeholder consultation into business areas. Our studies found that nearly all of the Executive Forum practitioners exploited opportunities to advance their agendas.

Incrementalism

A second factor in the catalytic process is the measured pacing of change. Lindblom, in his studies of public policy-making, depicted strategy as a fragmented process of serial and incremental decisions with little apparent coordination – a process he dubbed 'muddling through'.[14] Quinn, giving the process more shape, conceived of it as a process of 'logical incrementalism' whereby managers guide actions and events towards a conscious strategy through 'the simultaneous incremental process of strategy formulation and implementation'.[15] In the Executive Forum companies, managers adopted this incremental approach by frequently picking up on past or current initiatives and extending them into their domains.

One of Abbott's incremental moves towards integration has been the continued development and elaboration of its annual citizenship report. Abbott's Director of Global Corporate Citizenship and Policy, Kevin Callahan, opined:

The global citizenship report is a real catalyst for change, sometimes unbe-knownst to us. The report has brought people forward from many different departments saying, 'We're going to try to do something different in our department, and we want to check with you and see if you think this would be a good idea.' The citizenship report has become a mechanism through which initiatives to integrate corporate citizenship can be recognized, supported, and brought into alignment with Abbott's broad citizenship vision.

Emergence

A third factor in catalytic change is that it flows from multiple sources and that unpredictability is endemic to the process. Petro-Canada's managers reached for three separate handholds – a reputation team, aboriginal relations framework and total loss management system – to move their agenda forward. Only later were these separate initiatives harmoniously linked into a more integrative model of corporate responsibility. In the same light, Unocal's strategy – of conducting 'listening tours' to understand the needs of different business units – was designed to discover handholds to help move citizenship into business strategies. Ultimately, Unocal developed a 'player/coach' approach – using consultants with industry and citizenship expertise to coach business leaders how to liaise with stakeholders and then incorporate the input in their business plans. This general approach to navigating an unpredictable situation goes by the name of emergent strategy or, more aptly in this case, strategy-in-action.[16] This means that even as managers have a desired direction, their plans, actions and short-term goals continually shift depending on the situation at hand. Obviously it puts a premium on their capacities to flexibly adapt and creatively respond to changing circumstances.

Overall, this catalytic approach of leading from the middle acknowledges variability in 'readiness' in different parts of the companies, in senior management buy-in and in the relevance of citizenship initiatives depending on business issues, circumstances and needs. It also plays to the strengths of middle managers who are closer than senior managers to day-to-day operations and to front-line managers and staff and are better versed in the link between business and the social and environmental challenges encountered. While it is typical to characterize mid-management corporate staff as inflexible and bureaucratic, studies by Huy confirm that many have a surprisingly successful entrepreneurial bent when given the chance to lead change.[17]

In the end, this approach need not be any less systemic or strategic than its top-down counterpart. Indeed, by building connections among more bounded and localized initiatives and leveraging experience gained, practitioners can create momentum around more company-wide corporate citizenship activity without waiting for senior executives to generate or back an overarching plan. In fact, practitioners have found that when executives can respond to successful corporate citizenship initiatives, this strategy helps to generate more robust senior management buy-in and resources for action. What are the elements of this catalytic approach in practice?

Fundamentals for success

This combination of opportunism, incrementalism and emergence means that the change process towards citizenship across this sample of companies varied case by case. Nevertheless, we observed that the citizenship practitioners engaged in three distinct but overlapping classes of activities to move citizenship forward in their companies:

(1) *Building and transferring knowledge across the company.* The corporate citizenship managers gained broader and deeper knowledge of both their businesses and the context in which the business

operates so that they could approach functional and business unit
staff in conversations that focused on business problems and needs
rather than corporate citizenship per se.

(2) *Building relationships with corporate functional and business
unit managers.* Grounded in deeper knowledge of the business,
these managers opened new conversations, met people around
their companies, found new allies and established alliances in support of their goals.

(3) *Taking strategic action.* Finally, the managers took action, often
building on and extending existing efforts, to align citizenship
with the business, integrate it into the organization and institutionalize it in policy, mindsets and culture. Their knowledge and
relationships gave these actions relevance and affirmed that networks, rather than hierarchy, can also drive change.

Building knowledge

Decades of research into organizational change documents that the
more informed and knowledgeable people are about a current situation and the characteristics of a new course of action, the more recep-
tive they are to change.[18] This was received wisdom to the citizenship
practitioners studied here who built their own knowledge and stimulated knowledge-exchange around their companies.

Becoming familiar with business operations and issues. Often the
managers charged with advancing citizenship are from staff functions
and may not have much experience in business management. Located
typically in corporate communications, community relations, public affairs, the legal department, or environment, health and safety
(EH&S), they need knowledge about the business and the environment in which it operates to establish their credibility and understand
how line managers view the world.

Unocal's listening tour with line managers and Abbott's use of
select managers as a sounding board illustrate two ways practitioners
gained a general understanding of their business' strategies and goals.
At Agilent Technologies, the manager responsible for advancing corporate citizenship began discussions with product development managers and was included in their briefings on potential new product
ideas. At AMD, citizenship managers participated in strategic conversations about marketing on several key products and initiatives,

simultaneously gaining greater insight into marketing priorities and promulgating a citizenship perspective.

Locating and leveraging emerging issues. Petro-Canada's expansion into international markets for energy exploration motivated the company to take a fresh and comprehensive look at human rights, codes of conduct, contractor issues and improper payments. Stepping into this business arena, the leaders in its corporate responsibility function studied and detailed these new issues and updated policies and monitoring systems that were not attuned to global operations.

Equally important was the knowledge transfer from citizenship practitioners to line managers. The professional's awareness of anticipated legislation, emerging social issues and new trends in compliance, strategic philanthropy and the like, enabled them to educate managers around their companies and created more credibility for themselves as business partners. This ultimately informed AMD's launch of its 50/15 programme that aims to get 50 per cent of the world on the Internet by 2015 through a combination of new technology and supply-and-distribution channels, on the business side, complemented by community partnering and programmes to enlist and train users.

Bringing outside voices in. In a world where corporate scandals, media scrutiny and heightened activism are prevalent, the corporate citizenship managers studied worked to translate external pressure into internal motivation. As a former community advocate, Theresa Fay-Bustillos of Levi Strauss & Co. understood the need to bring stakeholder perspectives into the company. 'Who aren't we listening to?' she asked, meeting with NGOs and inviting them into her company One of the biggest problems she unearthed was that government law enforcement was weak in many countries in which Levi Strauss had manufacturing facilities, so she helped to build on the company's existing supply-chain practices to ensure:

(1) host government agencies had the resources to enforce the labour and environmental laws;
(2) local NGOs had assistance to advocate for better conditions; and
(3) local residents had access to micro-lending to create a more stable economic base.

Building relationships

Forging and fostering relationships and alliances are also strong predictors of garnering political support and successfully launching organizational change.[19] This was central for managers in advancing corporate citizenship in their companies. Indeed, because they typically operated without hierarchical authority over other corporate and business unit managers, and had scant budget and staff, they had to work through relationships to move the citizenship agenda in their firms.

Creating cross-functional alliances. Most commonly we observed alliances form between EH&S, community affairs and externally facing functions such as public affairs, procurement and communications. At AMD, for instance, Allyson Peerman, from the global community affairs function and Philip Trowbridge, part of the worldwide EH&S group, collaborated to strengthen initiatives that were 'owned' by their separate departments as well as to champion new citizenship efforts where they would work together.

Part of the reason they chose to collaborate was to minimize the resource commitment during a lean time for the company. 'From a resource point of view, and with a sea change of leadership occurring at AMD, it was not a good time to launch anything new', recalls Allyson Peerman, global community affairs director. 'And it certainly wasn't a good time to ask for more resources or schedule new meetings, because everyone felt overwhelmed as it was.'

In this and similar partnerships, we noticed that community affairs professionals typically demonstrate skills in, and have an affinity for, relationship building and are natural communicators. EH&S managers, by comparison, tended to be more introverted and have expertise in specific environmental issues and in the systems and processes that underpin their company's EH&S operations. Of course, both relational and technical skills are needed to expand the scope of citizenship into the other staff and business areas of a company. Not surprisingly, then, citizenship managers in these companies spent time developing their own relationships first.

Connecting key units and managers. Many practitioners believe that a bulletproof business case is required when soliciting support for citizenship from business units. Here, by comparison, we observed Executive Forum practitioners scouting for situations where managers had citizenship problems and building a business case with them. Several, for instance, found business allies in their supply chain areas – where a plethora of new supplier certification procedures and codes, as well as recognizable risks and threats, were all weighing down already overburdened managers. Abbott's global citizenship group, as one example, sought out the purchasing department as a partner because of issues of drug affordability, counterfeiting and the like that were troubling the entire industry.

As a result of positioning himself as an internal business partner, Abbott's Callahan helped the purchasing group to 'think about this as a part of their work' by conducting a supplier assessment and sending out risk-assessment questionnaires. Callahan also built bridges with the ethics and compliance function at Abbott. Now Abbott's citizenship group has connected these distinct functions into an informal working group that monitors societal expectations on a wide range of pharma issues.

Enlisting higher-level support. As noted, only a few of the Executive Forum practitioners had an explicit mandate from the CEOs or the leverage or influence provided by a top-down approach to change. Nevertheless, they faced situations where high-level support was needed to move their efforts forward. In some instances, this was accomplished by enlisting influential people and groups in an initiative, thereby influencing senior management. At Verizon, for example, the corporate responsibility manager worked actively with the company's Consumer Advisory Board to bring citizenship issues – involving everything from access to service to environmental standards – to the fore. This motivated Verizon's senior managers to form a corporate responsibility core team of twenty-five managers from all around the business to study the issues and develop an action plan. As a result, an issue formerly handled by corporate staff became a strategic priority for the company's leadership.

At Levi Strauss & Co., Fay-Bustillos recognized that employees are a key driver of incorporating citizenship into the business. 'Employees play an important role in asking questions about our practices and in consistently reinforcing the perception by executives that one of the top reasons people come to Levi Strauss & Co. is because they think we are a responsible company', she says, adding, 'They can't articulate specifically why we are responsible, nor do they need to. It's the consistency of the message that keeps corporate citizenship near the top of a business-focused agenda.'

Seeking out passionate supporters. Even as Agilent's Gail Brownell, quality systems manager, and Gene Endicott, from public affairs, began to collaborate on several business initiatives, their relationship stemmed more from mutual interest than professional mandate. An investor-relations manager connected Endicott and Brownell because of their personal interests in socially responsible mutual funds and their desire to become more involved in the measurement that fund questionnaires entailed.

As strategic partners, they are able to pursue a wider agenda than their individual efforts would allow. 'We just sensed that there was something we could work together on, and we are still figuring it out', says Endicott.

In addition, the company produces newsletters, sustainability training programmes and discussion groups that inform Agilent employees on citizenship trends and initiatives. Through these vehicles, the corporate citizenship practitioners have identified some impassioned individuals who seem to be willing to 'carry the torch' to the rest of the organization. 'It's just grassroots effort', remarked one manager, 'but it's a way to garner support from a division's management'.

Taking strategic action

Our research found that in these companies, without a sense of urgency or a concerted push from senior executives for corporate citizenship, managers had to calibrate when and how much to push the envelope, take leadership and be creative. While not always conscious of it, the corporate citizenship practitioners in our study adopted a dynamic and interactive approach to strategy – taking action on multiple fronts and operating as both strategists and catalysts for change.[20] We classify their action into three different, but related and sometimes overlapping, modes:

(1) Strategies for aligning corporate citizenship and business goals across a company.
(2) Strategies for integrating corporate citizenship into company structure, policies, processes and practices.
(3) Strategies for institutionalizing corporate citizenship in a company's culture and business philosophy, ensuring that it is sustainable.

Alignment strategies

Aligning corporate citizenship requires connecting it with corporate purposes and business objectives across the company. We've seen how Unocal managers used their business knowledge and AMD leveraged relationships to engage line managers in citizenship. What does it take to get citizenship and business aims aligned?

Creating a coherent context for corporate citizenship. In several of the cases, corporate citizenship managers worked to align a variety of existing company activities under the broader umbrella of corporate citizenship. Gene Endicott demonstrated this strategy in his work: 'I have to look at the whole collection of Agilent activities – operational practices, what we do as a business, our products', he said.

Part of assuming a leadership role in corporate citizenship entails pulling all this together to align it around corporate citizenship … I am not talking about something super complicated. It's about saying that our employee-relations practices are part of what we do as a corporate citizen. EH&S are part of what we do as a corporate citizen. Same with being involved in the community: align it and put it under a common heading.

Being able to articulate – in an inclusive and declarative way – how different functions, programmes and operations connect to corporate citizenship seems to be a key step to aligning corporate citizenship and business goals.

Because several Agilent products, such as air- and water-quality testing equipment, are marketed for environmentally responsible efforts, the next step has been to connect corporate citizenship and product development. 'It's a matter of getting others in the company to think that corporate citizenship is not a public affairs responsibility', Endicott says. 'Our business managers also play as a result of products and technologies we offer, which address issues that our stakeholders often care very passionately about.' Highlighting this connection has enabled Endicott to fit at least some aspects of product development under the citizenship umbrella.

Developing a common understanding of vocabulary and scope. While showing how citizenship encompasses a wide range of interests, actually 'naming' the thrust and clarifying its scope makes it a beacon for alignment. Reeta Roy and her colleagues had great success transforming 'issues management' into a citizenship function. When she was named vice-president for global citizenship and policy, however, both the title and change in name for the function gave the work a new identity in the company. She noted, 'We are not just managing issues but really trying to develop points of view and take action to address challenging issues facing our company and industry. (The new name) is more in keeping with our values and our mission and with how we support the business.'

AMD's Peerman and Trowbridge at first used their term 'sustainability' to encompass the social and environmental issues that fit under their purview. Then the company began to receive inquiries from socially responsible investing firms and from their B2B customers. This brought human resources, investor relations and marketing into the conversation. As a result, Trowbridge convened a cross-functional group. During one of their meetings, the group determined that 'corporate responsibility' was a term that more aptly described the company goals and best expressed its core values.

Using a cross-functional group to connect the business. AMD used its cross-functional group as a platform to discuss a variety of issues that were normally seen as the domain of 'the business'. The group compiled a comprehensive list of issues that surface in customer questionnaires, SRI surveys, supply chain audits, and the like. It then developed an 'issues matrix' to assess systematically any gaps in performance. 'We went through a SWOT analysis, looking at our strengths, weaknesses, opportunities and threats in each area', says Trowbridge. 'But we also asked the fundamental question: do we have a programme that addresses this issue? And if not, do we need one? How would people rank this issue in terms of importance to AMD?' He added, 'A healthy dialogue on an issue often results in people becoming more comfortable with change.' In addition, these conversations promoted a collective sense of corporate citizenship such that many individuals – not just the specialists – understood the core issues facing the company.

Integration strategies

Integrating corporate citizenship requires that it is embedded in the structures, processes and systems across business and functional areas of a company. Next are some of the integration strategies the managers we studied used effectively.

Leveraging existing structures, systems and processes. Integration can be accelerated when existing systems processes and structures are used or modified for purposes of corporate citizenship. Certainly Abbott leveraged its social reporting as a means to regularly convene people and interests throughout the business. Unocal, in turn, adapted its Country Risk Assessment Process. Previously concerned with commercial, political and environmental factors, the corporate responsibility team made sure this assessment included consideration of social factors when assessing countries for potential oil and gas projects.

Rather than reinvent the wheel, managers we studied sought opportunities to introduce citizenship into what already exists to lessen resistance, maximize efficiency and avoid redundancy. The managers were emphatic about the advantages and employed it as a central operating principle in their corporate citizenship-related work. They demonstrated creative range in finding opportunities to expand, revise and recalibrate measurement systems, planning processes and decision-making criteria to take account of the social and environmental dimensions of business.

Creating a high-level governance structure. Social and environmental initiatives at Petro-Canada were to this point led by three executives in community affairs, EH&S and human resources. Despite the best efforts of this trio, accountability for the range of citizenship-related activity was too diffuse and the group came to realize the need to coordinate and champion the integration of corporate responsibility across the company. This fragmented approach to citizenship was not consistent with the company's systems-oriented culture and several aspects of citizenship, such as attention to culture-specific issues in newly acquired international businesses, were falling through the cracks.

The trio conducted an assessment of Petro-Canada's corporate responsibility initiatives and operations in early 2002, with the intention, says Community Investment Manager Hazel Gillespie, of making 'a really strong move forward on corporate responsibility in the company'. The research process included:

(1) using a consultant to benchmark their company against best practices;
(2) conducting in-depth conversations with counterparts at other oil and gas companies; and
(3) meeting with internal stakeholders.

As a result of this research, the team favoured creating a top-level corporate responsibility governance structure and management system. Anticipating that achieving buy-in from the executives would be difficult, however, they made their case over the course of a year. In due course, their goals were achieved. Petro-Canada adopted a simplified corporate responsibility management system as a companion to the existing total loss management systems and created an Executive Corporate Responsibility Steering Committee that would set policy, oversee citizenship in the company overall and ensure accountability for compliance.

Establishing a formal corporate citizenship position. When the moment was right, some managers in our study proposed creating a formal, senior management citizenship position for their company. As a third outcome of their research, the team at Petro-Canada recommended creating a director-level citizenship position. They made the case that, among other benefits, a senior leader and integrated function would give the company a strategic approach; clarify accountabilities; reduce re-work and overlap; close gaps in management systems and align their positions and activities regarding related issues; and potentially reduce time spent in meetings and committees.

This required due diligence as to how this type of position functioned in other companies. Top leaders ratified this recommendation, too. As one of the leadership team commented, 'To have somebody who wakes up thinking about corporate responsibility every day is great – it (helps) to bring all the pieces together and to organize and coordinate and think more strategically about it.'

Institutionalization strategies

Institutionalizing corporate citizenship helps to ensure its durability by embedding it in a company's cultural identity and brand image. Firms like Johnson & Johnson, Herman Miller and Timberland seem to have citizenship 'DNA' that keeps their values and image constant in the face of changing economic, social and ecological pressures. What does it take to sustain the continued development of citizenship in a company?

Building citizenship on values. Although Levi Strauss & Co. has been a pioneer of many corporate citizenship activities, including responsible sourcing and workplace diversity, the company had not formalized its 'profits through principles' mantra through formal processes, operating models or progress measurement. Having noted that the company's brands used value propositions as a tool to define their qualities and character for consumers, Fay-Bustillos worked with the company's worldwide leadership team to develop a value proposition for corporate citizenship. Accordingly, and with the blessing of the CEO, she convened a cross-functional, multi-level working group around corporate citizenship, which included some top executives.

Fay-Bustillos, a lawyer and community activist, focused the group on understanding the company's 150-year legacy of corporate citizenship; listening to employees, executives and shareholders; and identifying current and potential future societal issues facing the apparel and textile industry. The group's work highlighted how citizenship was material to the company's strategic decisions. As Fay-Bustillos put it, 'It is about listening to the business people talk, boiling it down, and then using their own language to sell it back to them.'

Even as top executives struggled with the 'fast fashion' trends in consumer behaviour in the market, and launched a massive cost-cutting campaign, Robert Hanson, President of North America and of the US Levi Strauss brand, joined the working group's conversation and asked: 'Who are we?' Out of the discussions, a corporate citizenship value proposition emerged aligned with the company's values – empathy, originality, integrity and courage. The worldwide leadership team then pledged to educate employees on the new value proposition, incorporate it into the strategic business planning process and hold themselves accountable for making progress going forward.

Connecting citizenship to the brand

Another powerful force for institutionalization is to connect citizenship to a corporate-wide understanding of the brand and business. Certainly Petro-Canada used branding to leverage its citizenship efforts as it expanded globally. As Gillespie says, 'If you look at products or services from IBM, you can tell it's an IBM piece of information, but you couldn't tell that from Petro-Canada. Our message was fragmented. The whole idea was to create some key messages so that our stakeholders would understand what Petro-Canada is and define our reputation.' The focus on defining and communicating reputation gave these and other corporate citizenship practitioners a platform from which to internally promote the need for ramped-up citizenship efforts.

Agilent, spun-off from Hewlett-Packard, had a strong legacy in citizenship but it was not yet a part of the new company's internal identity or a brand differentiator in the marketplace. To build the case, its citizenship practitioners sought to demonstrate the importance of citizenship in a way that resonated with its analytically minded culture. They first gathered data from internal stakeholders about Agilent's corporate citizenship efforts and then included questions about it in the company's employee survey. By running correlations between questions about citizenship and loyalty, Endicott was able to demonstrate how the two are connected in employees' minds.

Though the employee survey information proved useful, Endicott knew that the case for citizenship would be enhanced if it could be cross-referenced with external, third-party data. He purchased GlobeScan's CSR Monitor data which showed, across companies in twenty-two countries, a link between CSR and reputation. He subsequently had Globescan conduct a customized survey in Agilent which personalized this link and also highlighted different key issues to address in the United States, Korea and elsewhere.

This bridge between citizenship and brand gave some resilience to the company's re-emphasis on citizenship. 'I'm starting to see corporate citizenship show up in more of the sales and marketing materials', Endicott says. 'Similarly, our brand management folks – who drive our corporate advertising – have also shown a real willingness and interest in highlighting corporate citizenship as a part of our overall advertising, and that's something I take some pride in. I can't claim to have ownership of it, but it's an example of how over time this concerted effort starts to permeate.'

Catalysing change: lessons from integrating corporate citizenship

While the research could to some degree differentiate between the more cognitive, relational and action-oriented interventions of these practitioners, it would be a mistake to attribute their success at integrating citizenship to any specific, discrete activities. Regrettably, some texts on organization change and many 'how to' books leave the impression that there are linear cause–effect relationships between interventions and their results, or specific problems and their solution. By comparison, there is a long literature and rich lore on patterns of organization change that emphasize its interactive and systemic character.[21] When practitioners confront a 'meta-problem' – like integrating citizenship into their firms – the force of change flows from multiple sources and moves in multiple directions. Thus, scholars today turn to models of non-linear dynamics to depict such processes of organization change and transformation.[22] In this framing, it helps to think of organizations as complex adaptive systems (CAS) that take in and dissipate energy. Attention turns, then, to how a mix of factors, in this case cognitive, relational and action strategies, together infuse and catalyse energy in a system and take it to a new state.

Broadly, the field of complexity science is concerned with the study of emergent phenomena – behaviours and patterns – that occur at the multiple levels of systems. What is key in the context of change theory is these emerge from non-linear interactions among complex systems that veer between equilibrium and randomness.[23] It is at this 'edge of chaos' that living systems are most dynamic and, in effect, naturally change. Such systems are characterized as 'complex adaptive systems' (CAS) – a term coined by theorists at the Sante Fe Institute.

Many of the CAS concepts neatly encapsulate the catalytic function of the efforts undertaken by the citizenship practitioners we studied. For instance, Prigogine's work in chemistry highlights the importance of disequilibria in a system because it 'dissipates' structure in order that the system might recreate itself in a new form.[24] The analogue in change management vocabulary is to 'unfreeze' existing patterns in a system through new inputs. Certainly the practitioners here promoted disequilibria by, for example, engaging external stakeholders and bringing their views into their companies, highlighting issues in the market and society that might bear on the firm, breaking through 'silos' to connect different people and interests, and more generally making a case for change.

Another practical implication is the need to confront tensions between the 'old' and 'new' way. In periods of high instability, complex systems hit a 'bifurcation point' or 'fork in the road' at which energies for change either dissipate in ways that allow an old 'attractor' to reassert itself or a new one to shift the system into a new form. This underscores the importance of a new or 'strange' attractor – like a future vision – in change management. Efforts to create a coherent context for citizenship, to 'name' the work and to link it to values, business strategies and the corporate brand are all aimed at shifting understandings and the profile of citizenship in a company. Wheatley, among others, suggests that the equivalent to an attractor in human systems is 'meaning'.[25]

CAS theory also offers some new ideas on the process of change. For example, a chemical process that both breaks down existing elements and recombines them in new forms involves catalysis. Knowledge has catalytic properties: it can simultaneously disconfirm old understandings and point to new directions. The forming of relationships and networks also has these properties: it can disrupt existing structural configurations and set new ones in motion. What are possible catalytic combinations of knowledge and relationships that can affect a change in citizenship in companies?

It is commonplace for organizations today to rely on boundary-spanning roles and scanning systems to monitor and signal turbulence in their environment. The socio-technical system idea, to create localized 'intelligent' systems where analysis can be undertaken and control exercised closest to the source of any 'disturbance' is being built into many work designs, specifically semi-autonomous work teams. The cross-functional teams many companies developed here, whose members scan internal and external issues, benchmark other company's practices, share and debate perspectives and operate as a 'sounding board', serve as an intelligent system to guide citizenship in a firm.

When citizenship practitioners serve as business partners to line managers they also gather and dispense intelligence and help their managers work through combined citizenship/business issues. Describing this boundary-spanning and bridge-building role, Kevin Callahan of Abbott says, 'It's not just about looking at what others are doing, but leading the company to help find solutions.' 'We help (managers) get through conflicting opinions and demands and work to provide leadership in the organization to stay ahead of these issues.'

At the level of the enterprise, developments in communication networks and the creation of communities of practice help to ensure that information flows across functional and hierarchical boundaries and that the right people can organize around it.[26] Through internal consultations, taskforces and involvement in supplier certification and social reporting, the citizenship practitioners built and fed an extensive communication network in their companies and created a corporate-wide community of practice. Interestingly, the Executive Forum extended that network across firms and broadened the practitioner's own community of practice.

CAS theorists have identified the importance of self-referencing in systems whereby small changes feed back on themselves and reverberate through the larger system.[27] The dynamic, called autopoieses or self-organization, involves a series of non-linear interactions that set the path by which a system evolves. What does this have to say about the practitioners and practices studied here?

(1) *The importance of small wins.* Most accounts of organizational transformation emphasize how interventions necessarily have to be bigger, deeper and wider to affect the 'system-as-a-whole'. CAS advises thinking again about small changes – the movement of a butterfly's wing – and thus the importance of small wins. At almost every Executive Forum company, the practitioners started small, advanced operational initiatives to demonstrate the value of citizenship, and then built on successes with more comprehensive efforts. As Petro-Canada put it, 'slow and steady wins the race'. More formally, this means that incremental additions of knowledge and modest new configurations of relationships together built a 'wave' for change to emerge.

(2) *The value of 're-using' structures.* Abrahamson's analysis of the value of more incremental, as opposed to transformational, change in organizations shows that by 'reusing' structures and/or 'recombining' processes managers can employ already culturally-approved mechanisms, build on past precedents, and thus allay at least some resistance to change.[28] The practitioners here 'piggy-backed' on existing measurement schemes, assessment and control systems, reputation projects, and the like by adding citizenship content and thereby moving their agendas forward. Adding new input into existing activities and new purpose to old structures set the system, in CAS language, on a new course. Practitioners prospected new areas of opportunity in their companies, such as, in one case, injecting citizenship materials into an executive development programme and, in another, experimenting with cause-related marketing.

(3) *The need for 'balancing acts'*. Brown and Eisenhardt's studies of complexity in strategy highlight several catalytic interventions that affect strategic change.[29] They frame these in the form of complex balancing acts, wherein managers have to, for example, balance past precedents versus future needs or movement towards intended directions versus available opportunities. In these citizenship cases, managers had to balance corporate interests against those of line managers, trade off the benefits of conforming to external codes versus developing ones unique to their own businesses, help their companies navigate through risks versus opportunities of taking a bolder stance on social issues, and formulate a business case for larger initiatives versus moving quickly to gain quick wins. This involved improvisation, time pacing, and what Brown and Eisenhardt term 'co-adapting' among the many interests in their companies.

(4) *The power of the passionate practitioner*. Deborah Meyerson's account of 'tempered radicals' shows how mid-level executives, often in staff positions in companies, can effect big change by building coalitions of supporters and leveraging many small wins.[30] Key to their success is their personal passion, which energizes a system, and personal commitment to 'being their true selves'. Her studies, and others like them, herald a fresh look at the power of the single individual in organizational transformation.

The managers studied here, each in their own way, were passionate about the possibility of a robust and integrated corporate citizenship programme for their company. For many of the managers, their passion was quite personal and not confined to their designated professional role. 'My passion and commitment are how I want to make a difference', says Agilent's Brownell. 'This is the kind of work I've wanted to do ever since I decided where to go to college.'

Similarly, Chris Lloyd, director of public policy and corporate responsibility at Verizon, related a similar longstanding commitment:

My interest in sustainable practices derives from my family background. My grandmother was always very pragmatic, using what meagre resources she had available to her. She also had a long-term focus, trying to develop ways of doing things that would still be valid in an uncertain future. The reason I first enjoyed my role in environmental policy for Verizon and now corporate citizenship is that both roles are true to my values. I have the unique opportunity of assisting the company to be conscious of its impact on others and to act responsibly.

Still the managers participating in the Executive Forum were pragmatic about the realities of corporate culture and organizational change. Most explicitly recognized that initiating and building momentum for corporate citizenship in their company is slow work. 'This is a slow-moving train', says AMD's Allyson Peerman, global community affairs director. 'You don't expect to reach your goals overnight. This work is about coalition building and that takes a long time. But at the end of the day, the results should be stronger and longer lasting than a fleeting programme.'

Social scientists are only beginning to identify how passionate practitioners, who are knowledgeable about their subjects and skilled at working through allies and building networks, can of themselves change the 'field' surrounding a new endeavour.[31] They also rely on these networks for intellectual and emotional support. In many respects, that was the true benefit of the Executive Forum for the practitioners. Referring to her involvement, Fay-Bustillos of Levi Strauss & Co. said:

This is a very collegial environment to work in. We don't always appreciate what we can accomplish just by networking and being part of different external organizations that are interested in moving the agenda. You learn. You get ideas. You get encouragement. You have a group of people you can call up, and they will help you. There are people at other companies who are more than willing to collaborate. Being a part of these external groups is a way to move the internal agenda at your company.

Notes

1 See N. Tichy, H. Hornstein and J.J. Nisberg, 'Participative Organization Diagnosis and Intervention Strategies: Developing Emergent Pragmatic Theories of Change', *The Academy of Management Review*, 1/2 (1976): 109–20.

2 See P.H. Mirvis, 'Academic-practitioner Learning Forums: A New Model for Inter-organizational Research', in A.B. Shani, N. Adler, S.A. Mohrman, W.A. Pasmore and B. Stymne (eds.), *Handbook of Collaborative Management Research* (Thousand Oaks, CA: Sage, 2007).

3 The sample companies were chosen to reflect different industries, sizes and customer bases and to encompass a variety of economic, social and environmental challenges. Each company had already developed some aspect of corporate citizenship and their representatives were eager to learn from one another to move their agendas forward. While the sample size was insufficient to provide a representative view of what is happening in any given industry, it did allow the research team an overview of some of corporate citizenship trends and activities common to many different kinds of companies today.

4 See D. Matten and A. Crane, 'Corporate Citizenship: Toward an Extended Theoretical Conceptualization', *Academy of Management Review*, 30/1 (2005): 166–79.

5 H.C. de Bettignies, 'Reviewing Meanings & Contexts of Role of Business in Society', presentation at the launch of the European Academy of Business in Society, Fontainebleau, 5 July 1992.

6 See J. Post and B. Altman, 'Models of Corporate Greening: How Corporate Social Policy and Organizational Learning Inform Leading Edge Environmental Management', *Research in Corporate Social Performance and Policy*, 13 (1992): 3–29; S. Zadek, 'The Path to Corporate Responsibility', *Harvard Business Review* (December 2004): 125–33.

7 P.H. Mirvis and B. Googins, 'Stages of Corporate Citizenship: A Developmental Framework', *California Management Review*, 48/2 (2006): 104–26.

8 See B. Googins, P.H. Mirvis and S. Rochlin, *Beyond Good Company* (New York: Palgrave Macmillan, 2007).

9 See P.H. Mirvis, 'Environmentalism in Progressive Businesses', *Journal of Organizational Change Management*, 7/4 (1994): 82–100; P.H. Mirvis, 'Transformation at Shell: Commerce and Citizenship', *Business and Society Review*, 105/1 (2000): 63–84.

10 D. Dunphy, A. Griffiths and S. Benn, *Organisational Change for Corporate Sustainability* (London: Routledge, 2003); W.B. Werther and D. Chandler, *Strategic Corporate Social Responsibility: Stakeholders in a Global Environment* (Thousand Oaks, CA: Sage, 2005).

11 F.E. Emery and E.L. Trist, 'The Causal Texture of Organizational Environments', *Human Relations*, 18 (1965): 21–32.

12 K.E. Weick, 'Small Wins: Redefining the Scale of Social Problems', *American Psychologist*, 39/1 (1984): 40–9.

13 D.J. Isenberg, 'The Tactics of Strategic Opportunism', *Harvard Business Review*, 65 (1987): 92–7.

14 C. Lindblom, 'The Science of Muddling through', *Public Administration Review*, 19/2 (1959): 79–81.

15 B. Quinn, *Strategies for Change: Logical Incrementalism* (Homewood, IL: Irwin, 1980), p. 145.

16 See H. Mintzberg, 'Patterns in Strategy Formation', *Management Science*, 24/9 (1978): 934–48; J. Moncrieff, 'Is Strategy making a Difference?', *Long Range Planning Review*, 32/2 (1999): 273–6.

17 Q.N. Huy, 'In Praise of Middle Managers', *Harvard Business Review* (September 2001): 73–9.

18 See G. Zaltman and R. Duncan, *Strategies for Change* (New York: Wiley, 1977); A.A. Armenakis and A.G. Bedian, 'Organizational Change: A Review of Theory and Research in the 1990s', *Journal of Management*, 25/3 (1999): 293–315.

19 N. Tichy, *Managing Strategic Change: Technical, Political, and Cultural Dynamics* (New York: Wiley, 1983); J. Kotter, *Leading Change* (Boston, MA: Harvard Business School Press, 1996).

20 J. Collins, 'Turning Goals into Results: The Power of Catalytic Mechanisms', *Harvard Business Review* (July–August, 1999); C. Markides, 'A Dynamic View of Strategy', *Sloan Management Review*, 40 (spring 1999): 55–63.

21 See L. Greiner, 'Patterns of Organization Change', *Harvard Business Review* (May–June, 1967): 119–31; P.H. Mirvis and D.N. Berg, *Failures in Organization Development and Change* (New York: Wiley, 1973); M. Beer and N. Nohria, 'Cracking the Code of Change', *Harvard Business Review* (September, 2000): 133–41; and L. Rising and M.L. Mann, *Fearless Change: Patterns for Introducing New Ideas* (London: Addison-Wesley, 2004).

22 See R.E. Quinn and K.S. Cameron (eds.), *Paradox and Transformation: Toward a Theory of Change in Organization and Management* (Cambridge, MA: Ballinger, 1988); K. Dooley, 'Complexity Science Models of Organizational Change', in S. Poole and A. Van De Ven (eds.), *Handbook of Organizational Change and Development* (Oxford: Oxford University Press, 2004), pp. 354–73.

23 J.H. Holland, *Hidden Order* (Reading, MA: Helix, 1995); S. Kauffman, *At Home In The Universe: The Search For Laws Of Complexity* (Harmondsworth: Penguin, 1996).

24 I. Prigogine, *Order Out of Chaos* (New York: Random House, 1984).

25 M.J. Wheatley, *Leadership and the New Science: Learning About Organization from an Orderly Universe* (San Francisco: Berrett-Koehler Publishers, 1993).

26 See E. Wenger, R. McDermott and W. Synder, *Cultivating Communities of Practice: A Guide to Managing Knowledge* (Boston: Harvard Business School Press, 2002).

27 See E. Jantsch, *The Self-Organizing Universe* (Oxford: Pergamon, 1980); H.R. Maturana and F.J. Varela, *The Tree Of Knowledge* (Boston: Shambhala Publications, 1987); P.M. Senge, *The Fifth Discipline: The Art and Practice of the Learning Organization* (New York: Doubleday/Currency, 1990).
28 E. Abrahamson, *Change Without Pain* (Boston: Harvard Business School Press, 2004).
29 S. Brown and K. Eisenhardt, *Competing on the Edge: Strategy as Structured Chaos* (Boston, MA: Harvard Business School Press, 1998).
30 D. Meyerson, *Tempered Radicals: How Everyday Leaders Inspire Change at Work* (Boston: Harvard Business School Press, 2003).
31 R. Quinn, *Change the World: How Ordinary People can Accomplish Extraordinary Results* (San Francisco: Jossey-Bass, 2000).

4 | CSR in search of a management model: a case of marginalization of a CSR initiative

AURÉLIEN ACQUIER

Introduction

A key trend of recent years is the emergence of CSR as a managerial field.[1] As noted by *The Economist*, 'Corporate Social Responsibility is now an industry of its own right, and a flourishing profession as well.'[2] This field involves the creation of a set of markets devoted to the communication, measurement and evaluation of CSR and Corporate Social Performance (CSP).[3] It is also marked by the multiplication of sectoral codes of conduct and other global standards.[4] It has also been accompanied by the emergence of new kinds of actors and CSR experts outside (CSR consultants and auditors) and within companies (sustainability or CSR departments have been created within most public companies) and the multiplication of educational programmes dealing with CSR management.

To some extent, this situation echoes the 'Corporate Social Responsiveness' era of the late 1960s and 1970s.[5] In a turbulent societal context, various companies had developed issues management departments to handle pressing social controversies, such as equal rights for minorities, consumer rights or environmental concerns. Researchers who studied those dynamics based their approach on the idea that CSR was not only a question of ethics, but that it also involved specific and difficult managerial problems. In itself, managers' will to increase the social good was not enough to implement efficient and sustainable CSR programmes. Rather, a key question was to understand how to select the most pressing issues, take relevant decisions, develop the appropriate management frameworks, tools and implementation approaches to respond to social pressures. Beyond individual ethics, CSR was thus to be considered as a managerial problem on its own.

To a large extent, these arguments are still valid today. For example, many uncertainties remain about the real impact of CSR practices[6] and the most appropriate ways to translate corporate commitment for CSR and Sustainable Development (SD) into management practices. There is both confusion and heterogeneity in the way companies manage their CSR and SD programmes.[7]

This chapter addresses this challenge by exploring *CSR management models*. A management model is a combination of:

(1) a definition of performance;
(2) a set of management objects; and
(3) organizational devices, processes and skills.

Owing to the current level of diversity in actors' approaches to CSR management, our research[8] has brought us to the conclusion that there is no general and commonly accepted CSR management model to date. However, the ability to develop appropriate and coherent CSR management models is critical to the institutionalization of CSR within firms. To illustrate this claim, we present a case study of a European energy company that we will call Energy Co. We demonstrate that in spite of an initially favourable organizational context, the failure to develop a coherent CSR management model led to the progressive marginalization of the company's CSR initiative.

The chapter is structured as follows: we begin by underlining two symptoms of the difficulty to account for managerial action in the field of CSR and present our definition of a management model. In a second part, we present a case study that reveals how the failure of Energy Co. to define and implement a coherent CSR management model led to the progressive marginalization of the CSR policy and a switch in corporate strategic orientations, from 'sustainable' to 'profitable' development. In a third part, we explore the implications of our case study and pose several questions related to CSR management models. In particular, we underline the importance of developing an innovative approach to CSR management.

CSR in search of management models

Adopting a managerial approach on CSR

Several symptoms suggest that in spite of broad social demands for CSR, it remains difficult to theorize CSR and its management implications. A first example is offered by the lingering controversies, both within academic and practitioner circles, about *the relationships between CSR and performance*. Within the academic circle, a review of the countless studies investigating the link between financial and social performance reveals the various conceptual weaknesses of this body of research.[9] The first difficulty relates to the definition and measurement of social performance or sustainability constructs. How can CSR or sustainability be measured? Do rating agencies provide meaningful measures of sustainability performance?[10] Should sustainability be linked to environmental performance? Are toxic-waste statistics a relevant measure of environmental performance and thus sustainability performance?[11] Beyond unavoidable debates about the relevance of statistical constructs to measure social or sustainability performance, the value of this research may also be limited by an inappropriate and oversimplified approach of what CSR is. Indeed, it is problematic to put such different conventions as 'social' and 'financial' performance at the same level and to define them in static terms. What is the value of a correlation between emergent, heterogeneous and contested 'social performance' indicators on the one side, and very standardized financial performance indicators on the other? Rather than defining corporate social performance as linked to financial performance, the value of the concept of CSR may lie in its ability to question and to reframe traditional financial measures. Since the content of CSR is constantly being redefined (owing to the most salient social debates), every measure of CSP is a specific, socially embedded, incomplete, subjective and temporary translation of CSR. The inability to account for the evolving nature of CSR constitutes a strong limitation of the various studies that try to discover the relationship between CSP and financial performance. Rather than simply taking CSR, sustainability and financial performance for granted, researchers should also investigate their dynamic interactions. Sustainability and CSR could thus be analysed in terms of the challenge of moving the frontiers of the economic game and to redefining corporate measurements of performance. Accordingly, the central challenge becomes the ability of sustainability and CSR issues to reframe the economic game through a dynamic of integration of externalities.[12] So far, such an approach has not been investigated. The inconclusive results of the studies that investigate the relationship between social and financial performance underline the difficulty of conceptualizing social performance and understanding the dynamics of CSR.

Those academic debates are echoed in the practitioner sphere, where intense debates concerning the 'business case' for CSR or sustainable development also illustrate the difficulty of theorizing CSR management. The 'triple bottom line' concept, which has played a central role in the contemporary diffusion of CSR, appears as a fuzzy and contested construct.[13] The real potential of the 'market for virtue' is also being put into question by various actors.[14] Today, both researchers and practitioners strive to develop a more contingent approach to the link between CSR policies and performance. They try to identify how certain CSR policies, in certain situations and specific organizational contexts, may be most appropriate to develop specific strategic resources.[15] Uncertainties about the nature of CSR and sustainability constructs, the definition of performance and the tenuous link between specific practices and performance, reveal the difficulty of conceptualizing action and developing a common representation about how such processes should be managed.

A second illustration of the lack of management models is illustrated by the ambiguity of sustainable managers' position within firms. Most publicly held firms in Europe and the United States have created CSR or sustainability departments over the last five years. Beyond a broad mission to communicate with external stakeholders (mostly through the development of a CSR reporting framework and the creation of a non-financial section in the annual report), there are wide uncertainties about the role, organization and internal position of a sustainability department within a company. Much of the problem comes from the fuzziness of concepts such as CSR or sustainable development and their link with other actors and activities within the firm. It is also difficult to understand the distinctive role of sustainability departments since other units (human resources and departments of environmental issues) are often already in charge of the field of activities covered by the 'triple bottom line'. How can the existence of new managers or departments devoted to sustainability be legitimized? How can a sustainability department be positioned vis-à-vis already established functional departments (finance, human resource management, environment) that already manage the interface between the company and its financial, social and environmental stakeholders? Should a sustainability department be placed under the responsibility of one of the above functional departments or should it be at the same hierarchical level? Should it take an operational role on specific issues or should it be positioned as a cross-functional actor, with the mission to develop policies and coordinate existing functions within the firm? Should a sustainability department develop privileged relationships with external actors (such as ethical investors or non-financial analysts) or should it focus on the internal aspects of the company and develop a new body of expertise related to the management of complex environmental and social issues?

Those questions illustrate the difficulty of systematically understanding the role of CSR in firms. Fundamental questions remain unanswered regarding what is to be managed, how issues should be managed and how to define and to evaluate performance. In this emerging and blurry situation, it is necessary to systematically analyse the concrete dynamics of CSR management within firms. We will now develop the notion of a CSR management model to systematically investigate managerial action in the CSR field. This notion will help us to consider SD or CSR management as domains of managerial action on their own, i.e. distinct from traditional environmental and human resource management. Taking seriously the idea of a systemic and integrative approach between economic, social and environmental dimensions conveyed by concepts such as the 'triple bottom line' or blended values approaches,[16] we will try to better understand the organizational dimensions of sustainability management.

Management models: definition and relevance for CSR analysis

We propose the concept of 'management model' to systematically account for corporate actions in the field of CSR. The notion of 'model' refers to a formalized and systematic representation of a set of practices. The idea of an interplay between action and representations (individual or collective) is quite common within social sciences[17] and constitutes a fundamental pivot within learning theories.[18] A management model regroups a set of representations, organizational structures and processes describing a dominant and coherent logic of action. A management model combines three elements that are necessary to develop and systematize a management approach within and outside a company. It regroups:

Table 4.1 *The 'external control' approach of CSR management*

	External control approach
Performance model	Increase corporate control by stakeholders by reducing information asymmetries. Extension of current governance models to a new range of stakeholders.
Set of management objects	All corporate activities. Establish and implement stringent standards concerning reporting and auditing activities.
Set of organizational devices, processes and skills	Standardization, reporting tools, top-down logic, performance evaluation protocols, regulation, external verification.

(1) a definition of performance;
(2) a set of management objects; and
(3) organizational devices, processes and skills.

To illustrate how the concept can be used in the field of CSR, we will characterize each variable and illustrate it with a CSR management model that, we believe, has been the dominant approach to CSR management so far. This model will be referred to as the 'external control approach'[19] (see Table 4.1) and relies on:

(1) a definition of performance: by nature, managerial action, with its intentional and purposeful character, relies on a definition of effective action. The definition of performance refers to the identification of objectives associated with business decisions. Those objectives may be multiple and vague, they need not necessarily be expressed in narrow terms. For example, shareholders may try to *reduce top management latitude* through more stringent standards of reporting; an engineer might seek to establish an experimentation protocol that would *maximize learning*; and a CEO may strive for his or her company to *acquire a dominant position* in a given business context. Very often, formal goal definition is the domain of action of corporate strategy. The external control

approach seeks to promote further control of corporate activities by external actors and promote corporate accountability to a wide array of stakeholders. In that case, performance can be defined as *the ability to increase transparency and reduce information asymmetries between the company and its stakeholders.*

(2) a set of management objects: management objects constitute the second pillar of a management model. They provide the 'targets' of action. In the field of CSR, an operational difficulty relates to the wide diversity of potential objects. The external control approach potentially involves *all activities of a firm* through the development of new reporting and auditing standards that need to be implemented within the firm.

(3) a set of organizational devices, processes and skills: finally, a management model relies on a set of actors, processes and skills, that are required to act according to the goals. A management model makes implicit hypotheses about the different actors involved in a managerial action and the way they should interact. From these hypotheses, it is possible to infer what actors' hierarchical positions should be, and the devices, processes and skills they require in order be effective. In the case of CSR management, the external control approach would underline the need to create *dedicated controllers within the firms and to implement a stringent form of reporting in a top-down logic.* This model would also give a very prominent role to regulation, external verifiers and auditing skills.

Several elements should be added to clarify our approach of management models. First, a management model can simultaneously result from and structure actors' behaviours. Such models can be implicit, evolutionary, inferred from practices and progressively systematized through a trial-and-error approach. Managerial action most often relies on explicit models which enable actors to legitimize themselves, establish and justify organizational routines, and which are necessary to formalize and form newcomers through educational programmes. Consequently, management models are not only designed within the firm. Business gurus, consultants, professional bodies and educational programmes also play an important role in the definition and diffusion of formalized management models.

It is also important to emphasize that all managerial actions should not be assimilated into a management model. For example, strategic planning or strategic decisions may provide an accurate performance model (a precise set of goals that should be achieved), but they may be difficult to translate and implement within a firm. Indeed, it may be hard to identify related management objects, viable organizational devices, processes and skills necessary to implement top-managers' objectives. Thus, a critical dimension of management models lies in their ability to combine in a viable, credible and coherent fashion the three dimensions (performance model/management objects/devices, processes and skills) presented above. Otherwise, a strong level of dissonance between strategic discourse and real performance measurement protocols and actors' behaviours may lead to discredit and undermine a change process.[20] Thus, the ability to develop a coherent management model is likely to play a key role in the institutionalization of a CSR initiative within a company. The second part of this chapter develops a case study that illustrates how the failure to develop an integrated and coherent CSR management model led to the marginalization of a CSR initiative. As we will see, a key element was the difficulty of aligning the three levels of the management model: i.e. strategic ambitions with appropriate actions, organizational devices and skills.

From 'sustainable development' to 'profitable development': a process of marginalization of a CSR initiative in an energy firm

Energy Co. is a European company focused on energy-related businesses such as production, trading, transmission, distribution, supply and services. It employs more than 100,000 people worldwide. Within ten years, the company has gone through profound transformation of its business environment, organization and leadership. Formerly a state-owned, monopolistic company operating in one dominant regulated market, it has recently opened its capital to private investors and faces the progressive liberalization of European energy markets (production, distribution and trading). In the meantime, it has experienced important external growth, has gone through important reorganizations and has quickly become a leading energy player in Europe, with a worldwide presence.

In 2001, the company decided to formalize a sustainability policy and to create a sustainability department. The company could build on a longstanding responsible culture, a good-citizenship institutional image, and numerous practices and activities related to CSR, developed throughout its history. The experience of Energy Co. in the field of sustainability exemplifies a process whereby a sustainability department became marginalized, i.e. the transition from a favourable organizational context to a situation where, a few years later, sustainability appears as loosely coupled, or, to a certain extent, in contradiction with the strategic orientations of the firm.[21]

Our analysis of this marginalization process underlines both the influence of unfavourable environmental evolutions, but also the central difficulty of identifying an appropriate management model for sustainability issues. In particular, a key problem lies in the ongoing and increasing dissonance between a strategic corporate discourse and its poor fit with the other elements of the CSR management model. In spite of the initial willingness of top-management, the failure to identify a coherent management model started a vicious circle and led to the progressive marginalization of the initiative.

An initially favourable organizational context

At the beginning of the process, Energy Co. offered a favourable context for the development of a CSR policy. The organizational context displayed several characteristics, generally recognized as critical factors of success of a CSR initiative:

(1) There was a *clear commitment of the CEO* on sustainable development issues and a strong personal involvement on such questions. He soon realized that sustainable development could play a pivotal role for modernizing and extending the culture of the company. SD appeared as a potential pillar to build and consolidate a European corporate culture after a period of rapid external growth.

(2) *Because of the company history, activity and legal structure, there was a widespread operational commitment to SD issues* inside the organization. Employees felt a strong link between the core businesses of the company (energy production and distribution) and environmental issues such as global warming or natural resources scarcity. Moreover, a long-term approach to business was the norm in an industry where investments in production

facilities are amortized over more than forty years, with strong technical irreversibilities.[22] As far as the social side of sustainability was considered, purpose of the state-owned company was defined as a public service mission. The link with public policy issues had also been a constant feature in its history: after the Second World War the company had been in charge of the electrification of the countryside. After national reconstruction, the public service mission was extended through principles of equal treatment for all customers (which implied a duty to provide energy to all customers at the same price, whatever their social status or geographic location). This public service mission played a great role in forming corporate culture. The vivid influence of the public service culture over employees' behaviour and initiatives was manifest during a crisis in late 1999, where hundreds of retirees spontaneously came back to fix large parts of the national distribution network after its collapse, due to an unexpected storm. For many people, CSR and sustainable development values were a part of the 'organizational genes', because of the company's history and culture.

(3) *Many formal practices and policies, in connection with the CSR/sustainability issues, had been developed throughout the history of the company.* In accordance with public-service values, several employees and managers had developed business sponsorship initiatives, but also innovative practices towards precarious customers or disabled persons. Those practices were first developed informally, at the local level (in close connection to the local context), thanks to organizational slack.[23] The company had also been active in terms of ethical codes and their implementation. In the environmental field, the company set up an environmental management system in order to get an ISO 14001 certification for all its operating capacities. In terms of competencies, the firm had developed strong R&D capabilities in various fields such as renewable energies, and developed innovative projects about vehicle motorization, energy efficiency or ecosystems biodiversity.

(4) In spite of one central dilemma related to the involvement of Energy Co. in nuclear energy generation,[24] communication surveys showed that the company enjoyed a very good public image. In 2000, the company was elected most preferred national company

in its home country and surveys showed that it was considered as a green and responsible company.

This diagnosis led the top management (CEO and executive committee) to create a taskforce and to mandate a study in 2001 for evaluating the necessity and opportunity to develop a structured policy and formal organization for SD issues. As far as the strategic objectives were concerned (see performance model in Table 4.2), the reference to sustainable development was seen as a potentially central strategic pillar for transforming both the company and its environment. As far as the internal transformation of the company was concerned, the challenge was to smooth the transition between a national organizational culture based on the public-service reference, to a more international reference (SD) still in the making, likely to cement and integrate the new European group. The CEO also perceived sustainable development as a way to further a culture of social and environmental responsibility and link it to new commercial services, new business models and enhanced corporate performance. The ultimate objective was to create a new corporate model, in between public and private logics, equilibrating both financial expectancies and the general interest. Outside the company, Energy Co. anticipated the transformation of its traditional stakeholders and the increasing role of new actors (financial institutions, the European Commission, NGOs, new competitors, local communities, etc.). In this context, CSR and SD represented a strategy for renewing the relationship between the company and its environment, moving it away from a state-centred, technical and paternalistic approach to a more transparent governance and a selective approach towards stakeholders. Last, energy breakdowns in California (in 2000 and 2001) and the Enron collapse in 2001 opened political debates related to the deregulation process and the organization of the energy sector in Europe. For the company, there was a window of opportunity to influence the deregulation process of energy markets in Europe and to put forth a new kind of integrated energy corporate model.

The company decided to launch a structured policy and organization dedicated to SD issues in 2001. However, this initial impetus, boosted by the CEO's commitment, could not be sustained within the company. An increasing dissonance emerged between an ambitious and strategic discourse about SD and the two other pillars of the CSR management model within the firm.

Table 4.2 *The gap between strategic intent and operational translation*

	Strategic intent	Operational translation
Performance model	SD as a lever of transformation for the firm and its environment. The ability to regenerate current business models, to influence the institutional environment. The invention of a new model of integrated energy firm, the renewal of the public service culture. Articulate CSR with the core business of the organization.	*Orchestrate an incremental dynamic:* Elaborate voluntary engagements, formalize corporate commitment. Increase employees' awareness of SD issues. Locate and communicate (internally and externally) good practices.
Set of management objects	Management objects were largely unspecified. Agenda 21, letters of intentions. *Innovative practices, new business models, renewal of traditional businesses, new concepts.* *Corporate communication and the institutional image of the firm.*	Elaborate letters of intentions, general policies. Coordinate various initiatives and elaborate management tools (evaluation). Report on heterogeneous internal initiatives related to environmental/social issues.
Set of organizational devices, processes and skills	Organizational devices, processes and skills were largely unspecified. *Coordination, but also the ability to structure, prescribe and stimulate organizational innovations.*	Multi-functional coordination. Low level of prescription. No dedicated means for action.

Notes:
Formal elements that can be tracked through explicit documents or practices are shown in normal text.
Unspecified elements, reconstituted and inferred to complete the two management models presented above are shown in italics.
We have added those elements to underline the differences and the dissonance between the two approaches.

The dissonance between management discourse and operational components of the CSR management model

Significant actions were taken in late 2001 and early 2002. First, an Agenda 21 was signed by the CEO. This encompassing document regroups twenty-one engagements subdivided into more than sixty sub-objectives. It still constitutes the official corporate roadmap and was considered as a major step of the company towards sustainable development. After its launch, an ambitious internal programme was set up for more than 300 executive managers of the company to increase their awareness of SD issues. Overall, this first stage was marked by a strong involvement of the top management (and in particular the CEO) of the company.

But those first actions (as well as the strategic positioning defined by top management), although useful to legitimize SD issues internally, did not provide an accurate framework of action or a complete management model. For example, beyond its ability to materialize and communicate the organizational commitment to SD, the Agenda 21 did not provide accurate guidelines for action. With its focus on general action and behavioural principles, its scope potentially covered all corporate activities and aggregated a very large number of heterogeneous issues and stakeholders. Giving no prioritization to certain stakeholders or issues over the others, it constituted a broad roadmap but was not easy to translate into clear objectives. Moreover, if orientations were made explicit, it was unclear what kind of practices were to be developed within the company, who should be in charge of them and what role the sustainability department should play in this process (see Table 4.2).

As a result, many questions remained in terms of operational management. Global objectives or strategic orientations did not provide a full-fledged CSR management model. Beyond a broad performance definition, the two other pillars of the CSR management model still needed to be defined. Thus, dedicated actors were appointed to design an appropriate organization and to define processes in order to implement the CSR policy. The choices they made reflected a rather common and standard approach to sustainability management. As defined by several reference documents, the mission of the department was to *coordinate and orchestrate an incremental dynamic within and outside the company.* Sustainability managers defined their mission as follows:

(1) *Elaborate voluntary engagements and formalize corporate commitment for SD.* With its mission to represent top-management's position on SD, one of the central tasks of the sustainability department was to develop various documents to formalize and prove corporate engagement both inside and outside the firm. Beyond the endorsement and support of general codes of conduct such as the Global Compact, the company took various voluntary engagements. Those engagements dealt with a wide array of environmental or social issues, diverse stakeholders and were mostly unilateral.

(2) *Increase employees' awareness of SD issues and orchestrate operational deployment.* Through letters of intent and engagement documents, top-management provided a global frame of reference. The sustainability department then had to increase managers' awareness of SD issues, but the responsibility to develop concrete policies was left to functional and operational top managers who had to translate general engagements into operational policies. At the corporate level, indicators and a reporting system were defined to track the firm's progress.

(3) *Identify and communicate (both internally and externally) good practices.* Given the proliferation of internal initiatives potentially connected with SD issues, a key challenge for the sustainability department was to identify, recognize and praise local innovation. To further this goal, an internal 'sustainability awards project' was set up to reward employees' initiatives for developing innovative solutions regarding environmental issues. External communication towards stakeholders was also central. The company established communications towards the general public (such as television adverts about the company policies and best practices), answered rating agencies' questionnaires to increase its presence within sustainability indexes and developed stakeholder collaborations at various levels, including the creation of a stakeholder council.

In terms of organization, the sustainability department reported to the top HR manager (who had been a strong supporter of the initiative) and to a sustainability executive board. A more operational network of 'organizational transmitters' was also created, formally coordinated on a two-month basis. In terms of staff, the new department regrouped former environmental managers who had kept their previous missions (environmental intelligence, lobbying and environmental management systems) and put five dedicated people in charge of the coordination of the sustainability policy.

The emphasis placed on coordination led to a low level of actual prescription over other actors' behaviours within the company. It enabled incremental changes but left possibilities for more radical change in the hands of operational management. A second limitation was its failure to develop a hierarchy of issues within the company. Moreover, the continuous improvement model and the adherence to former environmental practices limited the ability of sustainability managers to identify and work on emerging 'hot issues' that would resonate both inside and outside the firm. As a result, an increasing gap emerged between the *espoused theory* put forward by top management and the *actual theory in use* and related practices set up by sustainability managers. As shown by Table 4.2, the company implicitly set up two diverging models concerning CSR without managing to articulate them.

The vicious circle of marginalization

As dissonance became visible inside the organization, the sustainability initiative entered a vicious circle that led to its marginalization, whose logic is summarized in Figure 4.1. As noted above, the sustainability management philosophy combined a focus on: 1) defining and communicating broad engagements and on 2) defining a reporting framework to orchestrate an incremental logic of continuous improvement inside the organization. This model left a large place for operational initiatives. It relied on operational willingness to engage into the process, but it failed to identify clear priorities and objectives, allocate resources and develop an explicit hierarchy of stakeholder and salient issues. As a result, there was an increasing gap between a bold, ambitious and transformative strategic discourse on the one hand, and a management model which built on already existing practices. This dissonance was soon interpreted as a sign that sustainability was a green-washing initiative, i.e. an effort to communicate and to put an artificial strategic label on already existing initiatives that had been developed locally and informally. This feeling of green-washing was further reinforced by the belief that sustainable development had always been a part of employees' culture and practices.

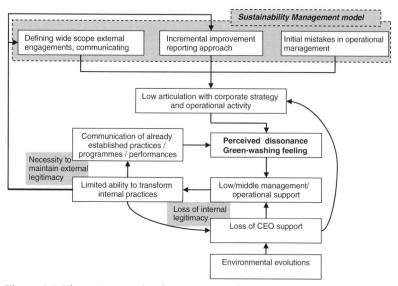

Figure 4.1 The vicious circle of CSR marginalization within Energy Co.

As this perception deepened, the initiative lost support from middle managers who did not make the match between broad corporate engagement and local issues. Middle managers progressively adopted a logic of symbolic conformation, doing the minimum to satisfy the hierarchical chain, but not granting much importance to it in their day-to-day activities.[25] From that moment on, the sustainability initiative progressively lost internal legitimacy. Having limited support within management and a low ability to transform internal practices, sustainability management then lost the support of the CEO, which further reinforced the scepticism of middle managers. This vicious circle was further amplified by unfavourable evolutions in the environment of the firm: because of its high level of debt and the forthcoming opening of its capital to financial markets, the company entered a stage of cost reduction and operational improvement. Rather than supporting the sustainability initiative, the CEO placed emphasis on improving the financial situation of the company. He was replaced later in 2004 by a new CEO who did not express his support for sustainable development. Rather, he emphasized the need to reinforce the financial situation of the firm. Thus, the reference to sustainable development in corporate communication was overshadowed by the objective of 'profitable development'. In this context, sustainability managers re-focused their action on former environmental issues (environmental lobbying, environmental management system). This decision tended to reaffirm a de-coupling between social, environmental and financial issues that was implicitly put forward by new corporate strategic orientations.

Interestingly, those internal evolutions were not perceived outside the company within the same timeframe. Thus, sustainable managers also tried to restore and leverage their internal position by underlining the need to respond to external stakeholder pressures. As a result, they tried to put forward a more stringent form of reporting and developed new forms of stakeholder engagement. For instance, a new strategic panel of stakeholders (with a good level of expertise in Energy Co.'s core businesses) was formed to develop ways to improve the company's CSR performance. This panel expressed explicit criticisms of the company's policy, but this externally driven approach of SD failed to restore the internal legitimacy of the initiative and to convince internal actors about the need for the company to develop and implement a more coherent and ambitious approach of CSR and SD.

Discussion and implications

Beyond its specificities, this case helps to underline more general issues related to sustainability and CSR management. It shows that in spite of a favourable organizational context, a company may encounter difficulties in formalizing, developing and implementing an integrated corporate CSR or SD policy. Our analysis underlines the central difficulty of developing a coherent management model on sustainability and CSR issues. For example, it shows that it is difficult for a new CSR department to develop a viable position by simply consolidating existing practices in the social and environmental fields.

The difficulties encountered by Energy Co. provide a good basis to understand the factors which contribute to reinforce or to marginalize CSR initiatives within firms. First, it helps to understand the fragility of CSR/SD departments and the difficulty of sustaining their organizational capacities. In particular, the case illustrates that top managers' support is necessary but never sufficient to initiate a true process of organizational change around CSR/SD issues. This support can be analysed as a temporary 'licence to operate', which may be removed quickly, as shown by the process of marginalization described in our case. Our case also reveals that the ability to identify an appropriate and coherent management model for SD constitutes a central challenge for SD managers if they are to institutionalize a SD initiative within a company. As a result, the ability to understand the characteristics of a management model that can sustain SD within the firm is a central question, both for researchers and practitioners. Building on the case study, we develop a few central characteristics that an appropriate CSR management model should contain.

First, *achieving coherence constitutes a central challenge to develop a credible management model.* In our case, the dissonance and the absence of fit between strategic objectives and actual management objects, processes and skills played a critical role in the loss of internal legitimacy. The alignment between 'espoused theories' (strategic intent and discourses) and 'theories in use' (actual implementation) is critical to maintain internal legitimacy.

In emerging managerial fields such as those of CSR and sustainability, several diverse approaches to CSR management may be identified. Thus, it may be worth investigating a range of management models in order to develop a more contingent approach to understand the articulation between organizational settings, objectives and CSR management models. To develop such a contingent approach, several variables should be investigated. These include organizational structures, hierarchical distance, sector of activities (which determines the link with consumers, the competitive structure of the value chain, etc.), internal awareness of sustainability issues and existing CSR practices – all of which are likely play a role in the adoption of specific management models.

The second dimension deals with the 'objects' of CSR managerial action. Since the legitimacy of a sustainable initiative derives both from internal and external support, the combination of internal and external dimensions appears as a central challenge when developing a CSR management model. Thus, *the ability to identify and act on issues that will resonate both inside and outside the company is a critical component of the viability of a CSR policy.* However, identifying objects and defining related modes of action that will garner both internal and external legitimacy is anything but an easy task: very often it involves playing two roles at the same time and in different timescales. As suggested by the case study, the mission to transform existing practices and to structure a business innovative approach of SD constitutes an essential component of the internal legitimacy of a CSR initiative. Although it is critical to embed CSR management within the organization, it is a long and exacting task requiring specific competencies, and may be hard to articulate with external time constraints and the need to communicate and send quick signals to external stakeholders and non-financial analysts. In this regard, time pacing strategies[26] and other strategies to couple internal and external sources of legitimacy should be investigated. This necessity to couple two – somehow competing – logics of action suggests that CSR/SD officers need to develop ambidextrous competencies, i.e. to be able to simultaneously set up stringent internal controls on specific social and environmental issues, excel at external communication (testifying that the company belongs to a group of responsible companies) and develop a more 'hands-on' and innovative approach to SD, stimulated in close contact with internal actors and specific stakeholders and articulated with operational issues. The ability to articulate those contrasting dimensions and the related modes of action represents a crucial way in which SD management can prevent a process of marginalization.

A third element relates to the *need to go beyond the pitfalls of a generic total quality management approach of sustainability management, and to the necessity to differentiate objects and related modes of action.* The idea that it is necessary to elaborate a management model able to couple external and internal logics of action suggests that it is necessary, for SD managers, to be able to distinguish various kinds of issues or objects and to adapt management models accordingly. In this context, the tendency of SD managers to set up a universal quality management framework[27] may be risky. Indeed, a natural drift from such approaches is that they tend to treat all issues in the same way. Setting up a Plan-Do-Check-Act (PDCA) approach, backed up with a reporting framework to track progresses made may be useful *when actors can manage decentralized improvement.* But PDCA approaches rely on the implicit hypothesis that action models are already available, i.e. that it is possible to know:

(1) how to set objectives;
(2) how to implement a policy;
(3) which internal actors and external stakeholders to mobilize;

(4) how to measure performance; and
(5) take corrective action.

Those hypotheses are often met for standard issues. But they do not constitute the norm, in particular in the case of CSR/SD issues. Most often, these issues blur the frontiers between public and private action: no existing regulations exist, no business model is clearly identified, and existing management and engineering knowledge is lacking or incomplete.

Take, for example, the issue of AIDS treatment for corporate employees in Africa.[28] When innovative companies decided to tackle this problem, they had to face radical uncertainties. Which actors and expertise should be involved within and outside the firms? With whom should managers collaborate? Who should bear the cost of such programmes? Who should be engaged or involved in those initiatives (the whole community, the employees, their families)? How should the costs, the social impact, the potential benefits, but also the risks of such policies, be balanced? To engage such problems, exploratory partnerships are often necessary to design and implement a solution.[29] Innovative practices in the field of sustainability reveal that the organizational and customer value of a sustainability initiative is rarely given *ex ante*. Very often, significant and meaningful approaches to SD issues involve the definition of new pieces of expertise, business models and to develop new systemic thinking and renew existing engineering models in the social and environmental sectors.[30] Thus, the ability to recognize and to manage innovative issues may be the true value-added of a CSR or SD department within a company.[31] Next to a generic and standardized approach of CSR organizational deployment, innovation involves a more 'hands-on' approach and specific skills to elaborate strategies, structure internal innovation processes and search for new business models. In such situations, where fields of expertise are not already established, the quality wheel may be turning in a vacuum, whatever the managers' ethics and goodwill.

Conclusion

In this chapter, we have investigated the patterns of CSR management and identified the difficulty of identifying a coherent CSR management model, distinct from existing environmental and human resource management models. We conclude with three observations about the value of our framework (the notion of management models) to analyse CSR dynamics. First, the definition and the identification of CSR management models are critical to understand the possible evolutions of the CSR management field, to move beyond pros-and-cons debate and ideological quarrels about CSR as a myth,[32] an expression of organizational hypocrisy,[33] managerial fad[34] or a new corporate revolution.[35] Acquiring a better understanding of management models will help to develop a more balanced and realistic view of what can be expected from such processes, both from corporations and other public bodies. Second, mainstreaming CSR does not necessarily imply more involvement of CEOs on this question. Solely relying on CEO engagement may make real institutionalization of CSR management difficult. As long as CSR management remain nothing but an emanation of top-management engagement, it will remain heavily dependent on a change in managerial fads and subject to environmental transformation or organizational change. Rather, we believe it is necessary to challenge the view that the involvement of CEOs is the key aspect of CSR management. In order to become institutionalized, CSR must identify appropriate management models, distinct from those already established in the environmental, finance or human resource functions. Third, the regeneration of existing environmental, social and financial functions within the firm may be a promising and ambitious way to conceptualize their activity. An innovative approach is likely to develop such a model. Following this approach, corporate sustainability should be analysed as a problem of redesigning core business functions and business models, and much more attention should be given to the collective design processes that give birth to innovative practices and policies in the field of sustainable development.

Notes

1 For a comprehensive approach of the development of a sustainability management field in Europe and several related case studies, see Franck Aggeri, Aurélien Acquier, Eric Pezet and Christophe Abrassart, *Organizing Sustainable Development* (Edward Elgar Publishing, forthcoming).

2 Clive Crook, 'The Good Company', *The Economist*, 20 January 2005, pp. 3–4.

3 So far, most studies have focused on a single CSR market (most of which have been focused on socially responsible investment and

rating markets: Frédérique Déjean, Jean-Pascal Gond and Bernard Leca, 'Measuring the Unmeasured: An Institutional Entrepreneur Strategy in an Emerging Industry', *Human Relations* 57/6 (2004); Céline Louche, 'Ethical Investment: Processes and Mechanisms of Institutionalisation in the Netherlands' (Doctoral dissertation, Erasmus Universiteit Rotterdam, 2004); Philippe Zarlowski, 'Translating Corporate Social Responsibility in the French Business Context: A Case Study of Social Rating Agencies', in Frank Den Hond, Frank De Bakker and Peter Neergaard (eds.), *Managing Corporate Social Responsibility in Action: Talking, Doing and Measuring*, (Chippenham: Ashgate, 2007)). A promising research avenue appears to be the analysis of the interdependencies of those inter-dependent markets, and to complete this market-level with an industry-level perspective (Aurélien Acquier and Franck Aggeri, 'The Development of a CSR Industry: Legitimacy and Feasibility as the Two Pillars of the Institutionalization Process', in Frank Den Hond, Frank De Bakker and Peter Neergaard (eds.), *Managing Corporate Social Responsibility in Action: Talking, Doing and Measuring* (Chippenham: Ashgate, 2007)).

4 Aurélien Acquier and Franck Aggeri, 'Institutional Work in Emerging Fields. Towards a More Distributed, Cooperative and Enabling Figure of Institutional Entrepreneurs. The Case of the Global Reporting Initiative (Gri)', paper presented at the 22nd EGOS conference, Bergen, Norway, 2006; Aaron Chatterji and David Levine, 'Breaking Down the Wall of Codes: Evaluating Non-Financial Performance Measurement', *California Management Review*, 48/2 (2006).

5 See Robert W. Ackerman, 'How Companies Respond to Social Demands', *Harvard Business Review* (July–August 1973); Robert W. Ackerman and Raymond A. Bauer, *Corporate Social Responsiveness* (Reston: Reston Publishing Company, 1976); William C. Frederick, 'From Csr1 to Csr2: The Maturing of Business-and-Society Thought' (Working Paper 1978 – Published in 1994), *Business and Society*, 33/2 (1994).

6 Joshua D. Margolis and James P. Walsh, 'Misery Loves Companies: Rethinking Social Initiatives by Business', *Administrative Science Quarterly* (2003).

7 In Europe, the concepts of Corporate Social Responsibility (CSR) and Sustainable Development (SD) are often considered as synonyms in corporate discourses and practices. British consulting firms (such as SustainAbility or AccountAbility), or professional associations (such as the World Business Council for Sustainable Development) have played a key role in the articulation of those concepts. Today, European companies edit 'CSR' or 'sustainability' reports, with little difference in the content of these reports. The triple bottom line (i.e. the idea to integrate economic, environmental and social performance, which is directly derived from the

SD concept), is often presented as an overhanging and integrative concept to organize CSR initiatives. Given the difficulty to clearly differentiate the concepts of CSR and SD in the corporate discourse, we will use the two concepts as synonyms in the rest of this chapter.

8 Cf. A. Acquier, 'CSR Management Models : From External Control to Innovative Design' (PhD dissertation, Center for Management Research, Ecole des Mines de Paris, France (in French)).

9 For a critical review of those studies, see A. Ullman, 'Data in Search of a Theory: A Critical Examination of the Relationships among Social Performance, Social Disclosure and Economic Performance', *Academy of Management Review*, 10 (1985); Timothy J. Rowley and Shawn Berman, 'A Brand New Brand of Corporate Social Performance', *Business & Society*, 39/4 (2000); Margolis and Walsh (2003); Jean-Pascal Gond, 'Constructing the (Positive) Relationship between Corporate Social and Financial Performance on Financial Markets', paper presented at the AIMS, Annecy, France, 2006.

10 Aaron K. Chatterji and David I. Levine, 'How Responsible Are Measures of Corporate Social Responsibility', paper presented at the conference 'Corporate Responsibility and Global Business: Implications for Corporate and Marketing Strategy', London Business School, London, 2006.

11 See Mark Starik, 'Childhood's End? Sustaining and Developing the Evolving Field of Organizations and the Natural Environment', in Mark Starik and Sanjay Sharma (eds.), *Research in Corporate Sustainability – the Evolving Theory and Practice of Organizations in the Natural Environment* (Cheltenham: Edward Elgar, 2002).

12 Michel Callon, 'An Essay on Framing and Overflowing: Economic Externalities Revisited by Sociology', in *The Laws of the Markets*, *Sociological Review Monograph Series* (Oxford: Blackwell, 1998); Aurélien Acquier and Jean-Pascal Gond, 'Building a Constructivist Perspective in Business and Society: Insights from the Anthropology of Markets', paper presented at the Proceedings of the International Association for Business and Society (IABS), Sonoma Valley, California, USA, 2005.

13 Wayne Norman and Chris MacDonald, 'Getting to the Bottom Line of the "Triple Bottom Line"', *Business Ethics Quarterly*, 14/2 (2004).

14 David Vogel, *The Market for Virtue – the Potential and Limits of Corporate Social Responsibility* (Washington, DC: Brookings Institution Press, 2005); Robert B. Reich, 'The New Meaning of Corporate Social Responsibility', *California Management Review*, 40/2 (1998).

15 Renato Orsato, 'Competitive Environmental Strategies: When Does It Pay to Be Green?', *California Management Review*, 48/2 (2006); Ans Kolk and Jonathan Pinkse, 'Business Strategy for Climate Change: Identifying Emergent Strategies', *California Management Review* 47/3 (2005); Sanjay

Sharma, 'Research in Corporate Sustainability: What Really Matters?', in Mark Starik and Sanjay Sharma (eds.), *Research in Corporate Sustainability – the Evolving Theory and Practice of Organizations in the Natural Environment* (Cheltenham: Edward Elgar, 2002); Juan Alberto Aragon-Correa, 'Strategic Pro-Activity and Firm Approach to the Natural Environment', *Academy of Management Journal*, 41/5 (1998); Juan Alberto Aragon-Correa and Sanjay Sharma, 'A Contingent Resource Based View of Proactive Corporate Environmental Strategy', *Academy of Management Review*, 28/1 (2003); Michael V. Russo and Paul A. Fouts, 'A Resource-Based Perspective on Corporate Environmental Performance and Profitability', *Academy of Management Journal*, 40/3 (1997); Dorothy Thornton, Robert A. Kagan and Neil Gunningham, 'Sources of Corporate Environmental Performance', *California Management Review*, 46/1 (2003).

16 John Elkington, *Cannibals with Forks – the Triple Bottom Line of 21st Century Business* (Oxford: Capstone, 1998); John Elkington, Jed Emerson and Seb Beloe, 'The Value Palette: A Tool for Full Spectrum Strategy', *California Management Review*, 48/2 (2006).

17 Peter L. Berger and Thomas Luckmann, 'From the Social Construction of Reality: A Treatise in the Sociology of Knowledge', in Frank Dobbin (ed.), *The New Economic Sociology* (Princeton and Oxford: Princeton University Press, 2004).

18 See Jean Piaget, *To Understand is to Invent* (New York: The Viking Press, 1972) and related organizational learning perspectives in organizational studies (Chris Argyris and Donald Schön, *Organizational Learning: A Theory of Action Perspective* (Reading, MA: Addison Wesley, 1978)). A common argument is that the individual, as he acts, develops mental causal representations to make sense of his environment, which help him organize the events in a coherent fashion and take action (see also Karl E. Weick, 'The Collapse of Sensemaking in Organizations: The Mann Gulch Disaster', *Administrative Science Quarterly*, 38 (1993)).

19 We qualify this model as an 'external conformation approach' because it is mainly put forward by external actors (institutional investors and extra financial rating agencies in particular) who theorize sustainability and CSR an extended model of governance, including a large range of stakeholders. This approach, which relies heavily on financial discourse, call for an extension and transposition of financial approaches and tools in the field of CSR (for a more accurate description and the identification of the potential limits of that approach, see Acquier and Aggeri (forthcoming)).

20 The dissonance between strategic discourse and concrete organizational devices may be interpreted as a difference between 'espoused theories' (reflexive justifications of the individual when he is asked to explain his

behaviour in certain circumstances) and 'theories in use' (the theory of action which actually governs his behaviour). See Argyris and Schön (1978).

21 It is important to note that the marginalization of the sustainability initiative does not necessarily mean that the social and environmental performance has decreased (for example the company continues to allocate very significant R&D budgets for renewable energy). It means that sustainability management have not succeeded in establishing themselves and developing a sustained and original dynamic within the firm. The marginalization implies that: (1) environmental and social performance are no longer articulated with the core strategy of the firm and that (2) sustainability managers have lost their influence over the main orientations in the social and environmental fields.

22 It should be noted here that although the internal culture was generally sensitive to SD, the switch to SD also implied strong evolutions, in particular concerning the relationships between the company and its stakeholders. The issue was to move away from a technical, state-centred and – to a certain extent – paternalistic approach to the relationship between the company and its stakeholders, to a situation of increased transparency and accountability towards the various stakeholders. This was quite new for a technical company which had not been accustomed to stakeholder dialogue and participation, and which had to face antagonistic associations which criticized the opacity of public information on some of its activities.

23 Richard M. Cyert and James G. March, *A Behavioral Theory of the Firm* (Englewood Cliffs, NJ: Prentice Hall, 1963).

24 There are various attitudes regarding nuclear technology in Europe, ranging from distrust and antagonism to social acceptance. Nuclear energy raises controversial debates worldwide, with supporters seeing it as a low CO_2 source of energy and pointing to the possibility of developing waste-free technologies in the medium term, and opponents underlining both the risks associated with plant operational command and the uncertainties related to the treatment and conservation of residual nuclear waste. Even if the company has to face several opponent NGOs (Greenpeace, Moving out of nuclear technology), it enjoys a good level of social acceptance in its places of operations.

25 John W. Meyer and Brian Rowan, 'Institutionalized Organizations: Formal Structure as Myth and Ceremony', *American Journal of Sociology* (1983).

26 Kathleen M. Einsenhardt and J.S. Brown, 'Time Pacing. Competing in Markets That Won't Stand Still', *Harvard Business Review*, 76 (March–April, 1998).

27 Sandra Waddock and Charles Bodwell, 'Managing Responsibility: What Can Be Learned from the Quality Movement?', *California Management*

Review, 47/1 (2004). Sandra Waddock, Charles Bodwell and Samuel B. Graves, 'Responsibility: The New Business Imperative', *Academy of Management Executive*, 16/2 (2002).

28 James P. Walsh and Walter R. Nord, 'Book Review Essay: Taking Stock of Stakeholder Management', *Academy of Management Review*, 30/2 (2005); Aggeri *et al.* (forthcoming).

29 Blanche Segrestin, 'Partnering to Explore: The Renault-Nissan Alliance as a Forerunner of New Cooperative Patterns', *Research Policy*, 34 (2005).

30 Scott R. Marschall and Darrell Brown, 'The Strategy of Sustainability: A Systems Perspective on Environmental Initiative', *California Management Review*, 46/1 (2003).

31 It can be argued here that once knowledge and management models are identified to tackle a specific issue, it will be transferred to existing actors (such as environmental and human resource managers) within the firm.

32 Michel Capron and Françoise Quairel-Lanoizelée, *Mythes Et Réalités De L'entreprise Responsable – Acteurs, Enjeux, Stratégies* (Paris: La Découverte, 2004); Vogel (2005); Deborah Doane, 'The Myth of CSR', *Stanford Social Innovation Review*, 1 (fall 2005).

33 Nils Brunsson, *The Organization of Hypocrisy – Talk, Decisions and Actions in Organizations* (Copenhagen: Copenhagen Business School Press, 2003).

34 Eric Abrahamson, 'Managerial Fads and Fashion: The Diffusion and Rejection of Innovations', *Academy of Management Review*, 16/3 (1991).

35 Thomas N. Gladwinn, James J. Kennelly and Tara-Shelomith Krause, 'Shifting Paradigms for Sustainable Development: Implications for Management Theory and Research', *Academy of Management Review*, 20/4 (1995); James Post, Lee E. Preston and Sybille Sauter-Sachs, *Redefining the Corporation: Stakeholder Management and Organizational Wealth* (Stanford: Stanford University Press, 2003).

PART II

Marketing and corporate responsibility

5 Global segments of socially conscious consumers: do they exist?

PAT AUGER, TIMOTHY M. DEVINNEY AND JORDAN J. LOUVIERE

Introduction

There is little doubt that corporate social responsibility (CSR) has gained in importance over the last decade leading firms to develop increasingly sophisticated CSR strategies for their organizations.[1] The challenges facing managers are nothing short of daunting given the vast number of issues that fall under the rubric of CSR and the equally large number of often conflicting groups pressuring companies to be more socially responsible.[2] The situation is even more complex for large and well-known multinational enterprises (MNEs) with operations that often span the globe and expose the organization to a wide range of economic, social, development and political conditions.

To help managers deal with this complexity, researchers in the CSR area have focused their efforts on the 'corporate side' of CSR with studies examining issues such as the relationship between CSR and financial performance, the different strategic and governance configurations to best deploy CSR initiatives, or the emergence of corporate philanthropy, among others.[3] This focus on the corporation is sensible given that CSR emerged as a field of study to investigate the response of organizations to the demands of civil society.

However, a number of researchers have argued that consumers play a critical role and are a driving force behind the emergence of CSR programmes.[4] This view posits that organizations have implemented CSR primarily as a response to consumer pressure, either actual or potential. From this perspective, a firm's CSR activities require a

This research has been supported by an ongoing series of grants through the Discovery Grants Program of the Australian Research Council. Additional support was received from the Alexander von Humboldt Foundation and the Rockefeller Foundation. We would like to thank AC Nielsen, Research International, and Heaton Quicktest for their assistance in conducting this research. All errors or omissions are the responsibility of the authors.

135

better understanding of the views and preferences of customers with respect to social and ethical issues. This consumer-driven view of CSR implies that researchers also need to focus some their research efforts on the other CSR: Consumer Social Responsibility (C_NSR).[5]

So far, most of the research on C_NSR (or, alternatively, ethical consumerism) has yielded mixed results in its quest to identify and characterize segments of socially conscious consumers, especially when the research is conducted in multiple countries. We believe that a significant obstacle to identifying socially conscious consumers has been in the methodology used to elicit the views and preferences of consumers. Specifically, the majority of the research findings on C_NSR are based on survey results that ask respondents to simply rate the importance of a list of social issues in a manner that is less than incentive compatible.[6] Such approaches do not force consumers to trade-off social features of products against traditional utilitarian features such as brand or price. Hence, it is not unreasonable to believe that traditional surveys may overstate the importance of social features, since there are clearly more socially acceptable answers.[7] For example, few people would answer that they do not care about the use of animal testing or the amount of pollution involved in the manufacturing of the products they consume when there is no cost in hiding their true preferences – a clear violation of incentive compatibility in instrument design. These survey instruments are thus unable to effectively discriminate between 'actual' socially conscious consumers and those who claim to be in surveys but do not behave accordingly at the checkout counter.

This lack of success at identifying segments of socially conscious consumers begs the question: do segments of socially conscious consumers really exist? Using data from a six-country choice experiment, we examined this important issue for two sets of products: AA batteries and athletic shoes. These experiments forced consumers to make trade-offs between functional product features (e.g. brand and price) and social product features (e.g. whether or not the product was manufactured by children). The two products utilized enabled us to examine a broad set of issues that covered environmental and labour issues. We used latent class finite-mixture regression analysis to identify and classify consumers into three distinct segments for each product, one of which was clearly populated by individuals who placed much greater value on socially acceptable products.

We also compared the segments on multiple dimensions to develop a better understanding of their basic nature and structure. We compared the sizes (number of respondents) and the composition (identity of the respondents) of the segments of socially conscious consumers for batteries and shoes. This allowed us to investigate the salience of different social issues across different product categories and different purchasing contexts. Using socio-demographic data gathered from each respondent, we compared the three segments for differences in demographic characteristics such as country of origin, age, gender, income and so on. Finally, we examined how respondents' knowledge of their most recently purchased batteries and athletic shoes differed between the two products and the three segments. We discuss several managerial and research implications based on the results of these and other analyses.

The search for the elusive socially conscious consumer

In its broadest form, $C_N SR$ can be defined as *the conscious and deliberate choice to make certain consumption choices based on personal and moral beliefs.* $C_N SR$ 'implies that individual consumers can have a significant role, through their daily purchase decisions, in promoting ethical corporate practices'.[8] Some of the ways by which consumers can accomplish this is by purchasing (or not purchasing) certain products and/or by paying more for more socially acceptable products. In general, research on $C_N SR$ has focused on the latter issue, namely the impact of ethical and social issues on the purchase behaviour of consumers. Most commonly, the issues under investigation have included environmental (e.g. use of recycled materials) and labour issues (e.g. use of child labour). Though some researchers have argued that research on $C_N SR$ is inherently unreliable,[9] most empirical studies have found that some consumers are willing to pay a premium for more socially acceptable products.[10] For example, Auger *et al.*[11] used choice experiments to examine the willingness of consumers in Hong Kong and Australia to pay for more socially acceptable products. Their results show that *some* consumers were willing to pay a premium for more socially acceptable products, especially for more sensitive issues such as the use of child labour and the use of animal testing. However, it was equally clear that consumers from both countries were not willing to sacrifice basic functional features for socially acceptable ones and this did not depend on whether they had supported social causes in the past.

Belk *et al.*[12] used video ethnography techniques with consumers from nine countries to get a deeper understanding of the underlying rationale for the purchase (or non-purchase) of socially desirable products. Their results yielded several relevant contributions. First, they found that culture had a much a smaller effect on perceptions of consumption ethics than expected. Ethical beliefs across the countries in their sample were fairly consistent in the sense that individuals understood the dilemmas present in their failure to act upon their beliefs. Second, ethical behaviour on the part of businesses can influence ethical behaviour on the part of consumers. That is, a large number of consumers in their sample cited the apparent lack of ethical conduct by business as a rationale for their own behaviour. Third, although the lack of ethical purchasing behaviour was similar across cultures, consumers in different cultures rationalized that inaction in very different, culturally consistent, ways. Once again, these results were seen to persist across all the countries in their sample.

Though some of the studies mentioned above were able to determine that some consumers were willing to pay more for socially acceptable products, few were capable of properly segmenting and characterizing these socially conscious consumers. Auger *et al.* found few relationships between socio-demographic variables (e.g. age, gender and income) and the willingness of consumers to pay for more socially acceptable products. They found no significant relationships between common personality measures used in ethics research (e.g. Machiavellianism, idealism and moral relativism) and the willingness to pay for social 'goods'. Hence, two key results emerge from the literature on $C_N SR$ that follow from this research: 1) socially conscious consumers appear to exist and 2) those socially conscious consumers cannot be easily segmented using observable socio-demographic measures.

Segmenting the socially conscious consumer

The results presented in this article came from experiments conducted in six countries – Germany, Spain, Turkey, the United States, India and Korea – with over 600 respondents. Our sample of consumers included only individuals who were representative of the middle class within their respective countries. The definition of 'middle class' was based on two criteria:

(1) matching with the median income of a dweller in the city of interest; and
(2) having the ability to purchase the products under investigation.

Table 5.1 *Selected demographic characteristics of respondents by country*

	United States	Germany	Spain	Turkey	India	Korea	Total
Age (median grouping)	30–39	30–39	30–39	30–39	30–39	30–39	30–39
Gender (per cent female)	60.6	52.5	59.4	50.5	49.0	70.0	57.0
Income (median grouping, $000)	25–40	15–25	15–25	15–25	15–25	15–25	15–25
Education (per cent uni-educated)	20.70	8.90	22.60	62.70	60.80	39.00	35.70
Marital status (per cent married)	39.80	33.33	50.90	31.33	50.00	66.00	45.30
Sample size	99	100	106	100	100	100	605

We focused on middle-class consumers since they facilitated comparisons across countries by reducing the variations in income and education between respondents from developed and developing countries (i.e. we compared apples to apples). The use of middle-class respondents also ensured that all respondents had the financial means to purchase the most expensive product in our experiments, athletic shoes (branded athletic shoes now frequently sell for over $100 putting them out of reach for a large number of consumers in developing countries). We selected the aforementioned countries to obtain variation in the level of economic development (i.e. developed, developing and middle income), geographical locations and cultures (i.e. languages, religions, etc.). These, and other similar variables, had been shown to affect social purchasing and ethical beliefs in prior research. Table 5.1 presents basic demographic information for our sample of respondents.

We used discrete choice modelling (DCM) to ascertain the degree to which socially responsible segments existed in those marketplaces. DCM allows researchers to infer the value consumers place on various attributes, not by asking them, but by looking at what they choose when presented with experimentally designed alternatives.[13] In our DCM experiments, described in Table 5.2, we created   products with different levels of functional attributes (e.g. whether an athletic shoe had good or poor ankle support) and social attributes (e.g. whether or not child labour was used to make the shoe). All of the choices forced consumers to make trade-offs – products never had the highest level of both functional and social attributes, so consumers implicitly had to make trade-offs and we were able to measure the trade-offs they made.

We gathered data for two types of products: AA batteries and athletic shoes. We selected these two products for the following reasons. First, they enabled us to investigate the importance of two different sets of social issues, namely environmental issues for batteries and labour issues for athletic shoes. Second, the products were familiar to and purchased by all the consumers in our sample. Knowledge of the product categories and prior purchase experience were important since we also asked respondents to tell us about the attributes of their most recently purchased athletic shoes and batteries. Prior purchase experience also facilitated the experimental tasks since respondents already understood the nature of the product attributes. Third, the products differed in their level of consumer involvement in the purchase process. Athletic shoes are considered high-involvement products compared to batteries since consumer search is more intensive and the price more noticeable to the consumer.

Figure 5.1 shows examples of product variations that the respondent would be asked to examine. In the case of Shoe A versus Shoe B the trade-off is between price ($40 vs. $100), brand (Adidas vs. Reebok), country of production (China vs. Poland), two of the ethical features (minimum wages and working conditions) and four of the functional features (weight, ankle support, sole durability and breathability). In the case of Battery A versus Battery B the differences no longer include price but do include brand (Eveready vs. Energizer) and country of production (Poland vs. China), three of the ethical features (mercury/cadmium free, hazardous production waste and material recycling) and two of the functional features (useful life and storage

Table 5.2 *Functional and social attributes for athletic shoes and batteries*

Athletic shoes	AA batteries
Functional attributes (levels of attribute):	
Shock absorption/cushioning (Low or High)	Useful life (15 hours or 30 hours)
Weight (Lighter or Heavier)	Storage life (3 years or 5 years)
Ankle support (Low Cut or High Cut)	Is the expected spoilage date on the battery? (No or Yes)
Sole durability (Short or Long)	On-battery or on-package tester (No or Yes)
Breathability/ventilation (Low or High)	Money-back guarantee (No or Yes)
Fabrication materials (Synthetic or Leather)	Rechargeable (No or Yes)
Reflectivity at night (No or Yes)	
Comfort/fit (Low or High)	
Country of origin (Poland, China, Vietnam, domestic)	Country of origin (Poland, China, Japan, domestic)
Brand of shoe (Nike, Adidas, Reebok, Others)	Brand of battery (Energizer, Duracell, two others varied by country)
Price ($40, $70, $100, $130)	Price ($1.30, $3.30, $5.30, $7.30)
Social Attributes (levels of attribute) (all are either Yes or No):	
Is child labour used in making the product?	Is the battery mercury/cadmium free?
Are workers paid above minimum wage?	Is the battery made from recyclable materials?
Are workers' working conditions dangerous?	Is the package made from recyclable materials?
Are workers' living conditions at the factory acceptable?	Was hazardous waste created from the production process?
Are workers allowed to unionize?	Is safe battery disposal information contained on the package?

Note: Each respondent received a series of eight experimental tasks for each product. Overall, there were thirty-two possible versions of product types that the individual could have seen based on a 2^N fractional factorial design. The experimental task was preceded by a short questionnaire pertaining to their knowledge of their last purchase and was followed by a standard battery of socio-demographic questions.

Features of the Shoes	Features of Shoe A
Shock absorption/cushioning	High
Weight	Heavier
Ankle support	Low cut
Sole durability	Short
Breathability/ventilation	Low
Fabrication materials	Synthetic
Reflectivity at night	Yes
Comfort/fit	Low
Is child labour used in making the product?	Yes
Are workers paid above minimum wage?	Yes
Are workers' working conditions dangerous?	Yes
Are workers' living conditions at the factory acceptable?	No
Are workers allowed to unionize?	Yes
Country of production	China
Brand of shoes	Adidas
Price	$40
1. If the shoes described above were available in your local shops now, would you consider trying it (Tick ONE box only)? ☐ No ☐ Yes	
2. If the shoes described above were available in your local shops now, would you buy it instead of or in addition to your current shoes next time you shop for shoes (Tick ONE box only)? ☐ No ☐ Yes	

Features of the Shoes	Features of Shoe B
Shock absorption/cushioning	High
Weight	Lighter
Ankle support	High cut
Sole durability	Long
Breathability/ventilation	High
Fabrication materials	Synthetic
Reflectivity at night	Yes
Comfort/fit	Low
Is child labour used in making the product?	Yes
Are workers paid above minimum wage?	No
Are workers' working conditions dangerous?	No
Are workers' living conditions at the factory acceptable?	No
Are workers allowed to unionize?	Yes
Country of production	Poland
Brand of shoes	Reebok
Price	$100
1. If the shoes described above were available in your local shops now, would you consider trying it (Tick ONE box only)? ☐ No ☐ Yes	
2. If the shoes described above were available in your local shops now, would you buy it instead of or in addition to your current shoes next time you shop for shoes (Tick ONE box only)? ☐ No ☐ Yes	

Figure 5.1 Examples of choice tasks for athletic shoes and AA batteries

life). In the case of all the products two questions were asked: a consideration question and a will-purchase-now question.

Figures 5.2 and 5.3 show the results of our primary data analyses for batteries and shoes, respectively. Our analyses consisted of a relatively sophisticated type of regression analysis referred to as latent class finite-mixture regression analysis (LCM). LCM allows for the classification of individuals into segments (called classes) and develops regression models for each of the segments simultaneously. These segments are referred to as latent segments since their formation does not depend on a group of pre-specified clustering variables (as is the case in traditional clustering methods). Instead, the latent segments are formed with discrete unobserved variables, which greatly improve the ability of researchers

Features of the Batteries	Features of Battery A
Useful life (in a CD or cassette player)	30 Hours
Storage life (how long the battery can last when not used)	3 years
Is the expected spoilage date on the battery?	Yes
On-battery power indicator or on-package tester	Yes
Money-back guarantee	Yes
Rechargeable	No
Is the battery Mercury/Cadmium free?	Yes
Was hazardous waste created from the production process?	Low
Is the battery made from recyclable materials?	No
Is the package made from recyclable materials?	No
Is safe battery disposal information contained on the package?	Yes
Country of origin	Poland
Brand of battery	Eveready
Price (4-pack)	$5.30

1. If the batteries described above were available in your local shops now, would you consider trying it (Tick ONE box only)? ☐ No ☐ Yes

2. If the batteries described above were available in your local shops now, would you buy them instead of or in addition to your current battries next time you shop for batteries (Tick ONE box only)? ☐ No ☐ Yes

Features of the Batteries	Features of Battery B
Useful life (in a CD or cassette player)	15 Hours
Storage life (how long the battery can last when not used)	5 years
Is the expected spoilage date on the battery?	Yes
On-battery power indicator or on-package tester	Yes
Money-back guarantee	Yes
Rechargeable	No
Is the battery Mercury/Cadmium free?	No
Was hazardous waste created from the production process?	Yes
Is the battery made from recyclable materials?	Yes
Is the package made from recyclable materials?	No
Is safe battery disposal information contained on the package?	No
Country of origin	China
Brand of battery	Energizer
Price (4-pack)	$5.30

1. If the batteries described above were available in your local shops now, would you consider trying it (Tick ONE box only)? ☐ No ☐ Yes

2. If the batteries described above were available in your local shops now, would you buy them instead of or in addition to your current battries next time you shop for batteries (Tick ONE box only)? ☐ No ☐ Yes

Figure 5.1 (cont.)

to identify meaningful segments in circumstances where observed variables (e.g. socio-demographics) have proven to be ineffective.

The figures present the standardized coefficients for the latent class models of product attributes on choice (i.e. the decision of whether or not to purchase a specific product). We also included six markers to indicate commonly-used levels of significance (i.e. $p = 0.05$; $p = 0.01$; $p = 0.001$) for easier interpretation of the results. Basically, all coefficients, with the exception of price, beyond the first marker ($p = 0.05$) are considered significantly different from zero (for price, we show price elasticity and all price coefficients were significant at the 0.05 level). For example, in the case of batteries (Figure 5.2), the brand Eveready is not significant for any group (it is below the 0.05 marker). Also, one group is enormously price sensitive (with a coefficient of nearly −6), with the other two groups quite low in terms of price

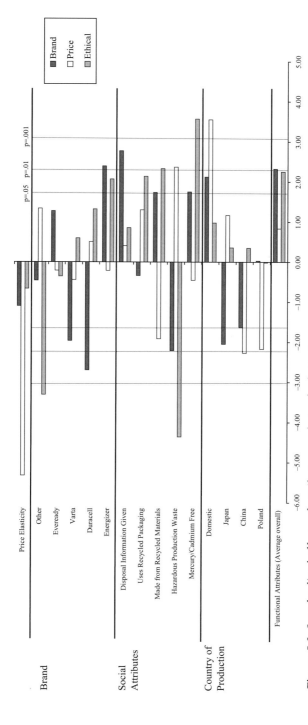

Figure 5.2 Standardized effects of attributes on choice for batteries

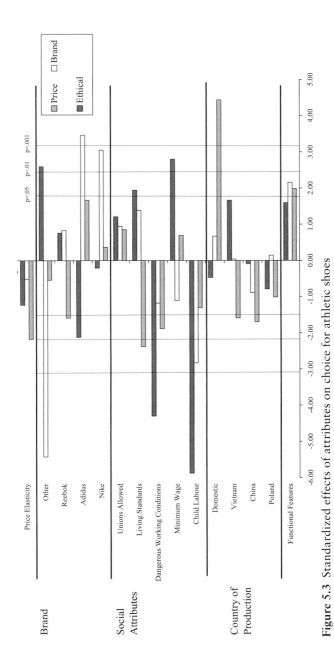

Figure 5.3 Standardized effects of attributes on choice for athletic shoes

responsiveness. In the case of athletic shoes (Figure 5.3), the fact that the product is made in Poland is also not significant for any group. In the case of child labour, one group reacts extremely strongly to the existence of child labor (the coefficient is approximately −6), one group moderately strongly (the coefficient is approximately −3) and one group not strongly at all (the coefficient is slightly above −1).

Our results show that respondents for both products can be categorized into three distinct segments. Intriguingly, the three segments for both products have very similar structures, allowing us to label them with the same descriptors, namely brand, price and ethical. These descriptors were selected by examining the dominant set(s) of attributes (i.e. the attributes with the largest standardized coefficients) within each segment.

Respondents in the 'brand' segment placed greater importance on brand (either positively or negatively) than respondents in the other two segments. This is especially apparent for athletic shoes where respondents in the brand segment valued the Nike and Adidas brands highly and also had high negative valuation for the 'other brand'. These individuals also display relatively low price sensitivity (especially for shoes), which is consistent with the brand-conscious consumer who is willing to pay a premium for his/her preferred brand.

On the other hand, respondents in the 'price' segment were very sensitive to price. This is especially the case for batteries. Respondents in the price segment also placed a much greater level of importance on the country of origin of the products, exhibiting a high level of positive domestic country bias.[14] This domestic country bias is especially pronounced for shoes, but is also large for batteries. Hence, this second segment is best described as highly price sensitive with a strong domestic country bias.

The third and most relevant segment from the standpoint of this chapter is the 'ethical' segment. Figures 5.2 and 5.3 deliberately present more details on the social attributes than the functional attributes to facilitate a more in-depth discussion of the former. We grouped all functional attributes (with the exception of brand and price) into a single category to simplify the presentation of the results. This is not to suggest that the functional attributes are unimportant, they are for both products. We present it this way simply to draw more attention to the social attributes given the focus of this chapter.

Interesting results emerge from a closer examination of the ethical segments. The first, and obviously more important, is the existence of the ethical segments. The two figures clearly reveal that respondents in the ethical segment for each product placed much greater importance on the social attributes than respondents in the other two segments. It is also important to note that the wording for the social attributes (see Table 5.2) is a mixture of 'positive' and 'negative' statements. We did this to ensure that respondents took the experimental task seriously and paid close attention to the levels of each attribute. All coefficients for the social attributes in the two ethical segments are in the correct and expected direction. That is, the signs of the coefficients indicate that the respondents in the ethical segments favoured products that were more 'socially desirable', no matter how expressed in the experiments.

Though we do not show the demographic break-up of the segments, there are no identifiable differences in demographic characteristics between the segments beyond some differences in nationality to be discussed in a later section. We found very few meaningful differences in age, income, education, marital status and gender between our three segments for both products. This confirms earlier work that simple segmentation strategies based on socio-demographics are not well-suited to understanding socially conscious consumers. It also highlights the strength of latent class finite-mixture regression analysis in tapping unobserved homogeneity based on behaviour and helps understand the relative lack of success at identifying segments of these consumers in previous research.

Second, the two products show very similar patterns with respect to the importance of the social attributes within the ethical segments. In fact, four of the five social attributes are considered to be relatively more important by the respondents in the ethical segments than by the respondents in the other two segments for both products. The only two social attributes that were not are 'the availability of disposal information' for batteries and 'the ability to form unions' for athletic shoes. Furthermore, each product has two social attributes that dominate the others within the ethical segments. For batteries, the two attributes are hazardous production waste and whether or not the battery is mercury/cadmium free. For shoes, the two most important social attributes are child labour and dangerous working conditions.

Though the specific nature (i.e. their identity) of the more important social attributes within each product category is only relevant for managers in those two industries, the differences in the relative importance of social and functional attributes have important implications for a much broader pool of managers. It is clear from our results that not all social attributes have equal effect on consumer purchase decisions. This is a somewhat obvious result, but one that has serious implications for managers designing CSR strategies. This result suggests that it is critical for managers to not only understand the social issues that are especially important for their customers but also to avoid CSR strategies that are too broad or try to cover too many issues. What our respondents demonstrated is that there are segments of socially conscious consumers, but that they do not value equally all social issues associated with a particular product. As such, our results would strongly favour a more 'focused' CSR strategy over one that attempts to do too much or does not address the more salient social issues.

Figures 5.2 and 5.3 also reveal that the functional attributes, including brand and price, are not irrelevant to respondents in the ethical segments. For example, respondents in the ethical segment for shoes still react to price as expected and to a much greater extent than for respondents in the brand segment. They also have a preference for alternative brands versus more well-known brands such as Nike and Adidas. Similarly, respondents in the ethical segment for batteries have a clear brand preference for Energizer and tend to value the functional attributes (as a group) as highly as the respondents in the brand segment (and much more highly than respondents in the price segment). What this suggests is that managers cannot simply ignore the core functional attributes of their products to create more socially acceptable ones. In other words, consumers do not appear willing to sacrifice functionality for social desirability. What these consumers are telling us is that they purchase products to fill a certain basic set of needs and that no amount of social desirability is likely to compensate for a failure to meet these basic needs.

Overall, this first set of analyses yielded three important results. First, segments of socially conscious consumers do exist and they exist for consumers who value products that are more socially desirable with respect to environmental and labour issues. However, these segments of socially conscious consumers do not differ from the other two segments with respect to common socio-demographic characteristics. Hence, segmentation methods that rely on traditional socio-demographics are bound to come up short in identifying these groups. Second, consumers within these 'ethical' segments placed different levels of importance on different social attributes. This implies that not all social product initiatives resonate equally

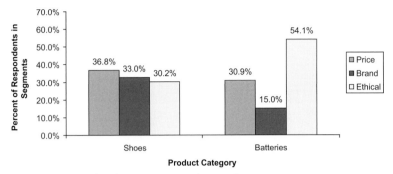

Figure 5.4 Membership in segments by product

well with consumers and that managers would be better off focusing on the one (or few issues) that has (have) the most potential. Third, functional attributes are important to the respondents in the ethical segments. Hence, managers cannot discount the basic needs that their products are fulfilling for their customers to create more socially desirable products. In effect, functional and social attributes must work hand-in-hand to create additional value for customers.

The size of the segments

As mentioned in the previous section, our methodology enabled us to classify each respondent into a specific segment. Figure 5.4 presents the distribution of respondents among the three segments for both products. For example, the results for athletic shoes indicate that 36.8% of respondents were in the price segment while 33.0% and 30.2% of respondents belonged to the brand and ethical segments, respectively. It is important to point out that these percentages for the ethical segments do not represent potential market shares for socially desirable products for two important reasons. First, our samples only included respondents from the middle class so that they were not representative of the entire populations of the countries under investigation. Second, social product features alone are not sufficient as was discussed in the last section. The ethical segments were populated by individuals who placed relatively greater importance on the social attributes, but they also valued brand and some of the other functional attributes as well.

What these percentages enable us to do is to comment on the relative sizes of the ethical segments between the two product categories since the same respondents took part in both experiments. It is clear

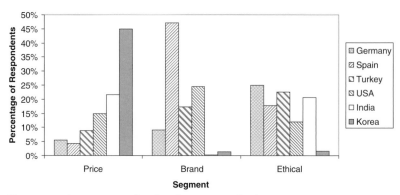

Figure 5.5 Country membership by segment for batteries

from Figure 5.4 that the ethical segment for batteries (54.1%) is much larger than the ethical segment for shoes (30.2%). Several possible explanations can help shed light on these differences and we now discuss two for illustration purposes. First, environmental issues tend to have a more direct impact on consumers than labour issues. For example, the consumption (and eventual disposal) of a battery with mercury or cadmium will have a direct effect on the consumer's physical environment by introducing these metals into the environment. By purchasing more environmentally friendly batteries, customers are thus contributing to the creation of a better environment for themselves. The same cannot be said of labour issues since the majority of consumers are not directly involved in the production of athletic shoes. As such, labour practices and conditions may often seem very remote for most consumers (something confirmatory of Belk *et al.*).

Second, environmental attributes tend to be more 'functional' than labour attributes. That is, environmental attributes can influence product performance and utilization (e.g. disposal of the battery). On the other hand, labour issues have little or no functional impact for the consumer. That is, it is impossible to tell the difference between two athletic shoes that were produced under different labour conditions. Hence, the additional functionality of environmental attributes could contribute to their higher relative valuations.

Differences in segment membership by country

Figures 5.5 and 5.6 show the distribution of respondents for the three segments by country. These analyses show that the segments are, in

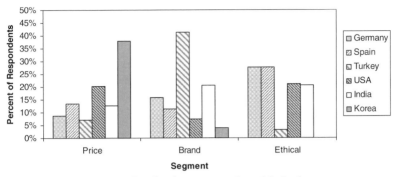

Figure 5.6 Country membership by segment for athletic shoes

general, not country specific. That is, all three segments have representatives from all six countries for both products with the exception of the ethical segment for shoes, which does not contain any respondents from Korea. However, the figures also show fairly large differences in the proportions of respondents from specific countries in specific segments. For example, the price segments for both shoes and batteries are clearly dominated by Korean respondents who comprise 38% of the segment for shoes and 45% of the segment for batteries. Similarly, Spanish respondents make up a much greater proportion of the brand segment for batteries (47%) while Turkish respondents dominate the brand segment for shoes (41%).

For their part, the ethical segments (for both shoes and batteries) show much more similar patterns of membership across the countries. Five countries – Germany, Spain, the United States, India and Korea – contribute very similar proportions of respondents to the two ethical segments. The first four countries contribute a relatively high and similar proportion of respondents to the two ethical segments while Korea contributes a relatively low proportion of respondents to both ethical segments. Turkey is the only country to show an inconsistent pattern of contribution, with a relatively high contribution for batteries (similar to Germany, Spain, the United States and India) and relatively low for shoes (similar to Korea).

Overall, our results show fairly consistent patterns in membership to the ethical segments across countries at the aggregate level. Furthermore, membership in the ethical segments tends to be more evenly distributed across the countries than for the other two segments. For example, the price segments tend to be dominated by Korean respondents for both products while Spaniards and Turks dominate the brand segments for batteries and shoes, respectively. These results suggest that preferences for social products may be much more global than previous research on C_NSR and consumer ethics has suggested.[15] In other words, cultural differences may not impact the importance consumers place on social issues as much as has been suggested in previous work. In fact, work by Auger *et al.*[16] using best–worst scaling methodology strongly supports the notion that the importance of culture may be overstated when it comes to views on social and ethical issues. They found that the preference orderings of consumers with respect to sixteen social and ethical issues showed very similar patterns across a number of countries. That is, the similarities in preference orderings for the social and ethical issues between countries far outweighed their differences. What is unique about their research is that they utilized experimental methodologies that are specifically designed to reduce erroneous differences due to inappropriate measurement instruments when comparing responses from multiple countries.

The results presented above show that the proportions of respondents from the different countries that make up the ethical segments are similar. However, these analyses only show the contributions from countries at the aggregate level. They do not show if the individuals in the two ethical segments (i.e. the ethical segments for shoes and batteries) are the same. In other words, are the individuals populating the ethical segments consistently showing preferences for social products? Or are the individuals in the two ethical segments different? These issues are discussed in the next section.

The socially conscious consumer

One of the more interesting and enlightening analyses is to determine to which segment each respondent belonged across the two product categories. To accomplish this we created nine pairs of segments that cover all possible combinations of segments between batteries and shoes. Figure 5.7 presents the distribution of respondents among these nine segment pairs. For example, the first pair on the left labelled 'price-price' signifies that respondents in that segment pair belonged to the price segment for both batteries and shoes. Hence, the figure indicates that 19 per cent of our sample was influenced primarily by price (and country-of-origin) for the purchase of both batteries and shoes. Similarly, the next segment pair, 'price-

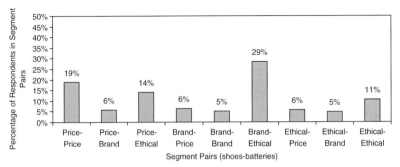

Figure 5.7 Memberships for segment pairs

brand', indicates that roughly 6 per cent of our sample belonged to the price segment for shoes and the brand segment for batteries.

Of greater interest is the segment pair at the righthand-side of the chart, the 'ethical-ethical' pair. Here, we see that only about 11 per cent of our sample was influenced primarily by social issues for the purchase of both batteries and athletic shoes. The implications of these results are important and consistent with some of the more recent research on C_NSR. First, the results strongly support the notion that individuals cannot simply be labelled as 'socially conscious' across product categories. That is, an individual who values environmental issues does not necessarily value labour issues, and vice versa. This suggests that social purchasing is most probably issue and context specific. That is, individuals may react positively to more socially desirable products given the right set of issues, the right product and the right purchasing context. This is critical for managers charged with designing CSR strategies. Our results reveal that consumers are concerned about very specific issues and are unlikely to react to social product features that are 'too broad' or lack functional relevance. Hence, it is important for managers to focus their efforts on a single (or very small number of) issue that can be linked psychologically to their product/service offering.

Second, these results support the use of more sophisticated research methods, especially 'incentive compatible' methods that force consumers to trade-off social features against functional features such as price and brand. We believe that simply asking respondents about their views on social issues with unconstrained survey instruments, such as simple rating scales, leads to an overestimation and muddled picture of the importance of these issues. Respondents may feel embarrassed or unwilling to reveal their true preferences for fear of being

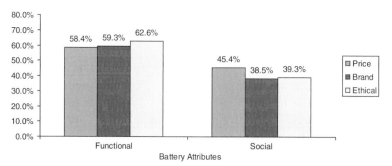

Figure 5.8 Percent knowing about most recent purchase by segment for batteries

judged negatively, leading to a social desirability bias.[17] Hence, forcing respondents to make 'hard choices' about purchases greatly reduces the chances that they will disguise their preferences and should lead to more reliable estimates. Managers should not only be concerned about the views of consumers with respect to social issues, but more importantly if these consumers are willing to pay for more socially acceptable products. Hence, the use of experimental methodologies, such as the ones presented in this chapter, could help reduce some of the problems associated with the social desirability bias. Furthermore, managers and researchers should be cognisant that the social desirability bias is not only problematic when studying social and ethical issues, but can be a factor whenever sensitive issues are under investigation.[18] Hence, researchers and managers should exercise caution when interpreting results from surveys about these sorts of issues.

Consumer knowledge about social issues

One of the tasks in our experiments required respondents to tell us about their most recent purchases. Specifically, we asked respondents to indicate the levels of attributes (the same attributes and levels as in our choice experiments; see Table 5.2) for their most recent purchase of batteries and athletic shoes. For this task, respondents also had the choice to answer 'don't know' if they did not know or were not sure about the levels of specific attributes.

Figures 5.8 and 5.9 show the percentage of respondents by segment who knew about the functional and social features of their most recently purchased batteries and athletic shoes, respectively (see

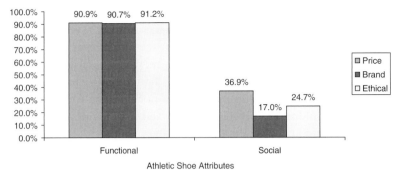

Figure 5.9 Percent knowing about most recent purchase by segment for athletic shoes

Table 5.2 for a list of functional and social attributes). The percentages presented are averages for the two groups of attributes and do not include knowledge of brand and price (almost 100 per cent of respondents remembered the level of these two attributes for both products).

A number of interesting results emerge from these two figures. First, the percentage of respondents who knew the functional attributes of athletic shoes (almost 91 per cent overall) is much greater than the percentage for batteries (roughly 60 per cent overall). These differences between shoes and batteries are consistent with high and low involvement products. Basically, an athletic shoe is a higher involvement product, which implies that consumers are more likely to spend time researching it. Hence, one would expect that consumers would be more knowledgeable about and better remember the features of the higher involvement product. Our data clearly support this conclusion and demonstrate that respondents were taking our experimental tasks seriously.

Second, the percentage of respondents who knew about the social attributes of batteries (about 40 per cent overall) is much greater than the percentage for shoes (roughly 26 per cent). Furthermore, there is much greater variation in the level of knowledge about social issues between the three segments for shoes than for batteries. For the former, the results are consistent with our earlier explanation about the greater percentage of respondents in the ethical segment for batteries versus shoes. Especially relevant here is the notion that environmental attributes such as 'mercury-free' are much more 'functional' than labour attributes such as the use of child labour. Moreover, the nature (or level) of environmental attributes is often revealed on the packaging. For example, it is unusual to see battery packaging that indicates if the packaging is made from recycled materials or if the battery is free of cadmium. On the other hand, one never sees a box of athletic shoes that specifies whether or not the product was manufactured by children or if employees involved in the production of the shoes were paid above minimum wage.

The results pertaining to the greater variation in knowledge about social issues for shoes are more difficult to explain. One possible explanation is that consumers who purchase products primarily on price tend to conduct more thorough research to identify the lowest priced products. Hence, these consumers become better informed about social features during that more extensive research process. This would explain why the respondents in the price segments for both batteries and shoes indicated a greater level of knowledge about the social attributes of their most recently purchased products. However, it would not explain the similar level of knowledge across the three segments about the functional features.

Another explanation is more specific to our sample and would suggest that our Korean respondents, who make up a large proportion of the respondents in the price segments, are simply better informed about social attributes of the products they purchase. Both of these explanations clearly require additional research.

What is clear from the results is that consumers are generally unaware about the social attributes associated with athletic shoes and moderately unaware about the social attributes of batteries. Hence, we can infer that individuals may not possess enough knowledge to make socially responsible choices. The implications are that managers need to communicate and educate consumers more effectively about their CSR strategy if they wish to impact consumer purchase decisions. As we discussed previously, more effective communication is especially important for issues that are more important to consumers. What we suggest is that consumers must be informed in a way that fits effectively with the issues they care most about. Hence, consumers concerned about child labour are more likely to respond to a campaign focused specifically on child labour than to a general labour rights issue campaigns emphasizing living conditions, wages, unionization *and* child labour.

Conclusions

The growing importance of CSR for companies around the world implies that consumers are increasingly expecting the corporate world to behave in socially conscious ways. This notion of consumer-driven CSR has received some support from the emerging literature on C_NSR with a number of studies showing that some consumers are willing to pay a premium for more socially desirable products. However, most of these studies have had less success at determining whether these consumers existed, and if they did, what characterized them.

This chapter presented the results of a six-country empirical study that aimed to identify segments of socially conscious consumers using a combination of choice experiments and latent class finite-mixture regression analysis. For the products studied, results suggest that these segments do exist and that consumers within these ethical segments placed different levels of importance on different social issues. The results also show that respondents in the ethical segments valued some of the functional attributes and did not differ significantly on socio-demographic characteristics than respondents in the other two segments (i.e. brand and price). This implies that managers need to utilize a focused approach to CSR strategy by stressing the one (or few) issues that are especially salient to their consumers. Our research also suggests that simple segmentation strategies may not be appropriate when trying to identify socially conscious consumers. It is also clear from our analyses that environmental issues tended to influence a greater number of consumers' purchase decision than labour issues. These results highlight the greater salience of social attributes that have a more direct impact on consumers and are more functional in nature.

One of the more interesting results seen here is that only a small percentage of our sample (about 11 per cent) belonged to the ethical segments for both batteries and shoes. This suggests that consumers cannot simply be labelled as socially conscious across product categories. It also highlights the importance of the specificity of social issues and purchasing context as determinants of social purchasing. Our analyses uncovered differences in segment membership between the six countries in our study, but fewer differences in the composition of the ethical segments than in the other two segments. In general, our results strongly suggest that culture may not affect social purchasing as much as has been reported in previous research.

Finally, our research uncovered large differences in the knowledge that consumers possess about the social attributes of the products they purchase. Our analyses showed that consumers had much less knowledge about labour issues than environmental issues. This was expected and easy to explain given the nature of environmental attributes. However, the relatively low level of knowledge about social issues in general (for both batteries and shoes) suggests that organizations need to communicate more effectively with their customers. Failure to do so may reduce the impact of their CSR strategy.

Overall, we have hopefully clarified and shed additional light on a number of issues associated with social purchasing and the search for the socially conscious consumer. We believe that three implications are especially important for managers associated with the development of CSR strategy and researchers in the CSR area. First, managers need to carefully select a single social issue (or a few at most) on which to concentrate their CSR efforts and ensure that the selected issue has relevance for their customers. The selected issue must also be tied psychologically to the product to make it more functional and hence more relevant. Second, managers and researchers must exercise great care when using the results of consumer surveys on social purchasing. Sensitive issues tend to lead to social desirability biases when the survey instrument does not force consumers to make trade-offs. Therefore, we believe that research must not only focus on the views of consumers, but more importantly, on their willingness to pay for more socially desirable products. Put differently, research must not only investigate attitudes, but more importantly, behaviour. Finally, a large number of consumers are unaware of the social features of the products they purchase. Hence, an important aspect of an effective CSR strategy is the communication, persuasion and education processes that are required to ensure that consumers understand the nature of the social attributes.

Notes

1   C.B. Bhattacharya and S. Sen, 'Doing Better at Doing Good: When, Why, and How Consumers Respond to Corporate Social Initiatives', *California Management Review*, 47/1 (2004): 9–24; S. Sen and C.B. Bhattacharya, 'Does Doing Good Always Lead to Doing Better? Consumer Reactions to Corporate Social Responsibility', *Journal of Marketing Research*, 38 (May, 2001): 225–43; T. M. Devinney, 'Is the Socially Responsible Corporation

a Myth: The Good, Bad and Ugly of Corporate Social Responsibility', *Academy of Management Perspectives*, 23/2 (2009): 44–56.

2 N.C. Smith, 'Corporate Social Responsibility: Whether or How?', *California Management Review*, 45/4 (2003): 52–76; J.G. Klein, N.C. Smith and A. John, 'Why We Boycott: Consumer Motivations for Boycott Participation', *Journal of Marketing*, 68/3 (2004): 92–109; D.L. Spar and L.T. La Mure, 'The Power of Activism: Assessing the Impact of NGOs on Global Business', *California Management Review*, 45/3 (2003): 78–101.

3 A. Harrison and J. Scorse, 'Improving Conditions of Workers? Minimum Wage Legislation and Anti-Sweatshop Activism', *California Management Review*, 48/2 (2006): 144–60; P. Mirvis and B. Googins, 'Stages of Corporate Citizenship', *California Management Review*, 48/2 (2006): 104–26; J. Peloza, 'Using Corporate Social Responsibility as Insurance for Financial Performance', *California Management Review*, 48/2 (2006): 52–72.

4 R. Harrison, 'Corporate Social Responsibility and the Consumer Movement', *Consumer Policy Review*, 13/4 (2003): 127–31; T. M. Devinney, P. Auger and G. M. Eckhardt, *The Myth of the Ethical Consumer* (Cambridge, Cambridge University Press, 2010).

5 Harrison (2003).

6 T. Mason, 'The Importance of Being Ethical', *Marketing*, 26 October (2000): 27; D. Rogers, 'Ethical Tactics Arouse Public Doubt', *Marketing*, 6 August (1998): 12–13.

7 P. Auger and T.M. Devinney, 'Do What Consumers Say Matter? The Misalignment of Preferences with Unconstrained Ethical Intentions', *Journal of Business Ethics*, 76/4 (2007): 361–83.

8 A. Crane and D. Matten, *Business Ethics: A European Perspective: Managing Corporate Citizenship and Sustainability in the Age of Globalization* (Oxford: Oxford University Press, 2004).

9 M. Carrigan and A. Attala, 'The Myth of the Ethical Consumer – Do Ethics Matter in Purchase Behaviour?', *Journal of Consumer Marketing*, 18/7 (2001): 560–77; P. Ulrich and C. Sarasin, *Facing Public Interest: The Ethical Challenge to Business Policy and Corporate Communications* (Boston: Kluwer Academic Publishers, 1995); E. Boulstridge and M. Carrigan, 'Do Consumers Really Care About Corporate Responsibility? Highlighting the Attitude-Behavior Gap', *Journal of Communication Management*, 4/4 (2000): 355–68; F.L. Simon, 'Global Corporate Philanthropy: A Strategic Framework', *International Marketing Review*, 12/4 (1995): 20–37.

10 K.A. Elliott and R.B. Freeman, 'White Hats or Don Quixotes? Human Rights Vigilantes in the Global Economy', Working Paper 8102,

National Bureau of Economic Research (2001); O. Uusitalo and R. Oksanen, 'Ethical Consumerism: A View from Finland', *International Journal of Consumer Studies*, 28/3 (2004): 214–21; Marymount-University, 'The Consumers and Sweatshops', www.marymount.edu/news/garmentstudy/overview.html (1999).

11 P. Auger, P. Burke, T.M. Devinney and J.J. Louviere, 'What Will Consumers Pay for Social Product Features?', *Journal of Business Ethics*, 42/3 (2003): 281–304.

12 R.W. Belk, T. Devinney and G. Eckhardt, 'Consumer Ethics across Cultures', *Consumption, Markets, and Culture*, 8/3 (2005): 275–89.

13 J.J. Louviere, D.A. Hensher and J.D. Swait, *Stated Choice Methods: Analysis and Applications* (Cambridge: Cambridge University Press, 2000).

14 M.K. Hui and L. Zhou, 'Linking Product Evaluations and Purchase Intention for Country-of-Origin Effects', *Journal of Global Marketing*, 15/3/4 (2002): 95–116; R.A. Peterson and A.J.P. Jolibert, 'A Meta-Analysis of Country-of-Origin Effects', *Journal of International Business Studies*, 26/4 (1995): 883–900.

15 J.A. Al-Khatib, A.D. Stanton and M.Y.A. Rawwas, 'Ethical Segmentation of Consumers in Developing Countries: A Comparative Analysis', *International Marketing Review*, 22/2 (2005): 225–46; J.A. Al-Khatib, S.J. Vitell and M.Y.A. Rawwas, 'Consumer Ethics: A Cross-Cultural Investigation', *European Journal of Marketing*, 31/11/12 (1997): 750–67; M.J. Polonsky, P.Q. Brito, J. Pinto and N. Higgs-Kleyn, 'Consumer Ethics in the European Union: A Comparison of Northern and Southern Views', *Journal of Business Ethics*, 31/2 (2001): 117–30; M.Y.A. Rawwas, G.L. Patzer and S.J. Vitell, 'A Cross-Cultural Investigation of the Ethical Values of Consumers: The Potential Effect of War and Civil Disruption', *Journal of Business Ethics*, 17/4 (1998): 435–48.

16 P. Auger, T.M. Devinney and J.J. Louviere, 'Using Best-Worst Scaling Methodology to Investigate Consumer Ethical Beliefs across Countries', *Journal of Business Ethics*, 70/3 (2007): 299–326.

17 R.T. Carson, T. Groves and M.J. Machina, 'Incentive and Informational Properties of Preference Questions', unpublished working paper, University of California, San Diego, 2000; N. Schwarz, 'Self-Reports: How the Questions Shape the Answers', *American Psychologist*, 54/2 (1999): 93–105.

18 R. Tourangeau and T.W. Smith, 'Asking Sensitive Questions: The Impact of Data Collection Mode, Question Format, and Question Context', *Public Opinion Quarterly*, 60/2 (1996): 275–304.

6 Impact of CSR commitments and CSR communication on diverse stakeholders: the case of IKEA

FRANÇOIS MAON, VALÉRIE SWAEN AND
ADAM LINDGREEN

For many researchers and observers alike, it remains difficult to understand fully how organizations design their corporate social responsibility (CSR) policies and communicate them to different stakeholders. They also have trouble determining different stakeholders' complex perceptions of and attitudes towards the organization, which means managerial guidelines are virtually nonexistent in this important area. Although prior work focuses on organizational commitment to and communication with customers, employees and prospective employees, and financial investors,[1] it often fails to consider other stakeholders, such as trade unions and non-governmental organizations (NGOs) whose influence over CSR policies continues to grow.[2] Furthermore, previous studies generally address one type of stakeholder, which prevents them from offering an overall analysis of the value of commitment and communication in CSR. We contribute to the literature by reporting on one organization's CSR commitments and communications; we achieve this by taking into account the influences and the reactions of an organization's different stakeholders.

Specifically, we report on IKEA's CSR commitments and communications and their relation to the organization's different stakeholders, which enables us to examine stakeholders' perceptions of and attitudes towards IKEA and its CSR policies and thereby gain an understanding of how stakeholders themselves influence CSR commitments and communication. By including a variety of stakeholders, our case approach provides insight into the dynamics that occur among stakeholders. We structure the remainder of this chapter as follows. First, we review the literature. Second, we provide details of the case organization developed for this study. Third, we present and discuss the findings. Fourth and finally, we identify some theoretical and managerial contributions and conclude with research limitations and opportunities for further research.

Literature review

Being a socially responsible organization is increasingly advocated like a necessary criterion to do business in the twenty-first century,[3] which in turn suggests that responsible management links with corporate survival. Together with the emergence of concepts such as sustainable development and global business citizenship, pressure from and demands by various stakeholders help explain the role of CSR during the last decades. In particular, various entities have gained ground, such as the anti-globalization movement, NGO campaigns, careful and thorough examinations of sustainable investments, changing consumption behaviours that promote ethical buying, city council participation and government oversight.[4]

Moreover, the widespread distribution of the World Wide Web as a global communications device provides individuals and organizations with nearly instant information about an organization, its products and its services, which increases their expectations.[5] A 1999 survey by NFO Research of 1,000 US consumers found that 54 per cent consider an organization's labour practices, business ethics, social role and environmental impact to be very important.[6] A 2004 survey of 6,350 European consumers by Sofinco-IPSOS similarly found that 53 per cent believe that if they are to change their consumption behaviour successfully then organizations must become ethically more responsible.[7] Consumers who adhere to certain ethical values or even a particular cause search for applicable information about the organization, its products and its services, including employee, social and environmental issues. Consumption can thus express not only product preference but also whether consumers feel they can relate to the organization's values or cause.[8] Yet some evidence also identifies a gap between what consumers say they will do – consciousness – and what they actually do – consumerism – with regard to CSR issues;[9] for example, 'value for money' remains the prime reason in most consumers' purchasing decisions, even as 'values' become more important decision criteria.

Pressure to become a better corporate citizen also stems from business customers who purchase components and raw materials from suppliers and want them to act in environmentally correct and ethically sound manners. Global organizations must ensure that their CSR policies extend to not only their overseas subsidiaries but also their suppliers, over which they have varying degrees of control. Several large organizations require suppliers to provide details of their own CSR policies or demand improvements, such as in the areas of employee matters or social and environmental performance.[10] These demands can provide strong incentives for suppliers to focus more on CSR. If they choose not to commit to CSR, they may lose contracts; conversely, by designing and implementing CSR policies, suppliers can differentiate themselves positively and thereby attract customers.

CSR and stakeholders

Since Bowen argued that businesses have a duty 'to pursue those policies, to make those decisions, or to follow those lines of action which are desirable in terms of the objectives and values of our society', few have questioned the importance of CSR.[11] As a result, CSR has mushroomed to such an extent that it comprises a vast plethora of theories and approaches, some of which use different terminologies.[12] With little consensus about meanings, CSR remains a hot and controversial research topic, but carefully distilling CSR literature suggests a general consensus that it is no longer enough for organizations to be concerned about increasing profits. In addition to their economic and legal obligations, organizations have ethical and discretionary responsibilities to society. In order to comply with these considerations, they develop CSR policies that endorse employee, social and environmental concerns.[13]

Carroll conceptualizes CSR as different obligations, which underlines the central role that stakeholders play.[14] That is, 'CSR represents societal expectations of corporate behavior; a behavior that is alleged by a stakeholder to be expected by society or morally required and is therefore justifiably demanded of a business.'[15] A stakeholder-oriented approach to CSR emphasizes that organizations exist within large networks of stakeholders, all of which stake claims on organizations. Within the organization, the interests of these various stakeholders meet and interact with one another and the interests of the organization. When organizations face demands from stakeholders to recognize the importance of CSR, they generally translate those demands into CSR objectives and develop CSR policies; sometimes, however, organizations attempt to change their stakeholders' expectations.[16] Within the organization, managers must integrate stakeholders into the decision-making process, convince them to support the corporate strategic course and facilitate multipartite participation.

CSR and communication

In responding to CSR pressure and demand, some organizations follow a substantive strategy, whereas others develop a symbolic strategy.[17] The former implies that the organization modifies its objectives and business processes; the latter refers to institutional, opportunistic CSR communication that does not alter the organization's criticized behaviour. In both cases, CSR communication represents an important issue for managers.

However, several questions remain unanswered in relation to the impact of CSR communication on stakeholders' perceptions and attitudes. On the one hand, previous studies report a positive impact of CSR on corporate image and consumer goodwill.[18] For example, information pertaining to CSR policies positively influences consumers' buying intentions, and an organization enjoys an enhanced reputation when stakeholders perceive it has contributed to the common social good.[19] A reputation as a socially responsible organization even can protect an organization during a crisis.[20] On the other hand, organizations engaging in the most CSR often are those criticized the most. Those that proclaim themselves socially responsible must be prepared to deal with criticism when stakeholders believe they have behaved irresponsibly,[21] and if they choose not to respond to that criticism, they can face a serious crisis, as Nestlé, Nike and Shell discovered. Finally, in certain conditions, a CSR initiative can decrease consumers' purchase intentions towards the socially responsible organization, for example when consumers' support for a particular CSR aspect or product quality is low.[22]

Taking these conflicting findings and lack of guidelines into account, we attempt three objectives with this study. First, we examine IKEA's CSR policies and their development in a wider context (i.e. employee, social and environmental) by considering the influence of multiple, various stakeholders. Second, we analyse how IKEA communicates its CSR policies and commitment to various stakeholders. Third, we study the value added by this commitment and communication and the effect on stakeholders' perceptions of and attitudes towards the organization.

Methodology

Qualitative methods are appropriate for complex phenomena and when numerous variables may influence the issue(s) at hand. We select a case study as our research methodology, in accordance with the principles outlined by Yin.[23] First, we obtain a comprehensive understanding of the case organization's contextual setting so that we may develop our theory in context. Second, we use secondary data and multiple interviews to gather rich insights and provide a basis for the greater generalizability of our findings, including in-depth interviews with two representatives from IKEA and twenty external stakeholders that might affect IKEA's CSR policies in some way. Third, 160 responses to a consumer survey provide insight into consumers' views on IKEA's CSR commitments and communications. To avoid interference with the readability of the text, the case organization is introduced next; the data collection and analysis section, however, is discussed in the endnotes.

In qualitative studies, the choice of cases is usually theory driven.[24] Our goal is not to capture all possible CSR scenarios, but to gain a deeper understanding of the particular case organization and, from this understanding, develop analytical concepts and framework. For the purposes of our study, IKEA, the world's largest multinational, flat-pack furniture retail chain, offers a remarkably fertile case for examining CSR. The organization has enjoyed high-profile marketing successes. Furthermore, it offers greater simplicity in terms of competitive scenarios and strategic responses compared with larger, more complex furniture manufacturers and retailers. In addition, the policies described in the case have largely been developed and entered an evolutionary phase, whereas during data collection, many other furniture manufacturers and retailers were undergoing substantial change processes with uncertain outcomes. The organization's retail turnover has increased by 400 per cent during the past decade. Its business model is based on gaining control over strategic resources, particularly through logistical coordination of a network that consists of 1,500 suppliers in fifty (often developing and emerging) countries. These suppliers ignore mediators and deliver directly to IKEA, which minimizes the retailer's costs so that IKEA can offer low-priced furniture. However, the seeming eradication of the world's forests has resulted in increasing pressure on IKEA from environmental activists, and its worldwide perspective has made it a target of anti-globalization protesters; as a result, IKEA now includes sustainability issues in its CSR policies.

Findings

The leitmotiv of IKEA's founder Ingvar Kamprad has been to offer the company's products to the mass market at a low price through a strong commitment to cost and resource effectiveness. This commitment is reflected in IKEA's vision to 'create a better everyday life for the many people ... and to offer a wide range of home furnishings with good design and function at prices so low that as many people as possible will be able to afford them', a vision adopted in the late 1970s. The IKEA vision supports the organization's ambition to integrate social and environmental considerations into its daily operations and to 'make products which have minimum impact on the environment and ... manufacture them in a socially responsible way'.[25] These CSR commitments derive from Kamprad's philosophy, as well as from the prevailing norms and institutional relationships of Nordic countries, which tend to think of ethical values, politics and economics as constituents of a virtuous circle.[26] Through this virtuous circle, IKEA believes it can reduce the conflict between CSR and profit functions, though its emphasis on cost-effectiveness and its engagement in emerging and developing countries has sometimes conflicted with its ambition of being a responsible corporate citizen. Since the 1980s, for example, IKEA has undergone scrutiny in relation to issues such as child labour, working conditions in emerging countries, the use of hazardous components in furniture production and wood procurement from questionable sources. Figure 6.1 provides an overview of the main CSR-related criticisms and issues faced by IKEA from 1980 to 2004.

Environmental issues in IKEA's supply chains

For many years, IKEA maintained a 'green' reputation, largely based on its roots in conscientious Scandinavia.[27] However, in the 1980s and the beginning of the 1990s, IKEA faced greater criticism about

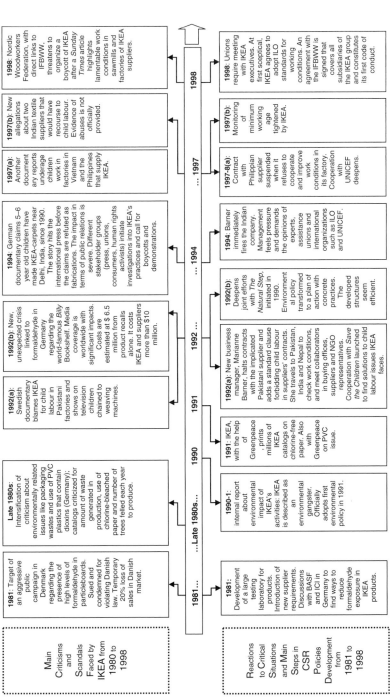

Main Criticisms and Scandals Faced by IKEA from 1980 to 1998

1981: Target of an aggressive public campaign in Denmark regarding the presence of high levels of formaldehyde in particleboards. Sued and condemned for violating Danish law. Temporary 20% loss of sales in Danish market.

Late 1980s: Intensification of criticism about environmentally related issues like packaging wastes and use of PVC plastics that contain dioxins (Germany); catalogs criticized for amount of waste generated in production, use of chlorine-bleached paper and number of trees felled each year to produce.

1992(a): Swedish documentary blames IKEA for child labour in Pakistani factories and shows on television children chained to weaving machines.

1992(b): New, unexpected crisis linked to formaldehyde in Germany regarding the world-famous *Billy Bookshelf*. Media coverage is worldwide with significant impacts. Costs are estimated at $ 6.5 million from product recalls alone. It costs IKEA and suppliers more than $10 million.

1994: German documentary claims 5–6 year old children have made IKEA-carpets near Delhi, India, since 1990. The story hits the international press before the claims are refuted as fabrications. The impact in terms of public relations is severe. Different stakeholder groups (press, unions, consumers, human rights activists) initiate investigations into IKEA's practices and call for boycotts and demonstrations.

1997(a): Another documentary reports underage children work in factories in Vietnam and the Philippines that supply IKEA.

1997(b): New allegations about two Indian textile suppliers that would have recourse to child labour. Evidence of abuses is not officially provided.

1998: Nordic Woodworkers Federation, with direct links to IFBWW, threatens to organize a boycott of IKEA after a *Sunday Times* article highlights lamentable work conditions in sawmills and factories of IKEA suppliers.

Reactions to Critical Situations and Main Steps in CSR Policies Development from 1981 to 1998

1981: Development of a large testing laboratory for products. Introduction of new supplier requirements. Discussions with BASF and ICI in Germany to find ways to reduce formaldehyde exposure in IKEA products.

1990–1: internal report about environmental impact of IKEA's activities: IKEA is described as an environmental gangster. Officially adopts first environmental policy in 1991.

1991: IKEA, with the help of Greenpeace, prints millions of IKEA catalogs on chlorine-free paper. Also with Greenpeace on PVC issue.

1992(a): New business manager, Marianne Barner, halts contracts with the implicated Pakistani supplier and adds a standard clause forbidding child labour in suppliers' contracts. She travels to Pakistan, India and Nepal to check work conditions, and meet collaborators in buying offices, suppliers and NGO representatives. Cooperation with *Save the Children* launched to find solutions to child labour issues IKEA faces.

1992(b): Deepens joint efforts with *The Natural Step*, initiated in 1990. Environmental policy transformed to a plan of action with concrete practices. The developed structures seem efficient.

1994: Barner immediately fires the Indian company. Management feels pressure and demands the opinions of experts, assistance unions and international organizations such as ILO and UNICEF.

1997–8(a): Contract with Philippian supplier suspended when it refuses to cooperate and improve work conditions in its factory. Cooperation with UNICEF deepens.

1997(b): Monitoring of minimum working age tightened by IKEA.

1998: Unions require meeting with IKEA executives. At first sceptical, IKEA agrees to adopt ILO standards for working conditions. An agreement with the IFBWW is signed that covers all subsidiaries of the IKEA group and constitutes its first code of conduct.

1981... | ...Late 1980s... | 1990 | 1991 | 1992 ... | ...1994 | ...1997 | ...1998

Figure 6.1a External stakeholders' influence on the development of IKEA's CSR policies from 1981 to 1998 (date of first code of conduct)

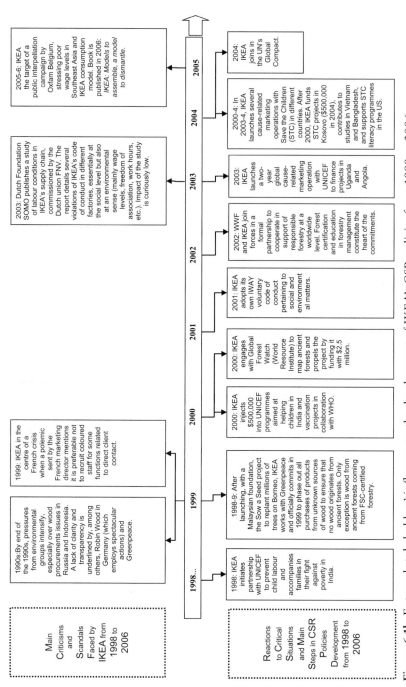

Figure 6.1b External stakeholders' influence on the development of IKEA's CSR policies from 1998 to 2006

the presence of formaldehyde – a suspected carcinogen – in its particle-boards, dioxins in the PVC it used, significant volumes of packaging waste and paper-consuming catalogues. In 1990, its first environ-mental impact internal report described the organization's environ-mental affairs department as an 'environmental gangster'.[28] In 1991, it adopted its first environmental policy, but by 1992, a new crisis had emerged in Germany, IKEA's biggest market. Worldwide media coverage of the high levels of formaldehyde in IKEA's top-selling Billy bookshelf led to costs of US$6.5 million for product recalls alone.[29] In collaboration with The Natural Step, an international, non-profit, educational and advisory sustainability organization, IKEA trans-formed its environmental policy in 1992 into a periodically updated action plan, after which the company suffers minimal further criti-cisms about its environmental impact. However, at the end of the 1990s, environmental groups exhort IKEA to clarify its wood pro-curement policies and stop using timber from intact natural forests. Even though IKEA was a member of the Forest Stewardship Council (FSC), these groups claim it failed to deal responsibly with timber. Therefore, in 1999, IKEA commits to phase out all purchases of prod-ucts from unknown sources of wood; the only wood allowed from ancient forests will come from FSC-certified forestry. In 2000 and 2002, IKEA then further engages with the World Resource Institute (WRI) and the World Wildlife Fund (WWF) to cooperate in support of responsible forestry worldwide; at the same time, it rejects the FSC label on its wood products and keeps using the IKEA logo, without making a 'green' distinction for its range of wood-based products.

Social issues in IKEA's supply chains

In the mid-1990s, a televised Swedish documentary showed Pakistani children chained to machines at an IKEA supplier, with which IKEA immediately stopped contracting. It also added a standard clause against child labour to all its supplier contracts and initiated a col-laboration with Save the Children. A German television documen-tary then alleged child exploitation by IKEA suppliers in India; these facts later were shown to be inaccurate. However, the impact on public relations was severe. Management responded by initiat-ing contacts with UNICEF and ILO and a UNICEF collaboration emerged. In 1997, after new allegations about child labour issues surfaced, IKEA tightened its monitoring of legal working ages in its supply chains. When a Philippine manufacturer refuses to cooperate to improve working conditions, IKEA suspends its contract. In 1998, the Nordic Federation of Building and Wood Workers (NFBWW), which is linked to the International Federation of Building and Wood Workers (IFBWW), threatens to boycott IKEA after *The Sunday Times* reveals the poor working conditions at Romanian suppliers. IKEA again partners with an outside group, committing to apply ILO standards for working conditions and signing a framework agreement about the promotion of workers' rights. Using this agreement as a basis, IKEA develops its own 2001 code of conduct – the IKEA Way on Purchasing Home Furnishing Products (IWAY) – that encompasses social and environmental policies for its whole supply chain.

Stakeholders in the CSR development process

The historical analysis of how CSR has developed at IKEA (Figure 6.1) indicates three elements:

(1) therole of external stakeholders in developing socially and environmentally responsible business practices and codes of conduct;[30]
(2) the role of NGOs in implementing and enforcing CSR agreements and codes of conduct;[31] and
(3) the mix of reactive and proactive actions taken by IKEA. We consider each element next.

Role of external stakeholders

External stakeholders play a key part in developing IKEA's CSR policies. For example, the IFBWW prompted changes to its code of conduct in 1998, based on an agreement reached between IKEA and IFBWW through negotiations among representatives from Greenpeace, Save the Children and the WWF. To gain knowledge about developments in the CSR field and facilitate its CSR commitments, IKEA has established relationships with various NGOs (see Figures 6.1a and 6.1b). For example, because wood represents 70 per cent of IKEA's raw materials, environmental issues related to forestry rank among the organization's major concerns, as evidenced by its certification efforts, planning operations and collaborations with Global Forest Watch, Greenpeace, a Swedish university and the WWF. In the area of child labour, IKEA now closely works with UNICEF and Save the Children and, as part of this process, has created a position within its organization that deals specifically with this issue.

Role of NGOs

IKEA's local purchasing departments monitor the implementation of their CSR agreements and codes of conduct, such as whether suppliers adhere to IKEA's requirements, while its internal compliance and monitoring group follows up with developments on a global basis. Monitoring is verified by independent auditing companies that simultaneously play consultancy roles for implementing codes of conduct. Third-party verification represents an important element of the internal audit process. In biannual meetings, IKEA communicates these audit results to the IFBWW and, in a reduced version, to the wider public through its annual social and environmental report. Independent organizations continuously assess and challenge the social and environmental measures implemented by IKEA; for example, Greenpeace, Robin Wood (a German environmental protection NGO) and SOMO (a Dutch research foundation) have repeatedly attacked IKEA for not respecting its environmental, social and human rights responsibilities. As recently as 2006, studies identified serious problems in the way that IKEA implemented its codes of conduct, such as in terms of freedom of association and collective bargaining, salary levels, work conditions and workers' rights.[32]

Reactive and proactive actions taken by IKEA

As a result of these external pressures, IKEA has integrated its CSR objectives more systematically into its management philosophy and business operations. For example, IKEA decided to adapt in response to social demands from public regulators (e.g. in Denmark and Germany), trade unions (e.g. IFBWW, FNV), the media and NGOs (e.g. Greenpeace, Robin Wood, Save the Children). Our findings demonstrate that IKEA reacts quickly when its image or reputation is challenged, such as when it recognized the high proportion of carcinogenic formaldehyde in particleboard sold in Denmark. The same year, IKEA's management established large-scale testing of its products and

introduced new requirements for its suppliers. Because of its success
in responding to such external criticism, IKEA has been nicknamed
the 'Teflon company'.[33]

However, IKEA also proactively seeks to anticipate stakeholders'
demands; for example, it increased collaboration with The Natural
Step and gradually transformed its environmental policy into an
efficient and adjustable plan of action with concrete business practices. IKEA also is a member of various business networks, including
Business for Social Responsibility and Global Compact.

CSR communication

Our analysis of IKEA's advertising to the general public through the
media indicates that the organization seldom includes direct references to its CSR commitments. There is, for example, no mention
of CSR in the nine key messages IKEA conveys to its customers: the
'IKEA concept', the 'IKEA product range', 'home furnishing spe-
cialist', 'low price', 'function', the 'right quality', 'convenient shopping', a 'day out for the whole family' and 'Swedish'.[34] Instead, IKEA
stresses its emphasis on the family and the environment, its Swedish
roots and, in turn, the solidarity and egalitarianism traditionally
associated with Sweden. Explains Jean-Louis Baillot, CEO of IKEA
France, 'people consider that IKEA has an environmental behavior'
because of its Scandinavian roots, which means that 'it is ultimately
not inevitably necessary to speak about it'.[35]

Traditional means of communication

Prior to 2005, IKEA used its stores, product catalogues and product
packaging to communicate its CSR policies to the public. For example,
the store's brochures contained information relating to various products' environmental impact and the 2004 catalogue included two
pages that centred on CSR themes. Inside stores, customers could also
read about IKEA's cause-related marketing campaigns and cooperative actions with Save the Children and UNICEF, as well as review
'green panels' that advised them about good consumption practices.
Since 2005 though, such descriptions of IKEA's environmental and
social efforts no longer appear in catalogues. In most countries, the
only ways to find information about the organization's CSR polices,

codes of conduct, brochures and annual reports are through the national IKEA websites.

Specific means of communication

IKEA's first social and environmental responsibility report was published in 2004 (for the year 2003). This report described how IKEA had incorporated CSR into its entire supply chain and its collaboration with various NGOs. Anders Dahlvig, CEO of IKEA, declared that IKEA's partners 'have been eager to start working seriously with these issues and have progressed step by step, but it is only now, when we have accomplished a little more, that it seems right to start telling the rest of the world about it'. The CEO also stressed that it was best to remain humble about what the organization had accomplished so far, 'because there is so much more that still remains to be done'.[36] Overall, this first report provided transparent communication about IKEA's CSR.

However, the report lists few numerical objectives and virtually no performance indicators. The 2005 and 2006 reports contain such information, though both objectives and indicators remain very general, which makes it difficult to judge the extent to which IKEA truly integrates CSR considerations into its business models. For example, its IWAY code of conduct contains several different performance levels, the first of which details the minimum requirements a supplier must meet to work with IKEA. But published reports do not clearly indicate the level of responsibility the organization and its suppliers have achieved in different areas. Approximations appear to be the rule rather than the exception in these reports.

When it comes to solutions it has implemented, IKEA remains vague in its descriptions, though it claims to have set up more CSR objectives and employed additional CSR indicators to guide its internal operations. On the basis of this description, the reports might best be regarded as a specific means of communicating with the general public.

Why has IKEA been so reluctant to place social and environmental labels on its products, even though the products meet criteria for products made of tropical wood materials? Our findings suggest the rationale is not rooted in cost and administrative considerations but rather in the organization's consciousness that the IKEA brand itself should 'be a guarantee of environmental consideration and social responsibility'.[37] Another reason IKEA has chosen to be cautious in communicating about its CSR is to avoid promoting 'itself as a target for anti-globalization organizations which focus on big brand names like ours despite our many community- and environment-friendly policies and contributions'.[38]

The next logical question pertains to perceptions of IKEA's communication. We find that the organization has not developed a particularly structured dialogue with its external stakeholders. Although IKEA states it collaborates with various external stakeholders throughout the world, NGOs and trade unions (except IFBWW) are not invited to participate in monitoring and auditing IKEA's CSR policies. Instead, these organizations receive completed audits and reports containing CSR information. Thus, these stakeholders (but not consumers) generally perceive a lack of transparency or clarity in relation to IKEA's CSR communication and consider it unsystematic, overly general and imprecise. In contrast, IKEA's communication with international partners or formal or legal partners, such as city councils and governmental organizations, is more transparent and comprehensive. Finally, even though 77 per cent of the surveyed consumers say they do not know much about IKEA's CSR initiatives, these stakeholders rarely ask for IKEA to communicate more about its CSR.

Impact of CSR commitments and communication on diverse stakeholders

Although generally appreciated, IKEA's efforts to reduce the negative environmental impact of itself and its products seem too slow to many stakeholders. Greenpeace, Robin Wood and other NGOs specifically assert that IKEA could be clearer and more transparent in communicating its CSR commitments. According to one researcher with an organization that analyses multinational organizations, including IKEA:

I would like to know what they are doing actually, but it's not very transparent, not even when we have spoken to them. They were open, but we didn't know what we could expect from them, they were not really clear.

Another observer, a member of an organization that advocates forest protection and has criticized IKEA's environmental practices, characterizes the organization's communication as:

A lot of words, but not very concrete! I'm not sure. But they communicate very little concrete stuff, and therefore it is hard to judge them. This is what they want. They want to be in the grey zone.

With regard to the supply chain, most stakeholders perceive IKEA positively but criticize those involved in auditing and reporting. Many interviewees, such as the Belgian trade unionist quoted next, consider the inclusion of trade unions and NGOs as highly important:

IKEA won't work with the unions in developing its CSR policies. However, it would really be better if they did. Likewise, they don't want to work with NGOs. They work alone.

Also, the manner in which suppliers are monitored seems not fully clear or evident to IKEA's stakeholders.

Frequently, IKEA further receives criticism that its stores destroy the local economy and put local businesses out of work. However, stakeholders also recognize that IKEA stores offer employment and access to a commercial network. These stakeholders remain concerned though about IKEA's labour contracts, which often offer work only when there is an actual need for it. On a general level, our investigation suggests stakeholders want to support IKEA in its CSR implementation efforts, even though most of them remain sceptical about its CSR commitments and communications.

Consumers

Although surveyed consumers feel they have little factual knowledge of IKEA's CSR commitments, they consider IKEA's commitments somewhat positively; only 5.4 per cent have formed unfavourable perceptions. Furthermore, 70.4 per cent of consumers, who remember having come across IKEA communication about its CSR initiatives, hold a favourable opinion; in contrast, only 30.3 per cent of those who do not remember such communication, hold a favourable opinion. Our analysis also shows that consumers who most associate social equity, ecology, responsibility and ethics with the image of Sweden (N = 68) have a more favourable opinion of IKEA's CSR initiatives than do consumers (N = 60) who least associate these terms with Sweden. This difference appears crucial, in that 95 per cent of the surveyed consumers actually named Sweden as the country of origin for IKEA in a multiple-choice question. Also, though 40.6 per cent of the surveyed customers indicated they would boycott IKEA if the organization performed badly on the CSR indicators they considered important, a positive impression about CSR initiatives was not sufficient reason for these consumers to buy IKEA's products. We cannot establish any significant relationship between appreciation for IKEA's CSR policies and behavioural intentions towards the brand. Our results reinforce the well-known assumption of the asymmetry between doing good and doing bad: doing good does not always help but doing bad hurts.

Long-term partners

Those NGOs and other organizations that collaborate, often internationally and formally, with IKEA on social, socioeconomic and environmental matters have some access to privileged information that is unavailable to the general public. Therefore, these partners maintain a positive view of IKEA's CSR commitments and regard it as a proactive organization that does not want to exploit its image as a responsible corporate citizen:

IKEA's CSR policies are good and serve as an example for other companies. They have very progressive targets, and a firm commitment and strategies in place to implement them (representative of an international nature protection organization).

Although IKEA has not realized its CSR policies fully, these partners believe the organization is on the right track and

expect more openness about how they are managing their suppliers in terms of working times, work conditions, salary, etc. More transparency! But, I don't feel that many companies do that (representative of a national division of an international child protection organization).

Partners also support IKEA's attitude towards CSR but simultaneously stress that they continue to observe the organization's CSR commitment and communication:

I believe they are on their way, but at the moment we would welcome more detailed communication on progress toward their social and environmental goals (representative of an international nature protection organization).

Organizations other than partners

In the past, organizations such as Oxfam Belgium, Robin Wood and Somo, with which IKEA has no partnerships, have criticized IKEA regarding its CSR commitments. Believing that much work still needs to be accomplished, these organizations blame IKEA's CSR guidelines for being unclear and its implementation for being too slow. More important, they regard the slow implementation of CSR policies as a sign of IKEA's lack of determination:

I think most of the work is still ahead of them and that they have taken some steps in the right direction. But it is still far away from our vision of what a really responsible corporation is supposed to be. (Representative of an international nature protection organization that has developed a regular, but informal dialogue with IKEA since the beginning of the 1990s)

In contrast with long-term partners, most of these other organizations regard IKEA as reacting more than acting when it comes to CSR:

They can't check their own labor conditions. What they call external verifications is not external. They hire them, they pay them, and they make them check their own labor. Obviously we would like another model as sometimes in other industries. (Researcher with an organization that analyses multinational companies' activities, including IKEA)

However, similar to long-term partners, other organizations are sceptical about IKEA's CSR communication, especially when it comes to transparency:

I would ask them to be more transparent ... I think that for a multinational organization like IKEA, which is sourcing all over the world, the customer should have the possibility to check what is going on in the shops. Also, the organization that claims to be socially and environmentally responsible should give the customer the opportunity to verify this. (Representative of a forest protection organization that has criticized IKEA's environmental practices)

City councils

Because of its socioeconomic impact, most city councils favour IKEA setting up stores in their neighbourhood; any potential loss for the traditional socioeconomic network gets compensated for by the creation of economic clusters around IKEA's massive stores. As one member of a Belgian economic affairs committee summarized it, 'At the social and socioeconomic levels, they first bring employment, which is valuable.'

IKEA's presence affects not only the level of employment (particularly among unskilled workers) but also regional visibility and commercial activities. Furthermore, city councils consider IKEA superior to other large organizations in terms of how it deals with social and environmental issues:

It's an organization that has proved to me, with facts, that they are for the environment and that they are engaged. I consider IKEA a lot more favorably than other organizations in the retail and in the furniture sectors. (Representative of a Belgian committee in charge of environmental and socioeconomic permits).

Trade unions

Trade union representatives working with IKEA regard the organization's CSR policies as more developed than those of other organizations. But they also consider IKEA's communication about its CSR policies insufficient:

The CSR policies are certainly interesting because they go deeper than in other organizations. But, they stay hidden, in the way that there is very little communication about them. (Belgian trade unionist)

These stakeholders want IKEA to develop their CSR policies further as well:

In a certain way, we can't expect a lot more in terms of CSR. Now, does it meet our expectations? It is clear that we would like to see them go further. (Belgian trade unionist)

Overall, the trade union representatives support and encourage IKEA in its CSR commitments, though they maintain their somewhat critical attitude.

Organizations specializing in CSR

Many organizations that specialize in CSR consulting, promotion and monitoring indicate a positive view of IKEA. They share the feeling that, when it comes to CSR, IKEA is more proactive than reactive, though they challenge the organization for focusing on very specific CSR issues, such as child labour and environmental concerns, at the expense of other issues, such as human resource management and workers' rights in developing countries. Similar to other stakeholders, these organizations also see weaknesses in IKEA's communication efforts:

They have much to develop when it comes to the interface with the consumers, on the marketing side, because they almost don't speak. Also, what they say seems to generate questions and, potentially, controversies. (Senior business consultant specializing in sustainable development issues)

These organizations also regret that IKEA rarely partakes in local programmes designed to share best practices in CSR. Although IKEA plays an active part in large, international, CSR-oriented networks, the organization still is perceived as weak in this area, as:

an organization that bases its philosophy around a responsible dimension, which sees itself as really responsible. But, I think it's an organization that doesn't look for communicating or sharing its strategy, its way of working. (Director of a European business and society network)

Even despite these complaints, these organizations generally respect IKEA for its CSR commitments.

This contrast among different stakeholders clearly demonstrates that, on the one hand, NGOs, city councils and trade unions maintain positive attitudes towards IKEA and its CSR commitments, largely because they stay in regular and direct contact with IKEA regarding social or environmental issues. On the other hand, other organizations, which have publicly criticized IKEA about CSR-related issues, express relatively serious worries and doubts about its implementation of its CSR commitments; some (former) partners share this view as well. Quite a few stakeholder groups express a critical view of IKEA's CSR communication and the transparency of this communication. This critique results in a sceptical attitude, especially if the stakeholder does not engage in direct dialogue with IKEA.

Managerial implications

This study examines how IKEA commits itself to CSR and how it communicates its policies to multiple stakeholders. In particular, we identify the important role that stakeholders play in IKEA's CSR policies and the added value associated with CSR commitment and communication. We also note that IKEA often develops its CSR policies in response to criticism. On the basis of the case study findings and our analysis of these findings, we draw several key managerial implications.

Listening to external stakeholders and acting both reactively and proactively

By letting IKEA know how they perceive the organization, whether by criticizing it publicly or entering into a collaborative, constructive relationship with it, external stakeholders have influenced IKEA's CSR policies significantly at various times. In response to external stakeholders' expectations or requirements, IKEA has changed its business practices. In some cases, IKEA has been quick to anticipate demands that external stakeholders may place on the organization, whereas in other cases, it has resolved a situation or a problem successfully after the crisis occurred and used communication to inform concerned stakeholders how it was dealing with the problem. IKEA's strategy thus involves carefully managing its CSR commitments in a strategic manner. Initially reactive to CSR complaints, the organization has gradually increased its proactive policies and coupled them with reactive responses when needed. This dual strategy partially explains why IKEA experiences crises but has never had to endure them for a prolonged period.

Demonstrating factual commitment and highlighting achievements

Scepticism constitutes a significant portion of stakeholders' perceptions of and attitudes towards an organization. When organizations communicate with or engage in dialogue processes with their stakeholders about CSR issues, they can reduce potential disbelief about their CSR statements and promises by developing reciprocal trust through the demonstration of credible and measurable organizational commitment. Conversely, a perceived lack of organizational deter-mination for CSR issues can lead stakeholders to question the organ-ization's commitment to its own CSR policies. In this sense, the IKEA case demonstrates that some level of transparency is necessary in dia-logue with stakeholders, so as to reduce their scepticism and create more positive attitudes towards the company. In this sense, as the organization implements its CSR policies, it is important to volun-tarily communicate on its progress and what remains to be achieved. Organizations should avoid being overly humble in their communica-tion, as IKEA often has been in the past, because such coyness could be considered an attempt to fool external stakeholders, which only generates suspicion and unwanted scrutiny. At the same time, organi-zations need to figure out what to say, how much to say, how to say it, when to say it and where to say it.

Communicating with external stakeholders using appropriate tools

IKEA has not felt the need to extensively advertise its CSR commit-ments. Rather, IKEA carefully selects specific CSR commitments such as children's rights and reduced environmental impact to communi-cate its responsibility stance. Furthermore, IKEA mainly maintains its image by using appealing elements including family, cultural and eth-ical values to indirectly portray its CSR commitments. With regard to organizational and institutional stakeholders, IKEA uses specifically adapted communication means, such as its annual CSR report. Our findings highlight the complexity associated with reaching decisions about the nature and level of communication. For example, the need to communicate varies depending on the type of stakeholder and the importance that the stakeholder places on CSR, as well as the stake-holder's potential influence. In the case of IKEA, NGOs and trade unions have been more influential than consumers, so communica-tion with these external stakeholders adds more value.

Involving external stakeholders in design and monitoring

Although its commitment to CSR and attempts to communicate that commitment positively influence IKEA's image in most cases, its decision to keep surveys confidential and exclude most external stakeholders from implementing and monitoring different CSR initiatives means it has missed some opportunities to improve its CSR policies. Organizations must realize that engaging with stakeholders in a constructive manner requires both time and effort. In the case of IKEA, for example, the organization paid considerable attention to its relationships with WWF and UNICEF. The parties entered into an ongoing dialogue, trusted each other and made compromises along the way, resulting in highly successful relationships. This example demonstrates the importance of involving external stakeholders in the design and monitoring processes when developing CSR initiatives, which indicates the organization is willing to change its CSR policies and thereby signals its credibility to the outside world.

Continuously developing CSR policies

The developments that have taken place in IKEA's external environment highlight the need to reconsider CSR policies regularly and through dialogue with the organization's various stakeholders, who want to be kept informed on how its commitments to CSR are being honoured or improved. If such adaptations do not occur, organizations risk significant criticism. To achieve successful communication, organizations should integrate external stakeholders in the way we depict in Figure 6.2. First, by including a feedback loop for stakeholders' perceptions of the organization, organizations acknowledge that their CSR policy involves a continuous process. Second, the framework awards a central role to external stakeholders whenever organizations revisit their CSR policies or communicate with the external environment. Third, stakeholders' attitudes towards an organization's CSR commitments depend on the nature and intensity of the dialogue between the organization and the stakeholders, as well as their perceptions of its honesty.

Conclusions and discussions

Drawing from our development of the case, we outline some key strategic implications for IKEA and organizations interested in CSR in general. The effective influence of stakeholders in the CSR development process and the variability of their perceptions about CSR activities and communication should prompt researchers to

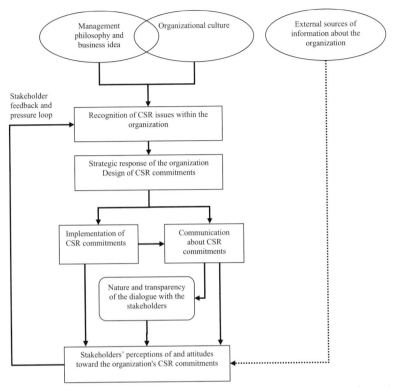

Figure 6.2 Stakeholders' role in the integration and development of IKEA's CSR policies

analyse CSR development issues and conduct impact analyses in a more comprehensive manner than currently exists. The crucial role of stakeholders' differential perceptions about the transparency and credibility of information about an organization's CSR commitments should remain central to any research effort; thus, our identification of different stakeholders' unique attitudes towards IKEA represents an important contribution.

As does most research, this study has several limitations that affect our interpretation of the findings and suggest directions for further research. First, our study is based on a single-case approach. Second, though we interviewed stakeholders from various European countries, the Belgian context predominates in the interviews of union representatives and local authorities and therefore may influence or bias the analysis. In addition, though we gathered information from a representative sample of external stakeholders, we could not address every category of stakeholder. Third, we only surveyed consumers through a convenience sample; also, we only used a questionnaire including mainly closed questions. In-depth discussions with consumers, as well as a larger survey on a representative sample could increase the validity of our conclusions. Fourth, our research is limited to an a posteriori analysis of CSR policies in a particular industry, which does not allow us to observe the formation or shifts in the key stakeholders' perceptions and attitudes directly. Real time and longitudinal data, rather than historical information and interviewee recall, would therefore extend our study effectively.

Moreover, follow-up case studies that address the entire CSR implementation cycle, as well as other industry contexts, are needed to generalize our results and establish a comprehensive framework of CSR commitments and communication. Further research also might consider additional cases to highlight any similarities and differences across cases and possible reasons for those differences. For example, researchers might analyse different organizations in different sectors to distinguish the roles of the content and nature of CSR policies, an organization's historical background in CSR in terms of stakeholder perceptions and attitudes and the organization's origin, as well as the respective influences of perceived CSR levels and CSR communication alternatives.

Other potential further research avenues include a comparative analysis of the role of various stakeholders in the organization's development of its CSR policies. In this sense, it would be worthwhile to evaluate comprehensively and systematically the influence of different stakeholder groups on organizational changes demanded by the integration of CSR principles into corporate strategy. Related CSR communicational choices thus might be revised and tailored to the expectations of each particular category of stakeholders. Also, the impact of organizational and strategic changes on the perceptions and attitudes of various stakeholders should be highlighted during different steps of the integration process. Finally, the critical role of transparency when implementing and communicating about CSR commitments warrants further research. For example, transparency may aid in the development of trust in the stakeholder dialogue processes, but it also may increase the level of expectations of the company, to the extent that the company is being criticized.

Companies should therefore determine the appropriate level of transparency when implementing and communicating about their CSR activities.

Acknowledgements

The authors contributed equally to this article. They offer sincere thanks to the organizations that participated in the study. They also thank Martin Hingley and Joëlle Vanhamme for critical comments to an earlier version of this chapter.

Appendix: data collection and analysis

We collected data for this case study using various methods. To increase our familiarity with the issues, we reviewed more than 200 pieces of written documentation, including promotional materials, previous case studies and IKEA websites. These data are comprehensive, particularly with respect to CSR elements and their implementation. We also rely on and refer back to this information during and following our in-depth interviews, which we describe next. Finally, to determine how IKEA communicates its CSR policies, we visited six stores in Belgium, France and the Netherlands on several occasions and analysed the 2004–5 media campaigns by reviewing all of IKEA's thirty-six national and international websites, IKEA catalogues for each individual country, English and French newspaper articles and advertising, television and billboard displays, and press releases from IKEA and its partner NGOs.

In addition to this document-based research, we interviewed in depth two senior IKEA managers. Twenty external stakeholders, who could impact IKEA's CSR policies in some way, participated in interviews as well. These stakeholders include nine NGOs (five international) that dealt with human rights and environment issues; two trade unions; one interest group for small and medium-sized enterprises; four organizations specializing in CSR consulting, promotion and monitoring; three city councils; and an international research foundation. These latter interviews serve to corroborate or challenge the findings we obtained in our in-depth interviews with the IKEA representatives.

For both types of interviews, we kept our questions deliberately broad to allow respondents as much freedom in their answers as possible.[39] For the interviews within IKEA, the questions focused on the organization's CSR commitments, the historical development of these commitments, issues raised by NGOs and trade unions, and CSR communication and marketing policies. The questions for the external stakeholders focused on the nature of the relationship between the stakeholder and IKEA, the stakeholder's perception and knowledge of IKEA's CSR commitments and communication, and the stakeholder's opinion about IKEA's CSR policies. Our interviews continued until we reached saturation, that is, when extra interviews yielded no more additional insights. Each interview lasted an average of one hour (range: thirty minutes to two hours). This process resulted in a transcript of 193 pages (twelve-point font, single-spaced). The IKEA interviewees, who had been involved in developing the organization's CSR policies, represent the richest source of information for investigating the issues at hand, whereas the external stakeholders make appropriate interviewees because of their work in dealing with a variety of CSR issues and, more particularly, because they had been critical of IKEA's CSR policies.

To obtain customer feedback, we distributed a self-administered questionnaire to 150 customers who had visited at least one IKEA store in the previous thirty-six months. We handed out the questionnaire to the general public – people in offices, on trains, or queuing (convenience sample). Our goal with this questionnaire is to determine how much customers know about IKEA's CSR policies, how they come to know about these policies, how they perceive these policies and what their attitudes towards these policies are.

Together, these data collection methods improve the robustness of our findings, compensate for the weaknesses of any one data collection method, improve the quality of our final interpretation and help ensure triangulation.[40] The unit of analysis we use is IKEA's CSR policies, commitment and communication. Therefore, we combine the information from each set of interviews and the secondary sources into one final case manuscript.

Next, we analysed the case using Eisenhardt's method.[41] That is, we first attempt to gain a richer understanding of the process IKEA underwent in terms of its CSR. Therefore, we create a timeline that includes information about how different stakeholders have influenced its CSR policies. Using open and axial coding procedures, we elaborate on the emergent theoretical categories.[42] Throughout the analysis, we tacked back and forward between the literature on CSR and the data, which enables us to develop five theoretical categories and 141 subcategories. In addition, our analysis relies on the software ATLAS-Ti to keep track of the data, facilitate coding and check for relationships. This software allows for a qualitative analysis of large bodies of textual, graphical, audio and video data; the software offers a variety of tools for accomplishing the tasks associated with any systematic approach to soft data, which cannot be sufficiently analysed using formalized, statistical approaches.[43]

Throughout this study, we adopted several methods to improve the quality of the research. Experts helped select the case organization and the external stakeholders; three independent researchers provided their individual interpretations of the findings; we conducted multiple interviews; and interviewees could provide feedback on our initial findings, all of which reinforces the reliability of our study. Although all the authors performed independent coding of the transcripts, the interviews were conducted by the same interviewer, which reduces the potential for bias.

Notes

1 See, for example, T.J. Brown and P.A. Dacin, 'The Company and the Product: Corporate Associations and Consumer Product Responses', *Journal of Marketing*, 61/1 (1997): 68–84; D. Greening and D. Turban, 'Corporate Social Performance as a Competitive Advantage in Attracting a Quality Workforce', *Business and Society*, 39/ 3 (2000): 254–80; P. Rivoli, 'Ethical Aspects of Investor Behaviour', *Journal of Business Ethics*, 14/4 (1995): 265–77.

2 See, for example, P. Argenti, 'Collaborating with Activists: How Starbucks Works with NGOs', *California Management Review*, 47/1 (2004): 91–116; T. Guay, J. Doh and G. Sinclair, 'Non-Governmental Organizations, Shareholder Activism, and Socially Responsible Investments: Ethical, Strategic, and Governance Implications', *Journal of Business Ethics*, 52/1 (2004): 125–39.

3 B. Altman, 'Transformed Corporate Community Relations: A Management Tool for Achieving Corporate Citizenship', *Business and Society Review*, 102–103 (1998): 43–51.

4 A. Crane and D. Matten, *Business Ethics: A European Perspective. Managing Corporate Citizenship and Sustainability in the Age of Globalisation* (Oxford: Oxford University Press, 2003).

5 M. McIntosh, D. Leipziger, K. Jones and G. Coleman, *Corporate Citizenship: Successful Strategies for Responsible Companies* (London: Financial Times-Pitman Publishing, 1998).

6 Environics International, *Millennium Poll on Corporate Social Responsibility* (Toronto: Environics International Ltd., 1999).

7 Canal IPSOS, 'Vers un consom'acteur européen', Sofinco-IPSOS survey (March 2004), available at www.sofinco.com/encyclo_conso/enquete_consox6.asp# (accessed 15 September 2006).

8 S. Lauer, 'La distribution est désemparée face aux alterconsommateurs', *Le Monde*, 25 July 2004, p. 23.

9 See, for example, M. Carrigan and A. Attalla, 'The Myth of the Ethical Consumer – Do Ethics Matter in Consumer Behaviour?', *Journal of Consumer Marketing*, 18/7 (2001): 560–76; E. Boulstridge and M. Carrigan, 'Do Consumers Really Care about Corporate Responsibility? Highlighting the Attitude-Behaviour Gap', *Journal of Communication Management*, 4/6 (2000): 421–33.

10 See, for example, M. Bhandrakar and T. Alvarez-Rivero, 'From Supply Chains to Value Chains: A Spotlight on CSR', in D. O'Connor and M. Kjollerstrom (eds.), *Industrial Development for the 21st Century* (London: Zed Books, 2008), pp. 387–414; A. Warhurst, 'Corporate Citizenship and Corporate Social Investment: Drivers of Tri-Sector Partnerships', *Journal of Corporate Citizenship*, 1/1 (2001): 57–73.

11 H.R. Bowen, *Responsibilities of the Businessman* (New York: Harper & Brothers, 1953), p. 6; A. McWilliams and D. Siegel, 'Corporate Social Responsibility: A Theory of the Firm Perspective', *Academy of Management Review*, 26/1 (2001): pp. 117–27.

12 See, for example, E. Garriga and D. Melé, 'Corporate Social Responsibility Theories: Mapping the Territory', *Journal of Business Ethics*, 53/1–2 (2004): 51–71; F.G.A. De Bakker, P. Groenewegen and F. Den Hond, 'A Bibliometric Analysis of 30 Years of Research and Theory on Corporate Social Responsibility and Corporate Social Performance', *Business & Society*, 44/3 (2005): 283–317.

13 A.B. Carroll, 'A Three-Dimensional Conceptual Model of Corporate Performance', *Academy of Management Review*, 4/4 (1979): 497–505.

14 Carroll (1979).

15 D.A. Whetten, G. Rands and P. Godfrey, 'What Are the Responsibilities of Business to Society?', in A. Pettigrew, H. Thomas and R. Whittington (eds.), *Handbook of Strategy and Management* (London: Sage, 2002), pp. 373–408.

16 J.O. Lamberg, G.T. Savage and K. Pajunen, 'Strategic Stakeholder Perspective to ESOP Negotiations: The Case of United Airlines', *Management Decision*, 41/4 (2003): 383–93.

17 M. Capron and F. Quairel, *Mythes et Réalités de l'Entreprise Responsable* (Paris: Editions la découverte, 2004).

18 A. Sen, 'Does Business Ethics Make Economic Sense?', *Business Ethics Quarterly*, 3/1 (1993): 45–54.

19 See Brown and Dacin (1997); C. Fombrun and M. Shanley, 'What's in a Name? Reputation Building and Corporate Strategy', *Academy of Management Journal*, 33/2 (1990): 233–58.

20 S. Tombs and D. Smith, 'Corporate Social Responsibility and Crisis Management: The Democratic Organization and Crisis Prevention', *Corporate Responsibility and Crisis Management*, 3/3 (1995): 135–48.

21 L.A. Mohr, D.J. Webb and K.E. Harris, 'Do Consumers Expect Companies to be Socially Responsible? The Impact of Corporate Social Responsibility on Buying Behavior', *The Journal of Consumer Affairs*, 35/1 (2001): 45–72.

22 S. Sen and C.B. Bhattacharya, 'Does Doing Good Always Lead to Doing Better? Consumer Reactions to Corporate Social Responsibility', *Journal of Marketing Research*, 38/2 (2001): 225–43.

23 R.K. Yin, *Case Study Research: Design and Methods*, 3rd edn (Thousand Oaks, CA: Sage, 2002).

24 A. Strauss and J. Corbin, *Basics of Qualitative Research*, 2nd edn (Newbury Park, CA: Sage, 1998).

25 IKEA Group, Social and Environmental Responsibility brochure 2006, www.ikea-group.ikea.com/corporate/PDF/Brochure.pdf (accessed 22 June 2006).

26 S. Christopherson and N. Lillie, 'Neither Global Nor Standard: Corporate Strategies in the New Era of Labor Standards', *Environment and Planning*, 37/11 (2005): 1919–38.

27 E. Lewis, *Great IKEA!: A Brand for All the People* (London: Cyan Books, 2005).

28 The Natural Step, *Organizational Case Summary IKEA* (1999), available at www.naturalstep.it/learn/docs/cs/case_ikea.pdf (accessed 15 September 2008).

29 G. Dauncey, 'Small Green Steps to Harmonize with Nature', *EarthFuture Eco News*, 85 (1999), available at: www.earthfuture.com/econews/back_issues/99-07.asp (accessed 25 September 2006).

30 I. Maignan and D. McAlister, 'Socially Responsible Organizational Buying: How Can Stakeholders Dictate Purchasing Policies?', *Journal of Macromarketing*, 23/2 (2003): 78–89.

31 J. Doh and T. Guay, 'Globalization and Corporate Social Responsibility: How Non-Governmental Organizations Influence Labor and Environmental Codes of Conduct', *Management International Review*, 44/2 (2004): 7–30.

32 O. Bailly, D. Lambert and J.-M. Caudron, *IKEA: des modèles à monter, un modèle à démonter* (Brussels: Editions Luc Pire, 2006); E. De Haan and J. Oldenziel, 'Labour Conditions in IKEA's Supply Chain – Case Studies in India, Bulgaria and Vietnam', Stichting Onderzoek Multinationale Ondermingen, Amsterdam, 2003.

33 K. Miller, 'The Teflon Shield', *Newsweek*, 12 March 2001, p. 36.

34 Lewis (2005).

35 Comité 21, Conference of IKEA, France's CEO Jean-Louis Baillot at the Meeting of the French Comité 21, 23 March 2004, www.comite21.org/rencontres_debats/rd2004/baillot.pdf (accessed 22 June 2006).

36 IKEA Group, Social and Environmental Responsibility 2003 report,www.ikea-group.ikea.com/corporate/PDF/IKEA%20Report2003.pdf (accessed 22 June 2006).

37 IKEA Group (2006: 11).

38 Marianne Barner, director of corporate communications at IKEA, quoted in Lewis (2005: 175).

39 B.G. Glaser and A.L. Strauss, *The Discovery of Grounded Theory* (New York: Aldine de Gruyter, 1967).

40 T.D. Jick, 'Mixing Qualitative and Quantitative Methods: Triangulation in Action', *Administrative Science Quarterly*, 24/4 (1979): 602–11; Strauss and Corbin (1998); Yin (2002).

41 Kathleen M. Eisenhardt, 'Building Theories from Case Study Research', *Academy of Management Review*, 14/4 (1989): 532–50; J. Hamel and S. Dufour, *Case Study Methods* (Newbury Park, CA: Sage, 1993); Yin (2002).

42 Strauss and Corbin (1998).

43 www.atlasti.com.

7 | *The relationship between corporate responsibility and brand loyalty in retailing: the mediating role of trust*

FRANCESCO PERRINI, SANDRO
CASTALDO, NICOLA MISANI AND
ANTONIO TENCATI

While the history of empirical research about the relationship between the social and the financial performance of companies has been studied for years, the literature still lacks, according to many, a convincing proof that corporate social responsibility (CSR) adds to the bottom line. J.D. Margolis and J.P. Walsh[1] emphasized that numerous empirical studies conducted in the last thirty years on the relationship between the social and financial performance of firms present serious methodological problems (in sampling, accurate measurement of social performance, absence of intermediate variables, absence of tests for the direction of the causal link). S.A. Waddock and S.B. Graves[2] had already pointed out that research on social and financial performance was replete with difficult obstacles:

(1) Social performance is hard to measure directly; proxy measures, such as social expenses, are more observable but are not necessarily desirable antecedents of social performance.
(2) The link between social and financial performance is mediated by many factors; this link could be embedded in a complex causal web in which the company's response to social issues comprise only part of the relevant considerations.
(3) The direction of the causal link cannot be easily assessed, because the most financially successful companies will always have resources to 'waste' on social investment, while companies in financial crisis will often be forced to curtail such investment.

In 2003, M. Orlitzky *et al.* analysed fifty-two studies published between 1972 and 1997 and concluded that the relationship between corporate social performance (CSP) and corporate financial performance (CFP) is bidirectional and simultaneous: 'the causation seems to be that CSP and CFP mutually affect each other through a virtuous cycle: financially successful companies spend more because they can afford it, but CSP also helps become a bit more successful'.[3] Even though the evidence collected by M. Orlitzky *et al.* supports the idea that, over the long term, social and environmental performance do not negatively impact the bottom line, such evidence does not provide a strong basis for orienting managerial choice in business practice.

In our study, we will tackle the issue from a different perspective. Instead of considering direct correlations between CSP and CFP indicators, we investigate whether companies perceived as socially oriented improve their relationships with key stakeholder groups. Consumers are one group expected to be particularly sensitive to a company's CSP. Many surveys suggest a positive relationship between a company's CSP and consumers' intentions towards that company and its products.[4]

Moreover, we argue that consumer perceptions that a company is socially oriented are associated with a higher level of trust in that company and its products. *Trust* in this case means the expectation that the trustee is willing to keep promises and to fulfil obligations. Trust literature has identified many antecedents, such as the competence, honesty and goodwill of the trustee.[5] Some of these antecedents clearly overlap with the attributes of a company perceived as socially oriented. Marketing literature[6] assumes that trust, when present, is translated into a consumer's intention to purchase. Therefore, we hypothesize that trust links consumer perceptions of CSP with intentions to purchase.

We suggest that, while there is no reason to expect that CSR *per se* will give companies a market lead, CSP can be leveraged to market products that cohere with positive ethical and social value systems. These products will primarily appeal to consumers interested in specific issues or who are particularly sensitive to the ethical aspects of purchasing. For these products, CSR can be a source of competitive advantage, because competitors with bad CSP will be unable to replicate the success of the leader. Even when they can replicate the products, their bad CSP will make it difficult for them to convince consumers that they will behave ethically and responsibly in all areas concerning their products.

To assess this idea, we conducted empirical research on a sample of retail customers who buy Fair Trade products. Usually, consumers are not able to verify that Fair Trade products are obtained according to the 'fair' terms alleged by the importer (with regard to price paid to local producers, working conditions and protection of environment). Therefore, trusted retailers selling Fair Trade products under their own private label should be considered a further guarantee that the relevant guidelines are actually respected. Consistent with this reasoning, we developed and tested a model in which consumer opinions that a retailer is socially oriented are related to trust in Fair Trade in general and to the consumer intention to purchase private-label Fair Trade products from that retailer.

Theoretical background

CSR

Despite the recent revival of interest, CSR is not a brand-new concept. The idea that business has a social role is centuries old.[7] The first modern definition of social responsibility was provided by H.R. Bowen,[8] who proposed that businessmen are responsible for the consequences of their actions in a sphere somewhat wider than that covered by their profit-and-loss statements.

Since Bowen's seminal work, several different approaches to CSR have been developed.[9] Despite criticism, policy-makers, citizens and companies are paying increasing attention to CSR. Among other institutions, the European Commission published a Green Paper[10] that defines CSR as 'a concept whereby companies integrate social and environmental concerns in their business operations and in their interaction with their stakeholders on a voluntary basis'. A related concept is CSP. Building on contributions by A.B. Carroll, S.L. Wartick and P.L. Cochran, D.J. Wood defined CSP as 'a business organization's configuration of principles of social responsibility, processes of social responsiveness, and policies, programs, and observable outcomes as they relate to the firm's societal relationships'.[11]

Traditional arguments in support of CSR underscore the benefits that should accrue to a socially responsible company from key stakeholder groups.[12] Many believe that consumers are particularly sensitive to a company's CSP. Numerous surveys suggest a positive correlation between a company's CSP and consumers' intentions towards that company and its products.[13] In particular, socially oriented companies should be able to differentiate among competitors, enhance customer satisfaction and improve their reputation.

While a positive relationship between CSP and purchasing intentions is expected, measuring the resulting benefits is difficult. According to T.J. Brown and D.A. Dacin,[14] CSR policies influence consumers' purchasing intentions only indirectly by creating a general context for their evaluation. Little research has been done on the real effects of CSP on consumers. Other studies suggest that 'consumer reactions to CSR are not straightforward and evident as the marketplace polls suggest'[15]; in fact, many factors should be taken into account both at the individual level (e.g. personal values of consumers and perceptions of adherence to a company's values) and at the company level (e.g. the specific domain of the company's CSP: community support, environment and operations abroad).

Fair Trade

According to EFTA (European Fair Trade Association), Fair Trade is 'a trading partnership, based on dialogue, transparency and respect, that seeks greater equity in international trade. It contributes to sustainable development by offering better trading conditions to, and securing the rights of, marginalized producers and workers'. The origins of the Fair Trade movement are related to the development of cooperative organizations in the second half of the nineteenth century. In its modern form, Fair Trade began to grow and become a real movement during the 1960s and 1970s.[16]

Today, Fair Trade importing organizations exist in Australia, Canada, Europe, Japan and the United States. Labelling organizations are generally broad coalitions of organizations (NGOs, church organizations and trade unions) that promote the label and the distribution of products. The labelling organizations offer commercial importers a register of monitored producer groups, a set of criteria about how to conduct Fair Trade and a social label to distinguish Fair Trade products from others. Since 1997, most Fair Trade labelling has been coordinated by *Fairtrade Labelling Organizations International* (FLO), a consortium of Fair Trade groups in Japan,

Canada, the United States and seventeen European countries. FLO has recently introduced a common label to be applied in all countries. However, different initiatives and labelling schemes still exist at local levels.

Typical Fair Trade products are bananas, coffee and other products that are usually produced according to local organic food standards. Fair Trade products are distributed through a variety of channels: Fair Trade shops, retail chains and mail order, including online retailing. In addition, there are other channels such as direct delivery; solidarity groups; wholesale, organic shops; and institutional outlets (e.g. canteens and public authority offices). In Europe, Fair Trade products are sold via more than 64,800 points of sale. In its report released in 2005, FLO estimated that overall retail value in 2004 exceeded 830 million euros. The aggregate estimated retail value of Fair Trade products (labelled and unlabelled) sold in Europe by retail chains and alternative channels is approximately 596 million euros.[17]

In Europe, the retail industry has played an active role in the growth of Fair Trade. Many retailers offer a large assortment of Fair Trade products. Most major retail chains have developed a range of private-label Fair Trade lines by dealing with Alternative Trading Organizations (ATOs) or directly with producers. Some observers fear the risk that, by going mainstream, Fair Trade may be taken over by large retailers and redefined in ways that advance private profits. At the same time many retailers have been at the forefront in developing and implementing CSR policies, as many success stories demonstrate: Coop and Migros in Switzerland, Kesko in Finland, Marks and Spencer and Safeway in the UK, the Musgrave Group in Ireland, Coop in Italy, Monoprix in France, Metro in Germany, Pick n Pay in South Africa, Coop and Ito Yokado in Japan and Whole Foods Market in the United States.

The role of trust in Fair Trade products

Trust is a fundamental asset in every business and non-business relationship. Indeed, this highly abstract construct can be applied to the analysis of many types of relationships (interpersonal, intra- and inter-organizational, social and business) that are studied from different perspectives.[18]

Trust is crucial to understanding business relationships when the trustor is in a vulnerable position (high risk). Trust literature offers a huge variety of constructs.[19] Trust has been generally defined as an expectation that the trustee is willing to keep promises and to fulfil obligations. The expectation is associated with antecedents such as the level of competencies, honesty and goodwill of the trustee, and also with non-opportunistic motivations to act.[20] As P.M. Doney and J.P. Cannon emphasized, trust includes both a perceived credibility and a perceived benevolence of the trustee.[21]

Some recent works have focused on the relationship between trust and other consumer-specific concepts, such as customer satisfaction, loyalty and brand image.[22] L.A. Crosby *et al.* developed the concept of relationship quality, a combination of trust and satisfaction, considering it as the fundamental element among those that reduce perceived uncertainties and the complexity of the choices related to the demand for services.[23]

The contributions by A. Chaduri and M.B. Holbrook and by D. Sirdeshmuk *et al.*[24] comprise the first empirical evidence of the relationships between intangible customer-based resources, that is, trust and loyalty, on the one hand, and a company's competitive performance on the other. The relationship between the concept of trust and other customer-based relational resources, in particular commitment, satisfaction and loyalty, was thoroughly investigated by E. Garbarino and M.S. Johnson, who ascertained the centrality of these concepts for customer relationships.[25]

Many typologies of trust have been proposed in literature. These typologies are based on the prevalence of the single dimensions of trust (e.g. cognitive, emotional and behavioural), on a variety of contents (and different drivers), on different analytical levels (interpersonal, inter-organizational) and various levels of consistency (thick vs. thin) producing a wide range of concepts.

One of the most common distinctions is based on the content of trust or, more precisely, on the nature of its antecedents.[26] From this perspective, it is possible to distinguish:

(1) the so-called calculative trust (or *rational* or deterrence-based);
(2) the trust based on knowledge of the trustee's profile (defined usually as *cognitive* trust);

(3) the trust based on identification and personal values (defined sometimes as *normative trust, goodwill trust,* or *value-based trust*).

The first typology refers to trust exclusively founded on economic
convenience. In some cases, it can be convenient to choose to trust
a third party, especially when the possible losses deriving from the
trust-based decision are less than the likely advantages deriving from
trust-based behaviour. Another case of calculative trust is apparent when the trustor believes that the trustee has an explicit interest
in fulfilling obligations. This example is closer to deterrence-based
trust.[27] Trust is granted with the knowledge that unreliable behaviour
by a trustee will harm its reputation when trustors react negatively.

The second typology is based on a specific knowledge about the
characteristics of the company in question – its behaviours and, above
all, its competencies and abilities. Trusting an individual means, above
all, recognizing the know-how needed to carry out, in a complete
and satisfactory manner, those activities demanded by the trustor.
Knowledge about the trustee's set of competencies underlies the decision to trust in a rational (but, in this case, non-economic) process.

The third typology of trust is based on identification and personal
values. This typology is the most abstract and the easiest to transfer to
other activities, tasks and businesses. Value-based trust is developed
normally in the more advanced stages of a relationship, when a high
level of interdependence has been built up between the parties. This
situation allows the individual to know the trustee's set of competencies as well as cultural values and ideas, without any necessary reference to specific activities. For this reason, the scope of activity, tasks
and performance increases, thus promoting the proliferation (exploitation) of such relationships.

Hypotheses

A company that is perceived to have a high CSP can nourish trust
of all typologies. As far as calculative trust is concerned, consumers
should conclude that a reputable company, which has been building
a positive relationship with the community and is generally appreciated as an ethical player, has strong incentives to maintain its good
reputation. Therefore, consumers can consider such a company less
probable to renege on its promises.

As far as cognitive trust is concerned, socially responsible companies usually subject themselves to increased disclosure. Social and ethical accounting, sustainability reports, codes of conduct, labels, and auditing and reporting initiatives are important sources of information that allow the community as a whole to monitor a company. Therefore, consumers can favour a socially responsible company over other 'non-CSR-oriented' companies.

Above all, as far as value-based trust is concerned, many CSR initiatives address issues of wide social interest. Since this type of trust is founded on personal values, the perceived CSP of a company can inspire consumers sensitive to ethical, social and environmental issues.

With regard to Fair Trade, we must emphasize that it appeals to consumers' social conscience. The price of these products is usually higher than that of comparable 'unfair-trade' alternatives. Clients are effectively asked to pay a premium price to contribute to an allegedly worthy social cause. In exchange, Fair Trade importers promise consumers that their purchases will finance more equitable business practices. This way refers primarily to such features as:[28]

(1) prices that cover the producer's costs;
(2) social premiums to fund development projects;
(3) partial advance payments to finance small producers;
(4) long-term contracts with predefined minimal prices;
(5) producers joining democratic cooperatives;
(6) producers' sustainable environmental practices.

Usually, consumers are not able to find out for certain whether Fair Trade products honour the 'fair' terms that the importers promise. 'Fairness' is simply not an attribute that consumers can verify in a product. Fair Trade products cannot be easily distinguished from those of competitors except by their labels. Besides, while in Europe organic food is subjected to an official process of certification, no such recognized process exists for Fair Trade products.

Consumers deprived of a direct informational channel are in a vulnerable position (risk of opportunism by the seller). In such cases, the act of purchasing is strongly dependent on the belief that the seller will maintain its promises (trust). For this reason, Fair Trade products usually involve third parties such as FLO and the other labelling organizations, which offer what they hope are credible guarantees that the labelled merchandise is produced according to Fair Trade principles.

However, none of these labelling organizations achieved much recognition in Europe until now. Their names and logos are relatively unknown to most consumers. But due to name recognition and their long-term relationship with clients, large retail chains are now in a better position to act as trust mediators.

In particular, in our study we hypothesized that the more consumers perceive a retailer as socially responsible, the more they will trust Fair Trade products sold by that retailer.

Hypothesis 1 (H1). Consumer perceptions of a retailer's CSP correlate positively with consumer trust in Fair Trade products sold by that retailer.

Currently, a significant share of Fair Trade products is sold by European retailers under their own private labels. The retailer's label is usually combined with the label of one or more Fair Trade labelling organizations. While it is difficult to obtain data about the turnover of private-label versus independent Fair Trade products, anecdotal evidence suggests that private labels are increasing more rapidly. Moore writes that one UK-based retail chain reports that nine of its top ten Fair Trade lines were private-label products.[29] Coop, the leading Italian retail chain, recently stated that its private-label lines alone account for 10 per cent of the total turnover of Fair Trade products in the country.[30]

Therefore, we hypothesize that such products should benefit from trust in Fair Trade.

Hypothesis 2 (H2). Consumer trust in Fair Trade products sold by a retailer correlates positively with consumer trust in the private-label Fair Trade products sold by that retailer.

Finally, we assume that trust should translate into an intention to purchase a product. This intention should determine brand loyalty as a direct consumer response. We follow the standard definition of brand loyalty as the tendency to be loyal to a focal brand, which is demonstrated by the intention to buy the brand as a primary choice.[31]

Hypothesis 3 (H3). Consumer trust in private-label Fair Trade products sold by a retailer correlates positively with brand loyalty to those products.

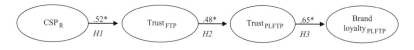

Standardized estimates are shown. $n = 400$. R = retailer. FTP = Fair Trade products. PLFTP = private-label
Fair Trade products.
* $p \leq 0.05$

Figure 7.1 Structural model

Results and discussion

Study

Our study was conducted by interviewing clients of retail chains in
two Italian cities (Milan and Florence). The study was completed in
June 2005. Four hundred valid surveys were collected (217 in Milan,
183 in Florence). Structural equation modelling (SEM) was applied to
test our hypotheses. Methods are described in the Appendix.

The resulting model (Figure 7.1) provided strong support for our
hypotheses. In accordance with hypothesis 1, consumers' perception
of CSR performance is positively and significantly related to trust
towards Fair Trade products ($\beta = 0.52$, $p \leq 0.05$). In accordance with
hypothesis 2, trust towards Fair Trade products is positively and significantly related to trust towards private-label Fair Trade products
sold by a retailer ($\beta = 0.48$, $p \leq 0.05$). In accordance with hypothesis 3, trust towards private-label Fair Trade products is, in turn,
positively and significantly related to brand loyalty to those products
($\beta = 0.65$, $p \leq 0.05$).

Findings

The literature on CSR has often emphasized that CSR should enable
a company to build better relationships with a variety of stakeholders. This emphasis predicts that a socially oriented company should
protect and increase trust, which is crucial to the company's success
in today's competitive marketplace. We focused our research on consumers and on the link between the perception that a company is
socially oriented and consumer intentions to buy products sold by
that company. We studied Fair Trade products sold by large Italian
retail chains with their own private label. Results of our structural
model are consistent with the prediction that CSR generates trust.

Consumers who perceive a retailer as socially oriented demonstrated more trust in the retailer, Fair Trade in general and private-label Fair Trade products. This trust translates into an intention to purchase the product (brand loyalty).

The results suggest that trust is a key mediator capable of measuring and explaining the success (or failure) of the CSR policies adopted by the company. Our findings support the idea that socially oriented companies can achieve competitive advantage in those business areas where trust is crucial in determining consumer choices. We showed that Fair Trade is one of these areas.

Limitations

Like all empirical research, our study is limited in several ways. First, our constructs relied on consumer perceptions. We did not discriminate between companies that are actually socially oriented and those that convincingly pretend to be. This is a problem in many studies on CSR, because consumers and other stakeholders cannot always know what happens behind corporate walls. Therefore, it is possible that consumer perceptions are distorted by contextual factors that are difficult to measure. One solution might be to look at the determinants of consumers' perceptions, as recently done by S. Du *et al.*,[32] who used consumer awareness of a company's CSR actions and consumer attributions of a company's motives (intrinsic or extrinsic) as antecedents of consumer beliefs about the CSR of the company.

Second, our data refer to a single industry (retailing) and to a single category of products (Fair Trade products): it is legitimate to ask whether the same results hold in other business environments.

Third, the technique we used to collect interviews (CATI) raises questions about whether interviewees were able and willing to articulate their actual preferences. Even though the questionnaire was designed to check for the consistency of the answers, individuals may be systematically biased towards verbally expressing 'pro-social' attitudes. Experimental settings may provide an interesting means by which to overcome the 'attitude–behaviour gap' we described above, although in this case there are problems relevant to external validity.[33]

Fourth, we conducted our survey among consumers who knew about Fair Trade products. It is therefore possible that they shared a special interest in Third World issues; there is no guarantee that the sample represents the broader public interested in social causes.

Fifth, variables that are not considered in our analysis may prove to be important moderators of the effects we measured.

Sixth, our data were collected in Italy, so that it is questionable whether our findings apply to other countries.

In summary, we see our study as a first step towards a new avenue of research on the interplay between trust, CSR and consumer behaviour. Further studies are needed to ascertain that our conclusions do not depend on national, industrial or other contextual factors involved in the particular case we examined. At the same time, we believe that we have proved that this avenue of research is a promising way to investigate the complex relationships between a company and its stakeholders.

Managerial implications

Even with the above limitations, our study yields several conclusions. First, the more a company is committed to developing a broad CSR policy, and able to correctly communicate this to stakeholders, the more customers reward its concrete actions through a specific consumer behaviour. From this perspective, socially oriented retailers seem to be appreciated by consumers for their environmental and social initiatives. Therefore, they can play a legitimate role in influencing their stakeholder networks towards sustainability objectives, that is, towards a superior economic, social and environmental quality. This finding is consistent with the notion that 'one of the most compelling ways to help firms succeed is by increasing the power of the linkages and networks they are part of'.[34]

In fact, retailers' intermediate place between producers and consumers provides them with a leading role in shaping consumers' and producers' decisions. Therefore, they are well positioned to drive new types of relationships in distribution channels. Sustainability needs innovative solutions: instead of the traditional approaches based on competition and zero- or even negative-sum games, it is crucial to foster cooperation and collaborative networks.[35] Furthermore, our results also indicate that retailers should be active in shaping consumer perceptions of specific categories of products.

A more immediate managerial implication is that CSR-oriented retailers should leverage their competitive advantage in selling trust-intensive products by extending Fair Trade lines (both private labels and others). Other socially labelled products such as organic food could also be marketed according to this same strategy.[36] At the same time, retailers should preserve their social orientation by actively and sincerely cooperating with importers and ATOs in the areas of Fair Trade and other sustainability principles.

Future research

The traditional approach towards analysing the relationship between CSP and financial performance has led to mixed results.[37] Studies usually focused on general objectives, such as investigating the links between social measures of performance (hard to define) and financial measures of performance (e.g. net income, earnings per share, market value), which are influenced by several contingent factors.

While the 'business case' is only one of many reasons that managers commit to social responsibility, clearer findings are needed about when and how social responsibility helps them to achieve their competitive and financial objectives. Our results suggest that trust plays an important role as a mediating variable in the CSP–financial-performance relationship.

Our study demonstrates that, while research on the direct relationship between social and financial performance might be useful, a business case for CSR can be built on a different approach. Business performance does not necessarily need to be assessed at the financial level; intermediate performance measures, such as brand loyalty, employee satisfaction or operational efficiency, may be better suited to a correlation with CSR policies and interventions.

With regard to Fair Trade, our study focused on trust. To pay the high price attached to Fair Trade coffee or bananas, customers need to believe that the retailer will respect the ethical promise implicit in these product labels and will effectively help Third World producers. As a rule, customers do not want to know the details, but they need to be sure that retailers will do what is expected. In a word, they need to *trust* the retailer. At the same time, trust is only one of the possible factors driving purchasing decisions. Further empirical research is needed on these other factors, and on determinants of ethical shopping in general.

Appendix: methods

Survey

Interviews were collected through CATI (computer-assisted telephone interviewing), a telephone interviewing technique in which interviewers follow a script provided by a software application. CATI enables customization of the questions based on the answers the participants provide, as well as of other information already gathered.

Before each interview, interviewers were instructed to verify that the respondent:

(1) had visited a chain store (full-service supermarkets or hypermarkets) in the last three months;
(2) had knowledge of Fair Trade products and was able to identify them from the specific names used in Italy (Fair Trade, Transfair, CTM Altromercato, Commercio Equo e Solidale) or the associated logos.

Measurements

CSP

Given the lack of generally accepted scales in the literature, we generated new scales based on a previous study reported by S. Castaldo and F. Perrini.[38] The study analysed the CSP of two multinational companies as perceived by a sample of 215 undergraduate students. An exploratory factor analysis was conducted on forty indicators surveyed. The indicators were based on a stakeholder framework and reflected the interests of the various stakeholder possibly involved in a company's operations. The analysis revealed that three dimensions of CSR play a dominant role in framing the perception of a company as more or less CSR-oriented:

(1) the environmental dimension, which refers to how much a company is considered sensitive to ecological issues;
(2) the consumer dimension, which refers to the perception that a company tries to satisfy consumer needs and protects rights and interests of the consumers;
(3) the employee dimension, which refers to equality of economic treatment, absence of social discrimination, health and safety.

A three-item scale was generated for each of the dimensions. Cronbach's alpha coefficients of these scales were 0.850, 0.800 and 0.908, respectively, for the environmental dimension, the consumer dimension and the employee dimension.

Trust

To measure trust, we started from the scale proposed by A. Chaudhuri and M.B. Holbrook.[39] The scale was integrated by items derived by A. Wong and A. Sohal, and by M.S. Kennedy *et al.*,[40] which are mainly based on trust measurements originally proposed by L.A. Crosby *et al.* and by R.M. Morgan and S.D. Hunt.[41] This scale was used to measure trust towards Fair Trade products in general and (with slight adaptations) towards private-label Fair Trade products. Cronbach's alpha coefficients were 0.922 and 0.926, respectively.

Brand loyalty

The three-item scale proposed by B. Yoo and N. Donthu, integrated with items introduced by M.S. Kennedy *et al.*,[42] was used to measure brand loyalty towards private-label Fair Trade products. Cronbach's alpha coefficient was 0.851.

All the measures consisted of items with answer options ranging from 1, 'strongly disagree', to 7, 'strongly agree'. The English translation of all the items used is in Table 7.A1.

Measurement evaluation

Before testing the hypothesized model, we assessed the adequacy of the measurement model for the criteria of overall fit with the data and discriminant validity. We ran immediately into a problem with the three CSP scales. Factor loadings for most items were low and some items were missing a large amount of data. Therefore, we decided to drop items with extensive 'holes' and to subject the remaining items to exploratory factor analysis (EFA) using principal factors extraction. From this analysis, a factor emerged. Three items were retained that loaded highly on it (all loadings exceeded 0.70). Cronbach's alpha coefficient for this factor, which we called 'CSR performance', was 0.843.

We used confirmatory factor analysis (CFA) to assess the quality of the resultant measurement model. CFA analysis was run with LISREL 8.72.[43] The measurement model had four latent variables and twelve indicators.

Table 7.A1 *Items used in this study*

CSP	*Environmental dimension:*
	___ is sensitive to waste recycling and recovery
	___ is sensitive to environmental protection
	___ is environmentally aware
	Consumer dimension:
	___ satisfies consumers' needs
	___ protects consumers' interests and rights on a voluntary basis
	___ assures quality along the whole supply chain
	Employee dimension
	___ guarantees equal opportunities to employees
	___ cares for occupational health and safety
	___ provides fair economic treatment to all employees
Trust	I trust ___
	You can always count on ___
	___ are reliable
Brand loyalty	___ are always my first choice
	If ___ were not available at the store, I would not buy other brands
	I consider myself to be loyal to ___

The CFA (χ^2 = 105.99, df = 48, $p < 0.01$) achieved adequate fit as assessed by the comparative fit index (CFI = 0.97), root-mean-square error of approximation (RMSEA = 0.055) and standard root-mean-square residual (SRMSR = 0.048). Except for one indicator, all the items loadings were above 0.70, which is an agreed threshold, with the exception of 0.67. Average variance extracted (AVE) for all constructs exceeded 0.50, which is the recommended level.[44] Results are shown in Table 7.A2.

Following the suggestion of C. Fornell and D.F. Larcker,[45] we assessed discriminant validity in order to verify that all constructs were more strongly correlated with their own indicators than with any of the other constructs. The most common test checks whether the confidence interval around the correlation between any two latent constructs does not include 1. Of the ten cases tested, none of the confidence intervals reached 1. The correlation matrix of the constructs is shown in Table 7.A3, along with descriptive statistics.

Table 7.A2 *Measurement properties*

Constructs	Items	Factor loadings
1. CSP	___ protects consumers' rights	0.70
	___ is sensitive to environmental protection	0.90
	___ is environmentally aware	0.82
	AVE: 65.75%.	
2. Trust towards Fair Trade products	You can always count on ___	0.89
	I trust ___	0.89
	___ are reliable	0.91
	AVE: 80.41%.	
3. Trust towards private-label Fair Trade products	___ are reliable	0.93
	You can always count on ___	0.92
	I trust ___	0.89
	AVE: 83.45%.	
4. Brand loyalty towards private-label Fair Trade products	___ are always my first choice	0.89
	If ___ were not available at the store, I would not buy other brands	0.67
	I consider myself to be loyal to ___	0.87
	AVE: 66.60%.	

Because of the high correlations that existed for the pair 'Trust towards Fair Trade products; Trust towards private-label Fair Trade products', the more conservative test of discriminant validity proposed by R.P. Bagozzi et al.[46] was performed. In this procedure, a pair of constructs is set up as a model with the correlation between the constructs set to 1 (constrained model) and then compared with the model without fixing the correlation (unconstrained model). The procedure involves comparing the chi-square values of the models and testing whether the constraint causes a significant decrease in fit. The fit of the unconstrained model should be significantly better than that of the constrained one in order to satisfy the discriminant validity criterion.

We applied this test to the pair 'Trust towards Fair Trade products; Trust towards private-label Fair Trade products': the chi-square of the unconstrained model resulted significantly lower than that of the constrained model, as required. The decrease was 101.71.

In summary, we concluded that the measurement model fits the data well and achieves discriminant validity.

Table 7.A3 *Means, standard deviations and correlations*

Variable	Mean	s.d.	1	2	3	4
1. CSP	5.52	1.21	(0.84)			
2. Trust towards Fair Trade products	5.19	1.40	0.47*	(0.92)		
3. Trust towards private-label Fair Trade products	5.32	1.37	0.46	0.84*	(0.93)	
4. Brand loyalty towards private-label Fair Trade products	3.60	1.70	0.34	0.50	0.66*	(0.85)

Notes:
$n = 400$. Cronbach's alpha coefficients are on the diagonal in parentheses.
* $p \leq 0.05$.

Hypotheses testing

In our baseline model (see Figure 7.1), we specified paths between the intermediate variables in conformity with the three hypotheses to be tested. Structural equation modelling (SEM) was applied to the model (again, LISREL 8.72 was used to run the analysis). Residuals were allowed to correlate.

As Table 7.A4 shows, all fit indexes of our baseline model emerged as good ($\chi^2 = 125.506$, df = 50, $p < 0.01$). Table 7.A5 describes the properties of the indexes.[47]

In order to verify that no alternative models provide a better fit to data, we tested four further structural models. Table 7.A4 reports the fit indexes of these models as well as the chi-square differences.

In Model 2, we drew a direct causal path from CSP_R to all the other three variables ($Trust_{FTP}$, $Trust_{PLFTP}$, Brand loyalty$_{PLFTP}$). Model 3 is like Model 2, except that Brand loyalty$_{PLFTP}$ received a causal path from $Trust_{PLFTP}$ rather than CSP_R. In Model 4, $Trust_{FTP}$ is treated as an exogenous variable and direct causal paths are drawn from it to the other three variables (CSP_R, $Trust_{PLFTP}$, Brand loyalty$_{PLFTP}$). In Model 5, $Trust_{PLFTP}$ is the exogenous variable; the other three variables (CSP_R, $Trust_{FTP}$, Brand loyalty$_{PLFTP}$) receive a causal path from it.

Table 7.A4 Comparisons of structural equation models

Model	χ^2	df	$\Delta\chi^2$	RMSEA	GFI	SRMSR	CFI	PNFI
1. Hypothesized model	125.50**	50		0.068	0.94	0.044	0.97	0.73
2. 'CSP$_R \to$ Trust$_{FTP}$'; 'CSP$_R \to$ Trust$_{PLFTP}$'; 'CSP$_R \to$ Brand loyalty$_{PLFTP}$'	251.80**	50	126.30	0.111	0.89	0.091	0.94	0.70
3. 'CSP$_R \to$ Trust$_{FTP}$'; 'CSP$_R \to$ Trust$_{PLFTP}$'; 'Trust$_{PLFTP} \to$ Brand loyalty$_{PLFTP}$'	152.77**	50	27.27	0.079	0.93	0.083	0.96	0.72
4. 'Trust$_{FTP} \to$ CSP$_R$'; 'Trust$_{FTP} \to$ Trust$_{PLFTP}$'; 'Trust$_{FTP} \to$ Brand loyalty$_{PLFTP}$'	221.79**	50	96.29	0.103	0.90	0.120	0.94	0.70
5. 'Trust$_{PLFTP} \to$ CSP$_R$'; 'Trust$_{PLFTP} \to$ Trust$_{FTP}$'; 'Trust$_{PLFTP} \to$ Brand loyalty$_{PLFTP}$'	158.79**	50	33.29	0.082	0.92	0.080	0.96	0.72

Notes:
$n = 400$.
** $p \leq 0.01$.

Table 7.A5 *Properties of the indexes*

RMSEA (Root mean square error of approximation) is an index of absolute fit that takes into account the error of approximation in the population; usually, values less than 0.08 are considered to represent a fair fit.[a]

GFI (Goodness of fit index) measures how much the actual input matrix is predicted by the estimated model. Usually, values above 0.80 indicate reasonable model fit.[b]

SRMSR (Standardized RMR index) is another typical index of absolute fit. Byrne suggests that this value should be smaller than 0.05.[c]

CFI (Comparative fit index) assesses which of two or more competing models provide a better fit to the data. Values above 0.95 indicate a good fit.[d]

PNFI (Parsimonious normed fit index) is concerned with the trade-off between the model fit and the degrees of freedom. PNFI is also used to compare competing models. There are no standard high or low values to indicate acceptable parsimonious fit.

Notes:
[a] R.P. Bagozzi and Y. Yi, 'On the Evaluation of Structural Equation Models', *Journal of the Academy of Marketing Science*, 16 (1988): 74–94.
[b] M.W. Browne and R. Cudeck, 'Alternative Ways of Assessing Model Fit', in K.A. Bollen and J.S. Long (eds.), *Testing Structural Equation Models* (Newbury Park, CA: Sage, 1993), pp. 136–62.
[c] B.M. Byrne, *Structural Equation Modeling with Lisrel, Prelis, and Simplis* (Mahwah, NJ: Erlbaum, 1998).
[d] P.M. Bentler, 'On the Fit of Model to Covariances and Methodology to the Bulletin', *Psychological Bulletin*, 112 (1992): 400–4.

As Table 7.A4 shows, the differences between the chi-squares between Models 2–5 and the baseline model are large. These models have more or less acceptable indexes of fit but are clearly worse than our baseline model.

Notes

1 J.D. Margolis and J.P. Walsh, 'Misery Loves Companies: Rethinking Social Initiatives by Business', *Administrative Science Quarterly*, 48 (2003): 268–305.
2 S.A. Waddock and S.B. Graves, 'The Corporate Social Financial Performance Link', *Strategic Management Journal*, 18 (1997): 303–19.

3 M. Orlitzky, F.L. Schmidt and S.L. Rynes, 'Corporate Social and Financial Performance: A Meta-analysis', *Organization Studies*, 24 (2003): 403–41, here p. 424.

4 N. Craig Smith, 'Corporate Social Responsibility: Whether or How?', *California Management Review*, 45 (2003): 52–76; C.B. Bhattacharya and S. Sen, 'Doing Better at Doing Good: When, Why, and How Consumers Respond to Corporate Social Initiatives', *California Management Review*, 47 (2004): 9–24.

5 B. Barber, *The Logic and Limits of Trust* (New Brunswick: Rutgers University Press, 1983); K. Blomqvist, 'The Many Faces of Trust', *Scandinavian Journal Management*, 13 (1997): 271–86.

6 F.R. Dwyer, P.H. Schurr and S. Oh, 'Developing Buyer-Seller Relationships', *Journal of Marketing*, 51 (1987): 11–27; R.M. Morgan and S.D. Hunt, 'The Commitment-Trust Theory of Relationship Marketing', *Journal of Marketing*, 58 (1994): 20–38.

7 A.B. Carroll, 'Corporate Social Responsibility. Evolution of a Definitional Construct', *Business & Society*, 38 (1999): 268–95; Smith (2003).

8 H.R. Bowen, *Social Responsibilities of the Businessman* (New York: Harper and Brothers, 1953).

9 E. Garriga and D. Melé, 'Corporate Social Responsibility Theories: Mapping the Territory', *Journal of Business Ethics*, 53/1–2 (2004): 51–71; F. Perrini, S. Pogutz and A. Tencati, *Developing Corporate Social Responsibility. A European Perspective* (Cheltenham: Edward Elgar, 2006).

10 Commission of the European Communities, *Promoting a European Framework for Corporate Social Responsibility*, Green Paper, Brussels: COM(2001) 366 final.

11 A.B. Carroll, 'A Three-Dimensional Conceptual Model of Corporate Performance', *Academy of Management Review*, 4 (1979): 497–505; S.L. Wartick and P.L. Cochran, 'The Evolution of the Corporate Social Performance Model', *Academy of Management Review*, 10 (1985): 758–69; D.J. Wood, 'Corporate Social Performance Revisited', *Academy of Management Review*, 16 (1991): 691–718.

12 T. Donaldson and L.E. Preston, 'The Stakeholder Theory of the Corporation: Concepts, Evidence, and Implications', *Academy of Management Review*, 20 (1995): 65–91.

13 Smith (2003); Bhattacharya and Sen (2004); T. Pigott, 'Tomorrow's Consumer', *UNEP Industry and Environment*, 27 (2004): 25–8.

14 T.J. Brown and P.A. Dacin, 'The Company and the Product: Corporate Associations and Consumer Product Responses', *Journal of Marketing*, 61 (1997): 68–84.

15 Bhattacharya and Sen (2004), here p. 10.

16 G. Moore, 'The Fair Trade Movement: Parameters, Issues and Future Research', *Journal of Business Ethics*, 53/1–2 (2004): 73–86.

17 FLO (Fairtrade Labelling Organizations International), *Delivering Opportunities. Annual Report 2004/2005*, www.fairtrade.net/sites/news/FLO_AR_2004_05.pdf.

18 P.S. Ring and A.H. Van de Ven, 'Structuring Cooperative Relationships between Organizations', *Strategic Management Journal*, 13 (1992): 483–98; P.S. Ring and A.H. Van de Ven, 'Developmental Processes of Cooperative Interorganizational Relationships', *Academy of Management Review*, 19 (1994): 90–118; A. Zaheer and N. Venkatraman, 'Relational Governance as an Interorganizational Strategy: An Empirical Test of the Role of Trust in Economic Exchange', *Strategic Management Journal*, 16 (1995): 373–92; A. Zaheer, B. McEvily and V. Perrone, 'Does Trust Matter? Exploring the Effects of Interorganizational and Interpersonal Trust and Performance', *Organization Science*, 9 (1998): 141–59; T.K. Das and B.S. Teng, 'Between Trust and Control: Developing Confidence in Partner Cooperation in Alliances', *Academy of Management Review*, 23 (1998): 491–513; T.K. Das and B.S. Teng, 'Trust, Control, and Risk in Strategic Alliances: An Integrated Framework', *Organization Studies*, 22 (2001): 251–83.

19 S. Castaldo, 'Meanings of Trust: A Meta-analysis of Trust Definitions', presented at *Second Euram Conference*, Stockholm, 2002.

20 J.B. Rotter, 'Generalized Expectancies for Interpersonal Trust', *American Psychologist*, 26 (1971): 443–52; Barber (1983); R.P. Dwyer, P. Schurr and S. Oh, 'Developing Buyer-seller Relationships', *Journal of Marketing*, 51 (1987): 11–27; J.M. Hagen and S. Choe, 'Trust in Japanese Interfirm Relations: Institutional Sanctions Matter', *Academy of Management Review*, 23 (1998): 589–600; Blomqvist (1997).

21 P.M. Doney and J.P. Cannon, 'An Examination of the Nature of Trust in Buyer-seller Relationships', *Journal of Marketing*, 61 (1997): 35–51.

22 B. Busacca and S. Castaldo, 'Brand Knowledge, Brand Trust and Consumer Response: A Conceptual Framework', presented at the 2nd Workshop 'Trust Within and Between Organizations', Amsterdam, 2003.

23 L.A. Crosby, K.R. Evans and D. Cowles, 'Relationship Quality in Services Selling: An Interpersonal Influence Perspective', *Journal of Marketing*, 54 (1990): 68–81.

24 A. Chaudhuri and M.B. Holbrook, 'The Chain of Effects from Brand Trust and Brand Affect to Brand Performance: The Role of Brand Loyalty', *Journal of Marketing*, 65 (2001): 81–93; D. Sirdeshmukh, J. Singh and B. Sabol, 'Consumer Trust, Value, and Loyalty in Relational Exchange', *Journal of Marketing*, 66 (2002): 15–37.

25 E. Garbarino and M.S. Johnson, 'The Different Roles of Satisfaction, Trust, and Commitment in Customer Relationships', *Journal of Marketing*, 63 (1999): 70–87.

26 R.J. Lewicki and B.B. Bunker, 'Developing and Maintaining Trust in Work Relationships', in R.M. Kramer and T.R. Tyler (eds.), *Trust in Organizations: Frontiers of Theory and Research* (Thousand Oaks, CA: Sage, 1996), pp. 114–139; D. Shapiro, B.H. Sheppard and L. Cheraskin, 'Business on a Handshake', *Negotiation Journal*, 8 (1992): 365–77; B.H. Sheppard and M. Tuchinsky, 'Micro-OB and the Network Organization', in R.M. Kramer and T.R. Tyler (eds.), *Trust in Organizations: Frontiers of Theory and Research* (Thousand Oaks, CA: Sage, 1996), pp. 140–65; M. Sako and S. Helper, 'Determinants of Trust in Supplier Relations: Evidence from the Automotive Industry in Japan and the United States', *Journal of Economic Behavior & Organization*, 34 (1998): 387–417.

27 Shapiro *et al.* (1992).

28 A. Hira and J. Ferrie, 'Fair Trade: Three Key Challenges for Reaching the Mainstream', *Journal of Business Ethics*, 63 (2006): 107–18.

29 Moore (2004).

30 Coop, 'Prospettive per il Commercio Equo e Solidale in Italia e in Europa', Convegno Coop, Genoa, 15–16 September 2005.

31 R.L. Oliver, 'Whence Consumer Loyalty', *Journal of Marketing*, Special Issue (1999): 33–44; B. Yoo and N. Donthu, 'Developing and Validating a Multidimensional Consumer-based Brand Equity Scale', *Journal of Business Research*, 52 (2001): 1–14.

32 S. Du, C.B. Bhattacharya and S. Sen, 'Reaping Relational Rewards from Corporate Social Responsibility: The Role of Competitive Positioning', *International Journal of Research in Marketing*, 24 (2007): 224–41.

33 M.J. Hyscox and N.F.B. Smyth, 'Is there Consumer Demand for Improved Labor Standards? Evidence from Field Experiments in Social Product Labeling', Working Paper, Department of Government, Harvard University, Cambridge, MA, 2007.

34 Commission on the Private Sector & Development, *Unleashing Entrepreneurship, Making Business Work for the Poor* (New York: United Nations Development Program, 2004), www.unep.org, here p. 30.

35 A. Tencati and L. Zsolnai, 'The Collaborative Enterprise', *Journal of Business Ethics*, 85 (2009): 367–76.

36 S. Zadek, S. Lingayah and M. Forstater, *Social Labels: Tools for Ethical Trade. Final Report* (Brussels: Commission of the European Communities, 1998).

37 A. McWilliams and D. Siegel, 'Corporate Social Responsibility and Financial Performance: Correlation or Misspecification?', *Strategic Management Journal*, 21 (2000): 603–9; A. McWilliams and D. Siegel, 'Corporate Social Responsibility: A Theory of the Firm Perspective', *Academy of Management Review*, 26 (2001): 117–27; Margolis and Walsh (2003); Orlitzky *et al.* (2003); C. Rubbens and C. Wessels, 'The Business

Case for CSR: In what way does CSR Contribute to Competitiveness?',
E-discussion, World Bank, 20–24 September, 2004; X. Luo and C.B.
Bhattacharya, 'Corporate Social Responsibility, Customer Satisfaction,
and Market Value', *Journal of Marketing*, 70 (2006): 1–18.

38 S. Castaldo and F. Perrini, 'Corporate Social Responsibility, Trust
Management, and Value Creation', presented at *EGOS 2004 'Trust in
Hybrids'*, Ljubljana, 2004.

39 Chaudhuri and Holbrook (2001).

40 A. Wong and A. Sohal, 'An Examination of the Relationship between
Trust, Commitment and Relationship Quality', *International Journal of
Retail and Distribution Management*, 30 (2002): 34–50; M.S. Kennedy,
L.K. Ferrel and D.T. LeClair, 'Consumers' Trust of Salesperson and
Manufacturer: An Empirical Study', *Journal of Business Research*, 51
(2000): 73–86.

41 Crosby *et al.* (1990); Morgan and Hunt (1994).

42 Yoo and Donthu (2001); Kennedy *et al.* (2000).

43 K.G. Joreskog and D. Sorbom, *LISREL 8: Structural Equation Modeling
with SIMPLIS Command Language* (Lincolnwood, IL: Scientific Software
International, 2002).

44 R.P. Bagozzi and H. Baumgartner, 'The Evaluation of Structural Equation
Models and Hypotheses Testing', in R.P. Bagozzi (ed.), *Principles of
Marketing Research* (Cambridge, MA: Blackwell Business, 1994).

45 C. Fornell and D.F. Larcker, 'Evaluating Structural Equation Models with
Unobservable Variables and Measurement Error', *Journal of Marketing
Research*, 18 (1981): 39–50.

46 R.P. Bagozzi, Y. Yi and L.W. Phillips, 'Assessing Construct Validity in
Organizational Research', *Administrative Science Quarterly*, 36 (1991):
421–58.

47 R.P. Bagozzi and Y. Yi, 'On the Evaluation of Structural Equation
Models', *Journal of the Academy of Marketing Science*, 16 (1988): 74–94;
P.M. Bentler, 'On the Fit of Model to Covariances and Methodology to
the Bulletin', *Psychological Bulletin*, 112 (1992): 400–4; M.W. Browne
and R. Cudeck, 'Alternative Ways of Assessing Model Fit', in K.A. Bollen
and J.S. Long (eds.), *Testing Structural Equation Models* (Newbury Park,
CA: Sage, 1993), pp. 136–62; B.M. Byrne, *Structural Equation Modeling
with Lisrel, Prelis, and Simplis* (Mahwah, NJ: Erlbaum, 1998).

PART III

Corporate responsibility and developing countries

8 Stretching corporate social responsibility upstream: improving sustainability in global supply chains

EMMA V. KAMBEWA, PAUL T.M. INGENBLEEK AND AAD VAN TILBURG

We, fishers, the lake is all we have to live on. We can make things change if we want to.

(Anonymous fisherman at Lake Victoria)

Introduction

While attention for corporate social responsibility (CSR) continues to grow,[1] firms are increasingly being held responsible for practices in their supply chains. In response, firms stretch their CSR programmes, which traditionally have focused on their internal activities, to include the activities of their suppliers. The example of Nike's corporate scandal on the use of child labour in its production facilities in developing countries shows that firms may be held responsible not only for the activities that are carried out within the walls of their firm, but also for those taking place in their supply chains.[2] If we adopt a relatively broad definition of CSR, such as the firm's 'status and activities with respect to its perceived social obligations', such programmes fall within the domain of CSR activities.[3]

As many companies have international or even global supply chains, the complexity and size of CSR programmes in these supply chains may increase exponentially – especially if they originate from developing countries. These channels have a triangle-shaped structure whose base consists of large numbers of small-scale primary producers that in the end replenish Western processing industries. Unilever, for example, is developing a programme in which it plans to reach out to 300,000 tea farmers in four countries in Asia and Africa to improve the sustainability of its Lipton tea production.[4]

217

Whereas actors in marketing channels often agree that current practices should change in order to sustain natural resources for future generations, existing governance mechanisms (such as spot-market prices) motivate actors to maximize their short-term profitability and overexploit natural resources. This is because the additional costs of over exploitation are not included in the market price. This might particularly be the case with common property resources (i.e. those that are communally owned, such as fisheries, forests, water and wildlife). As a result of common property rights (i.e. the right to use resources), users often do not take responsibility for managing resources, but instead rush to utilize them, which eventually leads to their destruction.[5] In short, firms find themselves confronted with marketing channels that seem to capture multiple global problems in a nutshell, from poverty and child labour exploitation to ecological degradation.

Nevertheless, despite the size and complexity of projects that stretch CSR to suppliers, firms seem to continue (or persist in trying) to learn about new solutions from stakeholders and from each other. For example, leading international food companies, such as Nestlé, Unilever and Kraft Foods, collaborate in the Sustainable Agriculture Initiative to search for governance mechanisms that may improve ecological sustainability. The aim of their collaboration is to share insights and practical experience on improvements in sustainable food production, predominantly related to activities in their supply chains.

This chapter indicates the major problems and opportunities that firms may encounter when stretching CSR to upstream channel partners indicating how these problems may help firms to find solutions. First, we sketch the background of the current trend to stretch CSR to suppliers. We describe the origins of this development and the reasons why firms engage in such programmes. Next, we portray the complexity of stretching CSR to suppliers by relating the case of a fish-marketing channel from Lake Victoria in East Africa to the European Union. This case recently drew a lot of attention because of the Academy Award-nominated documentary *Darwin's Nightmare*.[6] Using the results from interviews, desk research, focus group discussions and survey data on this case, we indicate the major problems that firms may encounter when stretching CSR to suppliers and suggest potential solutions. Finally, we make concluding remarks and sketch the implications.

Stretching CSR upstream

The emergence of upstream CSR programmes

The need for firms to stretch CSR to their suppliers is directly related to the fact that many firms can no longer oversee the global networks in which they operate. The business practices of suppliers, and certainly those of the suppliers' suppliers, are often hidden behind market mechanisms (such as spot markets) in which suppliers are anonymous. This applies particularly to firms that operate in an international environment. Driven by an insecure business environment (marked by two world wars, the economic crisis of the 1930s and the Cold War), international business had become concentrated among a handful of large conglomerates over the course of the twentieth century.[7] Unilever, for example, whose core business was the production of margarine and soap, owned virtually all stages of the production channel – from primary production to branding and packaging. It was the owner of the United Africa Company that ensured that palm oil was produced, traded and transported to Europe, and that goods manufactured in Europe (such as textiles) were transported to African countries and traded in return for the raw supplies that were needed for soap and margarine production.

Throughout the 1980s and 1990s, international business experienced dramatic changes.[8] Stimulated by the removal of trade barriers and a more secure business environment, international business activity increased. Facing growing competition in the many markets in which they were active, large multinationals were no longer able to maintain competitive advantage in all stages of the production channel. The general trend became to return to the firm's core activities and to outsource all other services. The firms became part of a continuously growing and increasingly complex business network.[9] While in the past such multinationals had full control over the entire production channel – and thus could also oversee the social consequences of their business across the entire channel, now their sight became increasingly blurred by the intricate network in which they operated.

At the same time, intensified competition compelled companies to become more efficient. Firms therefore increasingly pressed suppliers to reduce costs, switched to suppliers with lower cost positions, or made use of spot markets that increased the efficiency of their purchases. Such practices undoubtedly motivated suppliers to economize at the expense of, for example, natural, social and human resources, such as farmer incomes, the natural environment, diversity of ecosystems and child labour. The FAO notes, for example, that the pursuit of economic interests may imply that actors utilize the resources up until they are (in the case of fishing) 'commercially extinct; i.e. until there are too little fish left to warrant catching'.[10] Firms were often not aware of these consequences because they simply lost track of their supply system. For example, when Nestlé and other food companies were asked whether child slaves produced the chocolate in their ice creams, most could not answer the question and had to refer to their suppliers.[11]

In short, after two decades of returning to core activities, firms with global supply chains have begun to perceive the social and environmental drawbacks of these developments and have started to rediscover their (dramatically changed) marketing channels.

Reasons for stretching CSR upstream

Although it seems that an increasing number of firms stretch CSR to upstream stages in the channel, it is not yet clear why firms would do so. In essence, the reasons for stretching CSR to suppliers are similar to the reasons for engaging in CSR in general. First, firms that hold brands or clearly visible corporate images may be held responsible by their stakeholders (including consumers, employees and shareholders). Visibility on the consumer market makes these firms vulnerable to the campaigns of activists. McDonald's, for example, launched an animal welfare programme, in which it imposed criteria for animal welfare in livestock farming on its suppliers, after it became the target of animal welfare activists' campaigns. By responding to these pressures, McDonald's protected perhaps the most valuable assets it owns: its corporate image and brand name. Research has shown that a great majority of consumers are open to these negative claims.[12] Second, not only consumers, but also employees, may keep the firm responsible. Several studies have shown a positive relation between CSR and esprit de corps. Especially if the firm is critically dependent on human resources with specific skills, it may benefit from a strong position in the labour market.[13]

Next to these reasons for firms to engage in CSR in general, two other reasons for firms to stretch CSR to suppliers can be identified.

First, it has become clear that marketing assets (such as brands and customer relationships) may have a longer lifespan than the natural resources that are required for production. Unilever, for example, invested in the Marine Stewardship Council and other sustainable fisheries programmes because it owns several strong brands for fish products. It predicted that the ocean's fish resources might be depleted before the strength of these brands has eroded. Second, when going upstream in the marketing channels, firms may improve not only social and environmental aspects, but also efficiency and quality. African farmers that participated in a programme to become Eurep-Gap certified (a certification scheme for food safety, quality and several social and environmental issues) experienced, for example, higher efficiency. Similarly, coffee certification organization Utz Certified generates higher farmer incomes from, among other things, decreasing inefficiencies from the international marketing channels.[14]

In short, whereas the causes of – and reasons for – the current trend of stretching CSR to suppliers are clear, it is not yet clear which problems firms may encounter in their CSR programmes and how these problems may be solved. It has also become clear that stretching CSR to suppliers is typically related to firms with international marketing channels, because these are most complex. This, however, does not mean that this phenomenon belongs exclusively to global marketing channels, as is exemplified by the cases of stretching CSR to suppliers in domestic channels to improve animal welfare. Next, although many examples that we use are derived from food and agri-business, also firms in other industries may benefit from stretching CSR to their suppliers (consider the Nike example). Food and agri-businesses cope with issues like food safety that may have signalled a need to strengthen their influence on supply chains before the issue was raised in other industries. Many of these firms use food safety infrastructures to implement their social and environmental standards. The analogy between quality management and responsibility management may thus be felt more strongly in these industries.[15]

The Lake Victoria–EU Nile perch chain

The complexities that firms may experience when stretching CSR to suppliers are perhaps felt nowhere stronger than in the Nile perch chain from Lake Victoria to the EU. Over the past years, this chain has attracted controversies in the local and international media. The film, *Darwin's Nightmare*, for example, illustrates the complex problems related to fish catch and export from Lake Victoria. Such a complexity of issues surrounding the Nile perch channel is unlikely to become clear from desk research, journal articles or newspaper reports alone. What is needed is a walk along the lake, and conversations with (predominantly small-scale) fishers and traders, and large-scale processors. Across the borders, conversations should be held with importers and retailers about the Nile perch. Our approach for this study was a combination of these and other research methods.[16] We introduce the Nile perch channel through discussing its promising start, emerging problems and social decay that ensued, and we make some suggestions about a way out of these problems.

A promising start

Lake Victoria is the second largest freshwater body in the world. Located in East Africa, the lake is shared by Kenya (6%), Uganda (45%) and Tanzania (49%).[17] Nile perch – a freshwater fish- was introduced into the lake in mid-1950s from the Nile River to improve the productivity and economic value of the Lake Victoria fishery. The Nile perch is a predator fish (i.e. it feeds on other fish). It was not until the late 1970s that the first significant catch of Nile perch was made, signalling the beginning of the fulfilment of the objective – to improve the productivity of the lake. The bordering governments formulated policy objectives to guide the utilization of the booming Nile perch production:

(1) to increase the per capita consumption of fish;
(2) to increase employment opportunities through fishing, fish processing and trading;
(3) to enhance the living conditions of the fishers and their families by maximizing their economic benefits; and
(4) to maximize export- and foreign-exchange-earning capacity.[18]

True to the objective of introducing Nile perch into the lake, social and economic benefits manifested within a decade of the production boom. For example, by mid-1980s, regional employment in fisheries and support sectors more than doubled. Between 1970s and 1990s, the number of fishers in Lake Victoria increased from 26,000 to 105,000 (304%) and the number of boats increased from 9,643 to 21,986 (128%). By 2000, there were 123,986 fishers and 41,047 fishing vessels depicting 377% and 326% increases from the 1970s respectively.[19] More than half of these fishers earned their primary income from fishing. Although the income was low, it was fairly and evenly distributed. The spontaneous increase in the number of fishers was not only a result of the production boom but also the expansion of the export markets that led to the increased number of processing factories. This concurrent production boom and expanded export demand for Nile perch resulted in the increased competitiveness of the fisheries sector relative to other sectors such as small-scale agriculture thereby attracting many more entrants into the fisheries.

Food security and nutritional status improved among the communities following the high supply of table-size fish and a corresponding fall in fish prices. The annual per capita fish consumption in the Lake Victoria region based on total fish landing increased from 2kg in 1960s to 8kg in early 1990s.[20] The Luo men (one of the traditional fishing tribes in the region), in appreciation of the generous Nile perch food rations their wives gave them said that: *Mbuta* (Nile perch) taught women how to feed their husbands properly. In Tanzania, Nile perch was nicknamed a *Saviour* because of the dramatic improvements in the socioeconomic status of the rural communities.[21] The states bordering Lake Victoria moved from being net fish importers to net exporters in the mid-1990s, fulfilling the second objective of introducing Nile perch into the lake (to improve the economic value of the fishery) and the fourth objective of utilizing the Nile perch (to maximize foreign exchange earnings).[22]

Emerging problems

While the Nile perch production boom created unprecedented socioeconomic benefits, it also brought about economic and ecological problems. For instance, the increased fishing capacity and corresponding failure by responsible authorities to control the effort consistent with sustainable utilization of the fisheries, contributed to overfishing that in turn resulted in declining biodiversity and productivity. After a decade of intense fishing, fish catch and species diversity declined. About 300 indigenous species once believed to have been in the lake in the early 1950s, are feared to be extinct.[23] The decline in biodiversity is largely attributed to overfishing that erupted in response to the Nile perch production boom, increased export demand and predation by Nile perch.

As if decline in biodiversity was not enough, the overall fish production started to decline. The Nile perch catch and catch rate per unit effort have been on the decline since the 1990s. Average size of Nile perch at landing sites declined from 50–100kgs in the 1980s to about 5–10kgs in the mid-1990s. By 2000 the catch per unit effort had declined to almost the same levels as in the early 1980s before the Nile perch boom. Following the decline in supply, some processing factories closed down and those that continued to operate rarely do so at full capacity – sometimes operating at as low as 10 per cent of installed capacity.[24] In order to make up for the loss in catch, fishers resort to using destructive fishing gears – those that catch juvenile fish which has become a major problem in the declining trend of fish catch. The decline in fish supply means that juvenile fish finds ready buyers both in domestic markets and processing factories further providing incentives to fishers to catch juveniles.

The net increase in employment following the Nile perch production boom and expanded export-oriented industrial fish processing have been arguable. The expanded – export oriented – industrial fish processing displaced artisanal employment. Estimates show that in the late 1980s, when about 2,400 jobs were created in Kenyan factories, about 15,000 (predominantly women) were displaced in the artisanal processing and marketing sectors.[25] This signified not only loss of income and livelihoods among some local communities but also a skewed distribution of incomes in favour of the few that were not displaced. As Nile perch supply continued to decline, factories started to lay off personnel, further reducing employment benefits. It has been argued that fishers were earning less, which was nonetheless fairly and evenly distributed in the communities prior to the Nile perch production boom.[26]

Whereas these ecological problems are hard-hitting on the supply side, the channel was also hard hit from the demand side. The EU, which takes up about 80 per cent of Nile perch export volume, consecutively banned the imports of fish products from Lake Victoria for three times from the mid- to late 1990s due to alleged contamination by salmonella, cholera outbreak and fish poisoning. Although the channel continues to undergo restructuring to meet the EU food quality and safety standards, challenges remain enormous farther upstream. Landing sites lack adequate facilities such as cold storage facilities, electricity and hygienic landing jets – which are important to minimize post-harvest fish losses.

Social decay

Following the sustained decline in fish catch and supply, exacerbated by intense competition between domestic and export markets, there has been a dramatic reversal of the socioeconomic benefits once noticed among rural communities. Domestic fish consumption has declined over the years. In Kenya, for example, the per capita fish consumption based on the fish that was available to the domestic markets dropped from the earlier attained 8kg to about 3kg between early 1980s and late 1990s. During the same period (i.e. late 1990s), the lakeshore areas – the hub of fishing, fish trading and processing – registered among the highest levels of food insecurity and malnutrition (44%) and absolute poverty (48%) among rural communities.[27] While fish catch continues to decline, over 90 per cent of good-quality Nile perch catch goes to export markets and the remaining is sold in high-class domestic markets such as the hotels where the poor consumers and other low income people cannot afford to buy fish. Although export prices were probably higher than local prices, they didn't compensate for the loss in food security at the lake.

To make up for the loss in food, the poor communities, consequently, resort to eating factory by-products, including skeletons, skins and fats, the juveniles and fish that are spoiled due to lack of proper storage facilities. Ironically, in the early 1980s when fish supply was high, factory by-products were considered a waste and the factories incurred costs to dispose of them. The skeletons were then considered as a 'poor man's food' – implying that only the poor who could not afford the good quality fresh Nile perch could eat the skeletons.[28] However, with improved filleting technologies that literally remove all the flesh, the skeletons are left 'too naked' to be of any significant food value for human consumption.[29] Nevertheless, such skeletons have over time increased in price to an extent that some poor consumers no longer can afford them.[30] As evidenced in the *Darwins' Nightmare* documentary, buying, selling and eating such by-products signifies the state of desperation and lack of exit options rather than rational choice for the poor.

Moreover, the poor communities that rely on factory by-products compete with animal feed manufacturing companies for the supply of the by-products. Estimates show that about 59 per cent (17,000 tons/day) go to animal feed manufacturers – further depriving the local consumers.[31] An economist with the Kenya Marine and Fisheries Research Institute questioned whether the development of the Lake Victoria fishery, through the introduction of Nile perch, has been a boon or bane for food security. Further, some analysts wonder whether the local communities would have been better off eating the fish themselves (for food security), instead of focusing on exports, given that the benefits of fish exports have hardly improved the livelihoods of local (poor) communities.[32]

A way out

After realizing the extent of the ecological degradation, the increasing poverty in the region and the need to meet international standards for food safety and quality, the bordering states formed the Lake Victoria Fisheries Organization (LVFO) in 1999 to harmonize the utilization of the lake resources among the bordering states. The LVFO seeks to:

(1) foster cooperation among resource users;
(2) harmonize the national measures for the sustainable utilization of the lake resources; and
(3) develop and adopt conservation and management measures to ensure sustainability of the ecosystem.[33]

To achieve these objectives, the LVFO pursues a vision that encompasses infrastructure development, institutional and human resources development and provision of credit facilities to fishers. The LVFO continues to embrace an export-oriented Nile perch channel and seeks to harmonize the food safety and quality regulations for bordering states. The LVFO also seeks to minimize post-harvest fish losses in the primary stages of the channel.

While these upstream initiatives emerge, the challenges remain enormous. The export markets should generate export incomes not only for the processing firms, but also for the small-scale traders and fishers. So far, the market forces in the East African institutional environment have proven insufficient to solve the problems attached to the

Nile perch channel. Therefore, the upstream (African) actors of the East African–EU Nile perch channel must rely on the support of the downstream (European) counterparts.

A programme that stretches CSR upstream may help to stabilize food security for the rural communities, enhance the competitiveness of primary producers through enabling them to improve quality and meet safety standards, and to implement market mechanisms that reward appropriate behaviours rather than stimulate the depletion of the lake. This may require, among other options, that downstream partners such as retailers engage their suppliers in a manner that minimizes the complex obstacles that the primary producers face.

Problems of stretching CSR upstream

Based on our analysis of the Nile perch channel, this section describes the challenges that an upstream CSR programme may face:

(1) recognizing the upstream problems downstream;
(2) involving others in CSR;
(3) creating appropriate and sustainable market mechanisms; and
(4) implementing these mechanisms.

Recognizing upstream problems downstream

International marketing channels tend to involve physically and culturally disconnected, anonymous, partners. Consequently, there is no guarantee that firms that are willing to stretch CSR to their suppliers are well informed about the problems that surround their suppliers. Intermediaries may benefit from information asymmetry between suppliers and customers (consider price information). Therefore, concealing problems may be in the (short-term) interest of intermediaries or may be routine behaviour. In a situation in which firms may be held responsible for practices in their supply chains, a reliable stream of information from suppliers may be vital for the reputation and brand equity of downstream firms. The first problem for firms that are willing to stretch CSR to their suppliers may therefore simply be that they are unaware of what is going on upstream because suppliers choose the option of not-telling over the option of being the messenger of the bad news.

The Nile perch channel is a good example of obvious miscommunication and obfuscation of the problems by the intermediaries. In 2005, a large retailer asked an importer for information pertaining to the source of fish, including compliance with food safety standards like Hazard Analysis of Critical Control Points (HACCP) and social issues surrounding the upstream part of the channel. The importer went to Lake Victoria to collect information as requested. In return, the importer reported, 'everything was under control'; this implied that factories were complying with HACCP, that many people were employed in the factories and fishing sectors, and that their lives were continuing to improve. Shortly after receiving such feedback, the retailer (the quality manager is the respondent in this case) saw the *Darwin's Nightmare* documentary, which showed extreme poverty in precisely the same area where the importer had earlier reported differently. The example suggests that either the importer was protecting his image and business by concealing the right information in the event that the retailer would react negatively, and/or the importer was misinformed by the exporters who themselves want to protect their business, or choose to ignore what happens to the local communities, even when they see it.

Another example of concealing information became evident from interviews with another importer. The importer (a general manager being the respondent) could not acknowledge that Nile perch production was declining. The importer claimed that he had excess supply of processed Nile perch in the warehouse in the Netherlands from where he supplies to other parts of the EU. This counters the reality that the factories in the Lake Victoria region fail to operate at full capacity due to the insufficient supply of raw material. The importer's failure to acknowledge that Nile perch production was declining could be explained from a number of perspectives. He imports fish from a number of exporters from the bordering states, for example, such that the impact of the decline of fish supply at the importer's level is simply not felt. Alternatively, the importer may be aware of the threats to the sustainability of the Lake Victoria fishery, but tries to maximize the short-term benefits before the fishery collapses. Another possibility is that the importer declines to acknowledge publicly the problems of Nile perch degradation for fear of being held accountable.

In short, the reactions to and perceptions of the problems by the intermediaries in the Nile perch channel suggest that where many actors are involved, it may be difficult to make them recognize the problems for which they may be held accountable. Furthermore, dealing with the actors might also be difficult, particularly if they are thousands of miles apart and pursue their own self-interest. Pursuit of self-interest may drive what members of the channel do or what they wish to report about.[34] Moreover, each member probably has a different time horizon. Whereas one actor seeks to secure its business for the next generations, another may act to make quick money and retire. Firms willing to stretch their CSR programmes to suppliers may find it worthwhile to create a business climate in which channel members can freely communicate, rather than a climate that rewards information asymmetries.

Involving others

The second problem that firms willing to stretch CSR to suppliers may encounter is that of involving others to find solutions to problems. The traditional solution – to involve channel partners and make them comply with the new (CSR-based) requirements – is certification. Certification schemes such as Eurep-Gap, which is widely used in food retailing, impose standards on the channel members. An important disadvantage of this approach is that it motivates participants to do the minimum in order to obtain a certificate. Furthermore, mandatory requirements might exclude the (poor) small-scale actors (who may not be capable of certifying their products due to resource constraints) from participating in and benefiting from the global channels. For instance, although impositions of food-safety requirements may protect consumers in the Western developed economies, they are perceived as trade barriers for most developing economies.[35]

In contrast, some companies *motivate* participants to certify their products. Unilever, for example, allows its suppliers the voluntary option of certification. Indirectly, however, the multinational pressures its suppliers to certify their products by setting target dates by which it would purchase only certified products.[36] Most importantly, participants in such programmes that are willing to certify the products are given assistance in terms of resources and expertise. In this way, the members may not face any constraints to certify their products.

The approach of motivating rather than imposing certification on channel members may also have limitations. For example, the Nile perch channel, like other international food channels from developing countries, involves numerous primary producers. Fishers and middlemen are numerous, uncoordinated and operating in disparate units or as individuals. The sheer number of fishers in Lake Victoria, not to mention the middlemen, is itself a challenge to be met in involving all of them in CSR programmes. Furthermore, working with small-scale actors may be difficult for large-scale trading and processing companies because:

(1) quantities of products are small and heterogeneous in quality; and
(2) supply can be haphazard, where bulking-up of volume into a steady stream of good quality product might be difficult and costly to realize.

These may be serious problems when serving modern (and distant) marketing channels where timeliness, quality and quantity of delivery are critical issues for competitiveness. Furthermore, the organization of small-scale actors may be difficult, and firms that may be interested in organizing small-scale production and marketing systems may face high transaction costs.

In short, CSR programmes may require the involvement of – and investment from – all channel members (exporters, importers, retailers and primary producers). Because control is not an option, sustainable market mechanisms (i.e. those providing incentives for appropriate behaviour to stimulate quality and sustainability) are needed. Consequently, the issue is how appropriate market mechanisms can be created.

Creating sustainable market mechanisms for local traders and primary producers

The third problem facing firms seeking to stretch CSR programmes to suppliers is that of creating sustainable market mechanisms for local traders and primary producers. The traditional market mechanisms (i.e. the spot markets) often tend to motivate actors to deplete the resources. The overfishing that followed the expansion of competitive export markets and the information asymmetries in the Nile perch channel are typical examples of how market mechanisms can lead to the over-exploitation of the fisheries. Involving (poor) small-scale primary producers and communities in CSR programmes designed to protect the fisheries may require mechanisms that adequately compensate them for their contributions. This comes down to the question: what would small-scale primary producers perceive as adequate compensation for their contribution to CSR programmes, and what mechanisms would ensure that?

In agriculture, contract farming is common between small-scale farmers and large companies that help minimize market uncertainties and risks that farmers often encounter.[37] The responses we received in interviews and focus groups illustrate that money alone may not be what it takes to motivate fishers and traders to implement practices that may protect the fisheries. For example: (1) provision of sustainable fishing gear, (2) provision of quality improvement facilities such as ice to keep fish fresh and to minimize spoilage, and (3) provision of price information to minimize price and income uncertainties were, in order of importance, found to be the major factors motivating fishers to engage in contracts to implement practices that may protect the fisheries. The severity of enforcement mechanisms and legal sanctions for non-compliance with measures for sustainable fishing practices appeared to be of less importance in motivating fishers to enter into contracts that require them to implement sustainable practices.

Providing sustainable fishing gear: the importance of providing sustainable fishing gear – those that only catch large fish – can be understood from the fact that the use of unsustainable fishing gear – those that even catch juvenile fish – has contributed to the degradation of the fisheries. The use of unsustainable fishing gear is largely the result of ineffective enforcement by regulatory authorities and also the high approximate price of US$20 for sustainable fishing gear, which is considered unaffordable for many fishers. Ineffective enforcement of the legal requirement to use sustainable fishing gear implies that fishers willing to use sustainable fishing gear may not be motivated to do so. Those who use the sustainable gear ideally lose to those using unsustainable gear (who catch more fish, including the juveniles). During a focus group discussion, fishers admitted that relying on public institutions to enforce socially responsible fishing has not been effective thus far.

Consequently, some fishers have started to enforce social control among themselves through the traditional structures to help sustain the fishery. For example, fishers on a few beaches in Kenya implement socially responsible fishing practices under the leadership of some local institutions – the beach management units (BMU). The BMUs are local administrative institutions composed of fishers and traditional leaders in all landing sites along the lake. The BMUs oversee the activities of the landing sites, including enforcing responsible fishing behaviour to protect the fisheries. For a few years now, BMUs in a few beaches have been enforcing the use of sustainable fishing gear amongst respective fishers. These BMUs with the fishers in the respective landing sites resolved that they should only use sustainable gear. In order to help all fishers, especially those that cannot afford to buy sustainable gear, the BMUs run a self-help fund to which fishers contribute a small proportion of their daily fish sales. Any fisher facing problems such as loss or wearing out of gear or other emergency needs, may obtain loans from the fund. Our visits to such beaches confirmed that fish landings were consistently of large size. A secretary of one such BMU told us that: 'We – the fishers, the lake is all we have to live on. We can make things change if we want to, hiding behind poverty to destroy the lake will not help us. So we resolved to protect our resources.'[38]

Social control would be strengthened if the affordability of the sustainable fishing gear could no longer be an excuse. Therefore, stretching CSR to suppliers (fishers in this case) implies that downstream retailers and importers from the EU may need to support local initiatives (the BMUs in this instance) that ensure that all fishers can afford to buy sustainable fishing gear and to enforce social control to ensure sustainability of the fisheries. For example, if BMUs in all landing sites surrounding the lake are motivated and empowered to implement sustainable practices, they are likely to create a large public good (i.e. adoption of sustainable practices) in Lake Victoria for the benefit of all.

Providing ice: the importance of providing ice can be understood from the perishable nature of fresh fish and the implications of not having ice to keep fish. Observations at landing sites and interviews with fishers and traders revealed that fishers not only lose fish, but they also lose bargaining power. For example, fishers fail to bargain for better prices for fear of losing all of their fish. Hence, having ice or cold storage rooms in landing sites for keeping fish would not only minimize quality losses but, more importantly, strengthen the bargaining power of fishers. Although loss of bargaining power should theoretically reduce fishers' incentives to continue fishing, fishers in Lake Victoria, probably like many other small-scale primary producers in developing countries, face limited exit options into viable sectors of the economy. Instead, increasing fishing effort and the use of fishing gear that catch juvenile fish (to increase catch) to make up for the loss in income becomes the likely option, which unfortunately is more detrimental to sustainability.

Providing price information: abrupt and unpredictable price changes were of major concern to fishers, who often do not know the price of fish until they meet the buyers. In order to minimize price uncertainties, fishers prefer to have price information in the form of fixed prices. They are aware, however, of the risks of fixing prices, as one fisherman said during focus group discussions that it is better to know what he will get – whether little or more – and plan his activities, rather than not knowing anything and always have surprises. Other studies have also found that minimizing price uncertainties through provision of price information is a major determinant for choosing governance mechanisms among small-scale farmers.[39] The paradox, however, for stabilizing fishers' incomes is that it may make the fisheries more attractive, which would eventually attract yet more fishers as was the case when Nile perch production boomed. This will increase fishing capacity and rapidly deplete the fisheries. The challenge therefore is to find mechanisms that not only reward fishers to promote sustainable fishing practices but also ensure that they spend the additional income at the benefit of the rest of the economy, thus creating a multiplier effect.

In summary, identification of appropriate and sustainable market mechanisms is essential, although not straightforward. The characteristics of upstream stages of the channel, including the sheer number of actors, their asymmetric power relations, information asymmetries, poverty and common property rights, might make the implementation of the market mechanisms difficult – even if appropriate ones could be identified. This brings us to our last problem: how to implement sustainable market mechanisms.

How to implement sustainable market mechanisms

Even if solutions have been found, implementing them may be another challenge. Different implementation options could be considered:

(1) using a top-down approach;
(2) using a bottom-up approach; and
(3) using a market approach.

Top-down: certification institutions such as the MSC (Marine Stewardship Council) can help in the implementation of sustainable market mechanisms. These institutions provide codes of conduct for the sustainable utilization of resources. To ensure that channel members implement the codes of conduct, the certifying institutions undertake pre-certification assessment that qualifies actors to use a sustainability label in form of a logo (such as the MSC label for fisheries' products). To date, both the pre-certification assessment and post-certification audits entail rather substantial costs that limit the participation of small-scale actors from most developing nations. For example, since its inception in 1987, the MSC has certified only one fishery, the South African Hake, in Africa.[40] Making the certification process affordable to developing nations and also making the process suitable for fisheries under common property rights is therefore crucial for the effectiveness of the top-down approach.

Bottom-up: another way to implement sustainable mechanisms would be to follow local initiatives. In the Nile perch channel, emerging local initiatives through the BMUs offer opportunities to firms that are willing to stretch CSR to suppliers. For example, notwithstanding the newfound sense of social responsibility, the fishers in the few beaches that implement sustainable practices, like their colleagues in other beaches, still lack production facilities (such as ice, for example, to keep fish fresh). They equally suffer from the dominance of fish buyers in terms of price determination. Collaboration with such local institutions would make the implementation of the sustainable market mechanisms more feasible and would also encourage fishers to participate in and sustain the CSR programmes.

The emerging sense of responsibility among fishers to protect the fisheries is confirmed by our findings indicating that the severity of sanctions for non-compliance with the use of sustainable fishing methods is of least importance in motivating fishers to engage in sustainable practices. These results imply that, with proper incentives, third-party legal enforcement mechanisms might be less important in the enforcement of socially responsible fishing behaviour. This contradicts most of the literature on co-management, which emphasizes the enforcement of socially responsible fishing by regulatory institutions.[41]

The market approach: market forces themselves may support the implementation of sustainable mechanisms. Solving information asymmetry is, in this respect, a central issue in strengthening the bargaining power of small-scale actors. In the absence of fish auctions, price mechanisms are not transparent. Given that fishers do not have ice to keep fish fresh, buyers (who often form cartels to control the price) dictate the price to fishers. When prices decrease, fishers have no means to verify, say with other channel partners such as processors. To this end, attention should focus on information technologies. Increasingly, mobile phones are being used by fishers and other small-scale actors in developing countries to access price information, which enables them to decide where to buy and sell their commodities. *The Economist* argued, for example, 'Encouraging the spread of mobile phones is the most sensible and effective response to the digital divide.'[42] In Asia, the use of mobile phones is increasing; fishers access market information and then decide where to sell their fish.

In summary, there may be different options through which to implement sustainable market mechanisms. Most likely, a combination of the three approaches is used. Local initiatives provide a sound basis for bottom-up approaches. Top-down approaches such as certification offer standards for sustainable practices and mechanisms for ensuring compliance. Market mechanisms that minimize information asymmetries in the channel and amongst primary producers may enhance transparency. We are, however, mindful that a mere combination of the three approaches may not necessarily limit the possibility of uncontrolled new entry into the fisheries once the benefits become attractive. It is crucial that the sustainable mechanisms should be implemented parallel with building significant countervailing power for the local institutions (i.e. fishers) that, through group action from strengthened BMUs, can be instrumental in trying to continuously manage the threat of overfishing for the lake.

Conclusion

This chapter illustrates both the challenges and opportunities for firms willing to stretch CSR to suppliers. Firms may encounter enormous challenges and complexities that are interconnected – ranging from poverty and food insecurity to ecological degradation and social decay. Within the intricate network that international business has become, firms have lost track of the problems in their supply chains. Nevertheless, they may still influence the sustainability of the business activities of all channel partners – including downstream brand manufacturers and retailers. Firms that are willing to stretch CSR to suppliers should therefore implement appropriate information structures in order to recognize the problems; involve their channel partners and other stakeholders in finding solutions rather than adopting certificates that may be expensive and/or meaningless; and identify sustainable market mechanisms and find ways to implement them.

Similarly, downstream retailers and/or brand manufacturers going upstream in the Lake Victoria–EU Nile perch channel need to change the information exchange systems among channel partners, involve these partners, and provide fishers with price information, sustainable fishing gear and ice/cold storage facilities. Whereas the sheer number of fishers and traders in Lake Victoria may lead to coordination problems of both their activities and interests, collaboration with local institutions may reduce the costs and ease the problems of dealing with individual fishers. Collaborating with local institutions may both enhance the capability of primary producers to implement CSR programmes and increase their awareness of the benefits of their involvement in these programmes. With regard to the ecological sustainability of the fisheries, for instance, the motivation of fishers – the primary custodians of the fisheries – is paramount.

Firms that have already started stretching CSR to suppliers seem to be persevering. Stretching CSR upstream thus seems to be an emerging trend, rather than a short-lived fashion. These firms are involved in a learning process; they learn from their experiences, each other, their local and international stakeholders and channel partners how to make their business more sustainable in social, environmental and commercial terms. This learning process is just in its infancy, given the only recent recognition of the drawbacks connected with the intricate global networks that have emerged due to returning to core activities.

Stretching CSR to suppliers, therefore, promises to be an important step to a better future.

Acknowledgements

The authors would like to thank WOTRO and the Kenya Marine and Fisheries Research Institute for supporting the research, and Richard Abila, Tiny van Boekel, Ivo van der Lans, David Levine, Hans van Trijp and Ruud Verkerk for their constructive comments during the research process.

Notes

1 See, for example, the special issue of the *California Management Review* on social responsibility and marketing strategy: C.B. Bhattacharya, N. Craig Smith and David Vogel, 'Integrating Social Responsibility and Marketing Strategy: An Introduction', *California Management Review*, 47/1 (fall 2004): 6–8.

2 Sandra Waddock and Charles Bodwell, 'Managing Responsibility: What Can Be Learned from the Quality Movement', *California Management Review*, 47/1 (fall 2004): 25–37.

3 Tom J. Brown and Peter A. Dacin, 'The Company and the Product: Corporate Associations and Consumer Product Reponses', *Journal of Marketing*, 61/1 (January 1997): 68–84.

4 Paul Ingenbleek and Mathew T.G. Meulenberg, 'The Battle Between Good and Better, A Strategic Marketing Perspective on Codes of Conduct for Sustainable Agriculture', *Agribusiness: An International Journal*, 22/4 (2006): 451–73.

5 For problems of managing common property resources see the classical article, Garret Hardin, 'The Tragedy of the Commons', *Science*, 162 (1968): 1243–8.

6 *Darwin's Nightmare* is a documentary that has captured complex issues ranging from poverty, food insecurity, armed conflicts, HIV/AIDs, among others, around Lake Victoria. The documentary won sixteen awards before it was nominated for the Academy Award (Oscar) in 2005. The documentary illustrates in a nutshell how typical this chain is of global problems that may confront firms stretching CSR upstream. The documentary, however, needs to be interpreted with caution, as the IUCN and the Lake Victoria Fisheries Organization have warned that it distorts the reality of Lake Victoria fisheries (see open letter to the author posted on IUCN website: www.iucn.org/ IUCN News, December 2005).

7 Geoffrey G. Jones, *The Evolution of International Business* (London: McGraw-Hill, 1996).

8 Jones (1996).

9 Jones (1996).

10 Food and Agriculture Organization, 'Quality and Quality Changes in Fresh Fish', Fisheries Technical Papers – T348, 1995.

11 The Dutch Foundation for Nature and Environment sent mystery shoppers with this question to several supermarkets and ice cream producers. Nestlé (like most companies) answered that it didn't know where the chocolate precisely came from. It argued that measures against child slavery are the responsibility of local firms and governments. Unilever answered that it had a local system that controls for social and environmental aspects, including child labour and slavery. Wilma Berends, 'From Ground to Mouth: Transparency of the Food Market' (in Dutch) (Utrecht: Foundation for Nature and Environment, 2004).

12 S. Sen and C.B. Bhattacharya, 'Does Doing Good Always Lead to Doing Better? Consumer Reactions to Corporate Social Responsibility', *Journal of Marketing Research*, 38 (May 2001): 225–43.

13 Daniel B. Turban and Daniel W. Greening, 'Corporate Social Performance and Organizational Attractiveness to Prospective Employees', *Academy of Management Journal*, 40/3 (1997): 658–73; Isabelle Maignan, O.C. Ferrell and Thomas M. Hult, 'Corporate Citizenship: Cultural Antecedents and Business Benefits', *Journal of the Academy of Marketing Science*, 27/4 (1999): 455–69.

14 Ingenbleek and Meulenberg (2006).

15 Waddock and Bodwell (2004: 27).

16 We conducted focus group discussions and personal interviews with seventy-three fisherman, eight beaches, forty-one fish traders, managers of three fish-processing factories in Kenya and two importing companies; a quality manager of a large supermarket and fish specialty store. More details on our methods can be retrieved from the authors on request.

17 Lake Victoria Fisheries Organization, 'Strategic Vision for Lake Victoria (1999–2015)' (Jinja, Uganda, 1999).

18 Erik G. Jansen, 'Rich Fisheries – Poor Fishfolk. Some Preliminary Observations about the Effects of Trade and Aid in the Lake Victoria Fisheries', Socio-economics of the Lake Victoria Fisheries. IUCN, Report No. 1, 1997.

19 Eyolf Jul-Larsen, Jeppe Kolding, Ragnhild Overå, Jesper Raakjær Nielsen and Paul A.M. van Zwieten, 'Management, Co-management or no Management? Major Dilemmas in Southern African Freshwater Fisheries. Part 1: Synthesis Report', FAO Fisheries Technical Paper, No. 426/1 (Rome: FAO, 2003).

20 Crispin Bokea and Moses Ikiara, 'Fishery Commercialization and the Local Economy: The Case of Lake Victoria (Kenya)', Socio-economics of the Lake Victoria Fisheries, IUCN, Report no. 7, 2000.

21 Peter Gibbon, 'Of Saviors and Punks: The Political Economy of the Nile Perch Marketing Chain in Tanzania', Working Paper 97.3 (Copenhagen: Centre for Development Research, 1997).

22 For a review of the socio-economic benefits of Nile perch see Richard O. Abila and Erik G. Jansen, 'From Local to Global Markets. The Fish Exporting and Fishmeal Industries of Lake Victoria – Structure, Strategies and Socio-economic Impact in Kenya', Socio-economics of the Lake Victoria Fisheries, IUCN, Report No. 2, 1997; Bokea and Ikiara (2000).

23 See www.wildnetafrica.com, Bokea and Ikiara (2000).

24 Spencer Henson and Winnie Mitullah, 'Kenyan Exports of Nile Perch: Impact of Food Safety Standards on an Export-Oriented Supply Chain', University of Guelph and University of Nairobi, 2003, 84 pp.

25 Abila and Jansen (1997).

26 Abila and Jansen (1997); Henson and Mitullah (2003).

27 See Kim Geheb (ed.), 'Report of the LVFRP Nutrition Survey', LVFRP Technical Document No. 18. The Socio-economic Data Working Group of the Lake Victoria Fisheries Research Project, Jinja.

28 Richard O. Abila, 'The Development of the Lake Victoria Fishery: A Boon or Bane for Food Security?', Socio-economics of the Lake Victoria Fisheries, IUCN, Report No. 8, 2000.

29 Abila (2000).

30 Jansen (1997).

31 Abila and Jansen (1997).

32 Abila (1997).

33 Lake Victoria Fisheries Organization, 'The Convention for the Establishment of the Lake Victoria Fisheries Organization,' 2001, Jinja, Uganda; Lake Victoria Fisheries Organization, 'Lake Victoria 2000: A New Beginning, The Jinja Recommendation on the Way Forward', December, 2000. Lake Victoria Fisheries Organization (1999).

34 Emma Kambewa, Paul Ingenbleek and Aad van Tilburg, 'Improving Income Positions of Primary Producers in International Marketing Channels: The Lake Victoria-EU Nile Perch Case', *Journal of Macromarketing*, 28/1 (March 2008): 53–67.

35 Spenser Henson and Rupert Loader, 'Barriers to Agricultural Exports from Developing Countries: The Role of Sanitary and Phyto-sanitary Requirements', *World Development*, 29/1 (2001) 85–102; Spencer Henson and Bruce Traill, 'The Demand for Food Safety: Market Imperfections and the Role of Government', *Food Policy*, 18/2 (April 1993): 152–62.

36 For details of Unilever's CSR initiatives, see Unilever, Sustainable Fish Initiative, www.unilever.com.
37 For an example of contract farming, see FAO, 'Contract Farming, Partnership for Growth', FAO Agricultural Services, Bulletin 145, 2001; Oliver Masakure and Spencer Henson, 'Why do Small-scale Producers Choose to Produce under Contract? Lessons from Nontraditional Vegetable Exports from Zimbabwe', *World Development*, 33/10 (October 2005): 1721–33.
38 A Secretary of Wichlum beach in Kenya noted that fishers at the beach have agreed to protect the fisheries by using sustainable gear regardless of whether or not other beaches do the same.
39 Masakure and Henson (2005).
40 www.msc.org.
41 Jesper R. Nielsen and Christoph Mathiesen; 'Important Factors Influencing Rule Compliance in Fisheries Lessons from Denmark', *Marine Policy*, 27/5, (2003), 409–16; Jesper R. Nielsen 'An Analytical Framework for Studying: Compliance and Legitimacy in Fisheries Management', *Marine Policy*, 27/5 (2003): 425–32.
42 The use of mobile phones is increasingly being recognized as the best technology that fishers and farmers may use to get price information (see *The Economist*, 'Mobile Phones in India, Another Kind of Network', 1 March 2001; *The Economist*, 'Fishermen on the Net', 8 November 2001; *The Economist*, 'The Real Digital Divide', 10 March 2005; *The Economist*, 'Calling Across the Divide', 10 March 2005).

9 Breaking new ground: the emerging frontier of CSR in the extractive sector

V. KASTURI RANGAN AND BROOKE BARTON

Introduction

Commodities like copper, gold, oil and gas can be both the source of enormous profits for the companies that extract them and a magnet for the scorn and criticism of environmental and human rights activists the world over. However, in the fourteen years since the international furore raised by Shell's attempt to sink the Brent Spar rig in the North Sea and its alleged collusion with the Nigerian government in ignoring the rights of the Ogoni people, multinational extractive firms have arguably come a long way in reforming their CSR performance. Today, in response to activist – and increasingly investor – pressure, nearly all the global oil and mining companies have a CSR programme in place and seem committed to environmental stewardship and human rights. In fact many take part in international voluntary initiatives like the UN's Global Compact. And while debate may still rage in some corporate circles about the linkage between CSR and profitability, indeed CSR has become a prerequisite for business sustainability in the extractive industry, where a reputation for corporate citizenship could arguably make the difference between winning or losing multi-million dollar concessions.

However, in spite of the ever-ratcheting levels of corporate accountability that activist pressure has spurred in the extractives sector, we observe that many companies still struggle to gain and maintain their social licenses to operate.[1] Entrenched conflict with host communities in developing countries is on the increase and there is a growing list of corporations – Newmont Mining, Manhattan Minerals and Meridian Gold – that have lost multi-million dollar opportunities at the hands of well-organized campaigns run by NGOs and disgruntled host communities.

Where these companies failed was in grappling with the rising demands and socioeconomic complexities of the communities that lay beyond their fence lines. Host communities, increasingly empowered through global activist networks and a wave of democratization sweeping the developing world, are no longer satisfied with mere assurances that an extractive project will not create net negative social and environmental externalities. More and more, they are also demanding guarantees that these projects will impart long-term economic benefits through employment, growth and the allocation of monies for local development. The decision of local stakeholders to either accept or mobilize against a resource development project thus depends on their perception of the long-term benefits conveyed.

In this chapter, we argue that the challenge of building solid relationships with host communities in order to deliver long-term economic benefits represents the as-yet unconquered frontier of corporate social responsibility for extractives. At first blush, this challenge may sound simple, but, as we shall show, it is far from it. Indeed, delivering on this challenge falls far outside the current contours of most companies' CSR initiatives and involves new stakeholders, higher levels of complexity, and a host of externalities that most extractive MNCs are ill-equipped to address.

We first identify the core issue characterizing the long-term challenge of CSR. Then with the help of a case study we develop a framework to illustrate the challenges and provide guidance for managerial action. The chapter will point out that there is no magic bullet, and much of the work involves establishing a stakeholder-responsive process on the ground that allows management to approach the problem as a political one, even if this involves going outside the realm of what is in its immediate control.

Overview of the extractive sector

In 2006, the mining and metals business was a $249 billion industry (up 37 per cent from 2005).[2] It was also highly concentrated, with the world's top four mining companies (Table 9.1) bringing home 43% of total revenues and 47% of profit before taxes.[3] And, while global control over mineral production is increasingly concentrated in the hands of multinational giants headquartered in developed countries, the bulk of current production and exploration is found in the

Table 9.1 *2006 revenues of top mining and oil companies as a percentage of total industry sales*

Mining	%	Oil	%
Anglo American	13.3	Exxon Mobil	11.7
BHP Billiton	13.2	Royal Dutch Shell	10.7
Rio Tinto	9.0	BP	9.2
Companhia Vale do Rio Doce	7.9	Chevron	6.8
		ConocoPhillips	5.8
Total	43.4	Total	44.2

developing world.[4] Indeed, the majority of all new mining operations are sited in remote regions of developing countries and frequently on indigenous land.[5] In the oil and gas sector, the scenario is similar, if on a much larger scale. The 2006 revenues for the world's thirty-nine largest publicly listed oil companies were $2.79 *trillion*.[6] Here again, the top five companies accounted for a large chunk of this total, generating 44 per cent of total revenues.[7]

A brief look at the economies of those countries which are most dependent on mining for exports and foreign exchange illustrates the sometimes paradoxical relationship between high levels of resource extraction and economic development (Table 9.2). The world's top ten mineral-dependent countries (as defined by the percentage of their overall exports derived from ores and metals) are all developing countries and have a median per capita income of only US$421. In recent years, increasing evidence has come to light to suggest that a country's dependence on resource-extractive industries like mining and oil is strongly correlated with economic underperformance and slow growth.[8] Called the 'resource curse', this poor performance has at times been attributed to the historical decline in the terms of trade for primary commodities and the cycle of exchange-rate appreciation and economic stagnation linked to commodity exports known as the Dutch disease.[9]

But as highlighted by developmental economist, Paul Collier,[10] the root causes go far deeper. The weak internal functioning and corruption of the host-country governments often subverts the process of how the mineral wealth created is invested or redistributed to promote development and reduce poverty. Our point on weak

Table 9.2 *Top ten mineral-dependent economies*

Country	% of merchandise exports form ores and metals[a]	Transparency index[b]	GDP per capita (2004)[c]
Guinea	72	*	$380
Zambia	62	107	$336
Mozambique	55	97	$275
Niger	55	126	$156
Chile	54	21	$5,462
Papua New Guinea	49	118	$605
Peru	47	65	$2,206
Mongolia	43	105	$462
Central African Republic	36	*	$225
Georgia	25	130	$2,614

Notes: * Not available.
[a] Top ten countries by percentage of merchandise exports from ores and metals (corresponding to the commodities in SITC divisions 27, 28 and 68); World Bank's 2006 World Development Indicators Report.
[b] Drawn from Transparency International's 2005 Corruption Perceptions Index. Available at: www.transparency.org/policy_research/surveys_indices/cpi/2005.
[c] Constant 2000 US$, World Bank's World Development Indicators database.

governance can be seen from the ranking given on the corruption scale by Transparency International to each of the countries listed in Table 9.2. What is alarming is that foreign investors frequently abet the undesirable policies of the host government through signing concessionary agreements in which company payments and government receipts from resource extraction are couched in complex ways, and are mostly kept opaque for citizens of the host country or for that matter any interested third party. A lack of democratic processes in many countries perpetuates this tendency and ensures that the communities most affected by the negative social and environmental impacts of resource extraction often benefit the least from the revenues such activity generates. As Stiglitz[11] and others have variously argued, OECD governments often champion the business case of their corporations under the mistaken premise of free-market capital-ism without considering the repercussions of how the host-country's government would have to deal with the implicit social contract it has with its citizens. This is especially relevant if certain segments of the population further suffer as a result of the newly injected 'develop-ment capital' and the associated fiscal rules.

All this is not meant to deny that under a more inclusive and par-ticipative set of internal operating conditions, the mining industry could not contribute to significant human and economic development. From an analysis of thirty-three countries the International Council on Mining and Metals[12] advanced evidence that mining could pro-vide an important, and sometimes critical, contribution to economic development and poverty reduction in developing countries as long as the underlying conditions and policy frameworks were right. The ICMM study identified Ghana, Peru, Chile and Tanzania as four of the more successful countries. Peru is especially interesting because of the passage of the mining canon law (passed in 1992 and revised in 2001) that supposedly allocates 20% of the government's mining revenues to the local government, 60% to the provincial government, and only the remaining 20% to the central government.[13] It is inter-esting to note, however, that ICMM's report was unable to document any such gains for the other twenty-nine countries in the thirty-three-country sample.

The core issue: looking beyond the fence line

The script is familiar: when a global extractive firm sets up opera-tions in a developing country, the following scenario, or a variation of it, generally describes the local business context. At the outset, there seem to be handsome profits for the concessionary authority (usually the federal government) and the private developer. For the local people, the arrival of a new operation means losing their land, either through government expropriation or company negotiations in which they have little bargaining power, and thus their primary source of income. Once the project is in operation, the extraction and conversion of the natural resource almost always has environmental consequences. The economic benefits initially promised, in terms of jobs and secondary growth, rarely accrue to the people living closest to the project, who often remain impoverished. The tax revenue the project generates, millions of dollars every year, is siphoned off to federal treasuries and redirected to national rather than local priorities, if at all. Some may find its way into the hands of corrupt officials and investors.

These outcomes don't go unnoticed and increasingly local civil society organizations mobilize against the company, sometimes in a confrontational and contentious way. Because the host government is often unwilling or unable to address the grievances, these groups sometimes try to make their case heard in international forums. To do so, local groups seek out international partners, often Northern-based advocacy NGOs with global influence, who in turn publicly pressure the company in their country of origin. And in a few cases, when negotiations fail or dialogue cannot be established, local mobilization, sometimes peaceful, sometimes not, can halt development altogether. In the past five years, this scenario – that of discontent, mobilization and ultimate rejection – has become all too common.

Examples abound. In 2004, Newmont Mining, the world's largest gold miner by market capitalization, was forced to relinquish its permit to expand operations at its Yanacocha mine in Peru, instantly wiping 3.8 million ounces of gold reserves[14] worth an estimated $1.5 billion in future revenue streams from its books.[15] Massive protests by local farmers and representatives of the Catholic Church against the proposed expansion were fuelled by both environmental concerns and the perception that the mine had done little to alleviate local poverty. In 2003, opposition from local residents over a proposal by Canadian miner Meridian Gold to develop an ore body in Esquel, Argentina, led to protests and a community referendum against the mine. Opponents claimed that Meridian had failed to adequately consult the community in designing the mine's environmental plan and that it had underestimated the mine's long-term impacts on the community's well-developed skiing and fishing industries. As a result of losing the project, Meridian saw its stock price and total market capitalization take a dive of nearly 50 per cent in the first quarter of 2003.[16] In a similar case in Tambogrande, Peru, in 2001, Manhattan Minerals lost its mining concession when local citizens, concerned about the effect of mining activity on water supply and quality in this predominantly fruit-growing region, and convinced that they wouldn't benefit from tax revenues generated by the operation, overwhelmingly rejected the proposed mine in a community vote.

As these examples illustrate, host communities in developing countries do not oppose extractive operations simply on the basis of their short-term social and economic effects. In fact, their calculus is much more complex. They take account of a project's potential long-term economic contributions and weigh this against the contribution made by existing economic activities (such as farming, fishing or tourism), as well as against the risk that resource extraction will fundamentally imperil such activities (by diverting fertile land, polluting or overusing natural resources, or disfiguring the local landscape). They consider not only how the project will affect local employment and existing industries, but also whether or not the tax revenues it generates will end up benefiting national, rather than local, coffers.

This problem stems from the fact that, while nearly all major global extractive companies have developed sophisticated systems for managing and measuring their environmental and social impacts, most still take a 'beads and trinkets' approach to community economic development. Nearly all focus their efforts on meeting local short-term needs for basic infrastructure such as schools, community centres and health clinics. And while these are laudable and often much needed philanthropic projects, they are not sufficient to generate the kind of economic multiplier effect that will ensure growth beyond the life of the mine.

Case study: the Tintaya copper mine[17]

Background

Located 13,000 feet above sea level in Peru's Espinar province, the Tintaya copper mine had long been a source of intense friction between local Quechua-speaking community members and mine operators. Established in 1985 as a state-owned enterprise, the mine originally stood on 2,368 hectares (approximately nine square miles) of land expropriated from 125 families in Tintaya Marquiri, an indigenous farming community (see Figure 9.1).[18] In return for the land, the Peruvian government offered farmers ten *soles* per hectare (about $3 for 2.45 acres) and the promise of mining-related jobs.[19] In 1994, as part of Peru's structural adjustment programme, the mine was privatized and sold to US-based Magma Copper. In 1996, Australia-based BHP Billiton (at the time, Broken Hill Proprietary or BHP) acquired Magma Copper and, with it, the Tintaya mine.

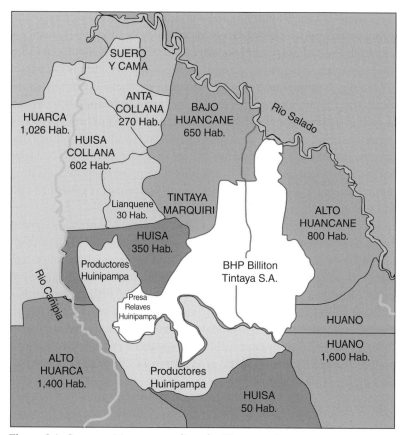

Figure 9.1 Communities surrounding the Tintaya mine

The Tintaya operation lost money until 2003, but spurred by soaring world prices for copper, turned a profit – nearly 25 per cent on revenues – of $284 million and $397 million in 2004 and 2005, respectively. BHP Billiton, with revenues of $31 billion in 2005, was the world's largest mining company.

One of the poorest provinces in the country, Espinar had 70,000 inhabitants and an economy that was highly dependent on the mine and related activities. In 2004, the mine provided employment to 615 direct employees and 236 contractors. Approximately 65 per cent of the mine's employees and contractors were from Espinar province, while the rest were from elsewhere in Peru. The mine also dedicated approximately 9% of its $139 million purchasing budget to local (provincial) suppliers, with 72% going to national suppliers and 19% to international. In addition to paying a federal income tax of $42 million in 2004, the company contributed nearly $1 million to address the grievances of communities directly surrounding the mine – known as the Dialogue Table Agreement – and a further $2 million to a provincial development fund known as the Espinar Framework Agreement, both of which will be discussed in detail in the following sections.

Key issues

Since 1996, the year BHP Billiton acquired the Tintaya mine, it faced a series of conflicts with communities immediately surrounding the mine and beyond. The conflicts came in three main waves. The first 'wave' of protests gained momentum in the late 1990s, when the five communities that had been displaced by the mine began demanding compensation for the land they had lost, for the harassment they had received when being evicted from their land and for environmental damage. Then, in early 2000, a second wave of protests arose from communities indirectly affected by current mining operations, but whose livelihoods were threatened by the construction of a new tailings dam. Here the concern was focused on ensuring that the company's activities did not threaten current livelihoods and long-term economic development. A third wave of protest originated in 2005 when local political groups demanded that the mine fund the construction of a highway and regional hospital. The conflict here goes beyond demands for sustainable development, to include issues of federal government investment and resource allocation for the concerned province.

First wave of protest

In addition to the original land that was expropriated from local villagers in the early 1980s by the Peruvian state, BHP Billiton had obtained 2,386 additional hectares throughout the late 1990s from adjacent communities to increase the mine's capacity and build a copper oxide plant and a tailings dam.[20] In some cases, community members claimed, company representatives had negotiated with, and purchased land from, community agents who lacked the authority to sell communal land. In the early 1990s, community members also began to complain about the mine's environmental impacts. Residents living near the company's operations reported that waste water from the company's processing plant had leaked into local rivers and springs, contaminating pasture lands and rendering the water unfit for human and animal consumption.

In 1999, unsatisfied with the company's response to their years of protests and complaints, the five displaced communities allied themselves with three NGOs:

(1) the National Coordinating Body for Communities Affected by Mining (CONACAMI), Peru's largest and most vociferous anti-mining organization;
(2) CooperAcción, a Lima-based NGO dedicated to helping indigenous communities gain the information and skills necessary to defend their rights; and
(3) Oxfam America, a US-based NGO and a member of Oxfam International, a confederation of twelve NGOs working to create 'lasting solutions to poverty, suffering and injustice'.[21]

At the behest of its Peruvian partners, Oxfam representatives met with corporate management at BHP Billiton's headquarters in Australia and asked the company to address the Peruvian communities' grievances. Finally in December 2001, at the prodding of headquarters, Tintaya's local management agreed to participate in a formal dialogue process with the communities and NGOs to look into the grievances.

It is instructive to ponder the rather laborious process by which BHP finally arrived at a forum for dialogue with the affected community. On the one hand, it can be argued that a private enterprise should not be asked to pay for the sins of its predecessors. Most of the communities' grievances stemmed from transactions that took place when the Peruvian government owned the mine. But on the other hand, while the ownership of the unfairly acquired assets transfer over, so do the associated social liabilities. The generally accepted standards on resettlement and compensation are only broad voluntary guidelines, but in the context of the current environment in which host communities and local and international NGOs are globally linked, regardless of the legality of the old agreement, what the NGO alliance demanded of the mine was 'fair' and 'reasonable' compensation.

The Dialogue Table. In preparation for the first meeting of what became known as the 'Tintaya Dialogue Table', the company and the community-NGO coalition carefully prepared their respective positions. At the Dialogue Table's inaugural meeting the ice was broken with the help of a respected and neutral facilitator, who led community members, NGO representatives, local government officials and BHP Billiton staff through an iterative 'issues identification' process. At the end of the process, consensus was reached on the need to address four key issues of concern to the communities – land, human rights, environment and sustainable development.

Dialogue Table participants agreed to form four working commissions to investigate grievances, formulate recommendations and implement changes in each of the four areas. Each commission was composed of the communities' elected leaders and interested residents, municipal and NGO representatives, and BHP Billiton corporate and local staff. Commission members would meet privately on a frequent basis to review findings and formulate recommendations, then periodically report back to all parties at regularly scheduled plenary meetings.

Dialogue Table participants identified several key principles and ground rules to guide the process – participation, consensus-seeking, joint fact-finding and confidentiality (see Table 9.3).

The local NGOs, by serving as advisors and advocates for the communities, bridged the cultural and economic chasm that had long separated the communities and the company and ensured that both parties were speaking the same language. Over time, and through repeated interactions at commission and plenary meetings, mutual understanding and respect between community leaders and BHP Billiton officials slowly grew. Many observers to the process saw this iterative learning process and ongoing exchange of perspectives as an element that facilitated remarkable personal transformations on the part of both community members and company managers.

On 21 December 2004, an agreement between BHP Billiton and the five Dialogue Table communities was signed. The agreement, which had been approved and ratified by each community's general assembly, represented more of a consolidation than a conclusion to the Dialogue Table's three-year negotiation.

The central aspects of the agreement related to the acquisition of new land for community members, the management and development of this land, the creation of a $1 million community development

Table 9.3 *The four pillars of the dialogue process*

Participation. Making the Dialogue Table a fully participatory
process was a priority shared by all parties. As development advocates,
the Oxfam organization insisted that the 'right to be heard' was one of
the fundamental rights of the community members affected by the mine.
BHP Billiton management, taking a perspective informed by the
practical difficulties of stakeholder negotiation, considered broad
participation vital to heading off the emergence of new claims later in
the process, which could slow or derail negotiations.

Consensus-based approach. Consensus-based decision-making was a
second key principle of the Dialogue Table. All decisions made by the
working commissions and at the plenary meetings were reached through
consensus, rather than a voting procedure. The rationale for this choice
lay in a shared belief that by reaching consensus over contentious issues,
trust would be built between parties and a shared interpretation and
joint vision of the conflict would be forged.

Joint fact-finding. From the outset, all Dialogue Table participants
agreed to jointly investigate community grievances and to implement the
recommendations of all outside experts hired by the Dialogue Table.
The working commissions contracted these experts through a
consensus decision-making process and asked them to provide
independent assessments of many of the Dialogue Table's most hotly
contested issues, including accusations of contamination and human
rights abuses.

Confidentiality. From the start, participants agreed to keep the Dialogue
Table's proceedings confidential in order to minimize the risk of
grandstanding and build trust between the parties. Participants decided
that public reports about the Dialogue Table would be vetted and approved
by all parties before being released.

---

fund and the ongoing work of the Human Rights and Environment
Commissions. It also affirmed that all future exploration and development activities by BHP Billiton would require the prior, informed
consent of the community or individual property-owners.

By the spring of 2005, the company had purchased 80 per cent of
the land that had been promised to community members as compensation. In addition, the company had begun to finance several community initiatives including irrigation, technical skills training and other
agricultural improvement projects. The company and community

leaders had also established community-based environmental monitoring teams and agreed to hold joint environmental impact assessments to be held on a regular basis.

Second wave of protest

Even as BHP was discussing the displacement and compensation issues with the affected communities, in May 2003, more than 1,000 people from the nearby Ccanipia basin stormed the Tintaya mine site. Their issues had nothing to do with displacement. At the heart of the conflict lay the fact that the Ccanipia communities had been inadequately consulted about the company's construction of a new tailings dam close to their lands. The new tailings dam was scheduled to be operational in the second half of 2003, when the mine planned to scale up its production. Although a public hearing on the proposed dam construction was held by the Ministry of Energy and Mines in May 2001, leaders from the Ccanipia communities claimed that they had not been told of the meeting and were not present for the consultation. An important dairy region in Peru, the Ccanipia basin was home to a large community of relatively well-off farmers who viewed the tailings dam as an imminent threat. Many believed that the dam, which would contain potentially toxic waste left over from the mine's processing of copper ore, would pollute their land and affect their livestock, and thus their production of milk. As a result of the entreaties and protests from this relatively wealthy community, BHP initiated a parallel set of discussions with their representatives, even as it was attempting to work through a settlement with the communities directly affected by the mine's various activities.

When the communities who felt potentially endangered by the pollution of the Ccanipia River joined in protest, BHP Billiton officials asked the leaders of the newly affected communities to join the ongoing Dialogue Table as a means of resolving the conflict, but they refused to participate and continued to press the company for compensation. Eager to bring the new copper-oxide plant and the tailings dam into operation, BHP Billiton managers addressed the Ccanipia communities' concerns by taking several steps to improve the environmental safety of the dam. The conflict with the Ccanipia communities also pushed the company to move ahead with a broader benefits agreement that provincial officials had been pressuring the company to consider.

Espinar's new provincial mayor, Luis Álvarez, took a pragmatic approach to working with the company. His central ambition was to move Espinar's economy from one entirely dependent on a non-renewable resource, which would be depleted in twenty-five years, to one capable of sustaining economic growth and creating employment well beyond the life of the mine.

Álvarez had long wanted the company to make a financial commitment to the long-term economic development of the entire Espinar province. Given the financial demands made by the Ccanipia communities, and their unwillingness to participate in the Dialogue Table, BHP Billiton sought to resolve the conflict by wrapping these demands into a larger agreement with the province.

The terms of the agreement, known as the Espinar Framework Agreement, were signed in September 2003. It established a development fund to which the company would annually donate up to 3 per cent of the mine's income (before interest and taxes) or, alternatively, when profits were low, a minimum of $1.5 million. The fund was to be managed through a coordination committee made up of local government officials, community organizations and mine representatives that would prioritize and facilitate the projects funded under the agreement. Unlike the development fund that the mine had discussed with the five Dialogue Table communities, this fund would provide support for economic development projects in any of Espinar's sixty-eight rural communities, plus its urban areas – not just the communities located near the mine.

The kind of issues raised in the second wave were qualitatively different from those during the first wave of protests. Even though the issues were largely anticipatory, they had the potential to cause harm to their local economy. Producing a scientific document to rebut their fears was likely to be less compelling to the community then actively engaging them in the solution, and even awarding them a role in its monitoring. Interestingly, the mine had assumed responsibility for community development that went beyond those directly affected by the mining operations. If the company's submissions were to be believed, all adequate environmental safeguards were in place, yet it chose to address the communities' grievances, real or imagined. All the projects chosen as part of the Espinar Framework had the singular aim of developing skills in the community to enable the enhancement of their livelihoods.

Third wave of protest

In spite of these achievements, which provided conditions for uninter-rupted operations, in May 2005, at a time of increasing copper prices, protests broke out again and the mine was invaded and overtaken by over 2,000 people. This time it was neither the displaced people nor those from the Ccanipia basin who were heading the charge, but rather student groups and members of political parties, protesting on behalf of the larger Espinar community. In addition to demanding a more generous allocation under the Espinar Framework Agreement ($20 million instead of the agreed-upon $2 million) protestors also demanded that the mine pave a fifty-mile regional highway and build a regional hospital. To protect its workers from the protesting mobs, BHP Billiton was forced to shut down and evacuate the mine, a rather difficult decision given the excellent market conditions.

Two important set of events determined how the conflict would play out. One, because the company had proven itself both open and responsive in dealing with the first and second waves of protests, it had garnered significant trust and goodwill in the region. Two, those immediately affected by the mine's shutdown were contractors and ancillary business personnel in the Espinar community whose liveli-hoods depended on providing products and services to the mine and mining community at large. Combined, these two events provided a groundswell of support for the mine, which was echoed by the local press. The protestors may or may not have had a valid point regard-ing the company's contributions to the development fund; neverthe-less, it was clear that their true grievances were fundamentally rooted in issues around the provincial and federal government allocation of mining revenues towards local infrastructure. In essence, the protes-tors were using the mine as a lightning rod for gaining resources from an otherwise unresponsive federal government.

New sets of negotiations were initiated, and the federal and pro-vincial governments were all parties to an agreement which required resource commitments on their part to the region. The federal gov-ernment had commissioned a feasibility study for a local hospital, the construction of which the company agreed to fund for $2 million out of existing monies in the Framework Agreement. Once the hos-pital was built, the provincial government would fund its operating costs. On the issue of the road, the company had made clear that this was the government's responsibility. In response, the Peruvian Transportation Ministry agreed to review the project. It was also agreed that Framework Agreement funds would be used to build a dairy-processing plant that would serve the farmers of the province. The mine was reopened within three months of the protests.

A framework for analysing the CSR frontier

To understand the root causes underlying the three waves of protests, it is useful to first consider the three main categories of impact that most extractive operations exert on their host communities in developing countries. For the purposes of simplicity, we will specify the framework with reference to the mining sector only, but it is equally applicable to analysing oil and gas projects. As shall be explained in more detail, these categories of impacts – displacement and environment, sustainable development and resource allocation – make up a hierarchy in which each successive level corresponds to a more diffuse set of stakeholders, weaker international standards and less firm control (Table 9.4) Although these three levels of impact do not remain neatly compartmentalized in real-world conflicts between companies and communities, the salience of each level of impacts typically changes throughout the mine's lifecycle.

Level I issues

Displacement refers to both the involuntary physical relocation (loss of homes and land) and the economic displacement (loss of assets leading to loss of income or livelihoods) that occur when a company acquires land for extractive purposes. Since the early 1980s, multilateral lending institutions like the World Bank have been under the gun by civil society forces to create clear standards for mitigating the devastating impacts of displacement brought about by the large-scale development projects it finances. In response, the World Bank, the IFC (the Bank's private-sector lending arm) and several other multilateral development agencies have created guidelines and requirements for loan clients acquiring land for development projects. Today, the World Bank Operational Directive on Involuntary Resettlement has achieved the status of a global standard and has been adopted by the world's top three mining firms (BHP Billiton, Rio Tinto and Anglo

Table 9.4 *The hierarchy impacts associated with mining*

Impact	Existing international standards or norms	Stakeholders affected	Level of firm control
Level I: Displacement and Resettlement	World Bank Operational Directive on Involuntary Resettlement. IFC Performance Standard on Land Acquisition & Involuntary Resettlement. The Asian Development Bank Involuntary Resettlement Policy. Inter-American Development Bank Operational Policy on Involuntary Resettlement.	Individuals and communities living on or near resource to be extracted. Individuals and communities whose income depends on assets affected by land acquisition.	High
Level I: Environment	ISO 14001. IFC/Equator Principles.	Communities located on or near impacted natural resources, or upwind/downstream of them.	High
Level II: Sustainable Development	International Council on Mining and Metals (ICMM). Sustainable Development Framework.	Employees, suppliers and distributors; local government.	Medium
Level III: Resource Allocation	Extractive Industries Transparency Initiative.	Local, provincial and national government authorities, local communities.	Low

American).[22] On the whole, these standards place primary responsibility with companies for ensuring that people potentially displaced by a mining operation are consulted and given the opportunity to participate in the planning and implementation of their own resettlement. Although local laws may permit expropriation with minimal compensation based on eminent domain, firms must go further by ensuring that the individuals and communities most directly affected by operations take part in a transparent process of consultation that delivers fair and adequate compensation benchmarked against the quality of life and livelihoods of the displaced at the time of the acquisition.

Though qualitatively different, a related first level of impact also relates to the *environment*. A mining operation's initial environmental impact relates to the destruction of virgin natural environments to build roads and other infrastructure for operations. Rare species of flora and fauna may be destroyed or put at risk.[23] In the course of the average mine's life, millions of tons of ore are extracted, processed for the desired mineral and then dumped – either in contained, above-ground 'tailings dams' or at sea. The run-off from these tailings becomes toxic when oxidized minerals from the mining waste come into contact with water, producing sulfuric acid. This run-off can damage watersheds, rivers, lakes and related wildlife, which in turn can hurt both the incomes and health of local peoples. Moreover, in the development of the infrastructure and in the mining operations itself, the soil that lies above the ore will have to be excavated. Storing the soil for such operations poses further risks of forest destruction as well as problems of instability of the ground where it is stored. Finally, the industry's potential for environmental impact is heightened in the context of gold mining, a process that makes heavy use of cyanide for extracting gold from ore.

Although by law most mining companies are required to meet local environmental requirements, global companies like BHP Billiton are inevitably held to higher standards because of their international connections. Activist pressure to prevent an environmental 'race to the bottom' has given rise to a plethora of corporate, industry and multilateral environmental standards.

Today, subsidiaries of extractive MNCs are nearly always accountable to a set of corporate policies and standards that are set high and often informed by industry and international norms. For example, BHP Billiton's environmental management approach is based on 'industry practice' as well as international environmental management standards such as ISO 14001.[24] Increasingly, mining companies are aligning their corporate environmental performance standards with the criteria set out by the IFC's Equator Principles. The Principles, which provide social and environmental guidelines for financing large development projects, have been adopted by forty-one financial institutions from sixteen countries.

Level II issues

While there has been considerable debate, discussion and formulation of common standards with respect to both displacement and environmental impact, the new twist has been the growing calls by stakeholders for mining to contribute to sustainable development, which we term a Level II issue. Sustainable development is best understood by the Bruntland definition as 'development that meets the needs of the present without compromising the ability of future generations to meet their own needs'.[25] Although mining is an economic activity with a finite lifecycle, companies have a responsibility to leave in their wake something more than the dependent and devastated company towns of eras past. Instead, international NGOs like Oxfam are calling for extractive companies to help build local capacity for alternative economic activities based on local renewable resources, competencies and skills that will sustain economic development beyond the life of the mine. Both direct employees and those supplying the mine should be able to find gainful employment after the business shuts down. The physical environment surrounding the mine should be managed to ensure that the land can and will be restored to other productive uses going forward.

International guidance on the role of extractive industries in promoting sustainable development is scant. The ICMM, the largest mining membership association, recently committed its fourteen member companies to implementing a 'Sustainable Development Framework', which entails the application of ten principles, a commitment to public reporting, independent assurance and sharing of good practice (ICMM). While the framework is an important step towards increasing transparency in the sector, the ICMM's sustainable development principles are vaguely worded and provide no concrete guidance on how companies should approach the process of creating long-term economic value in the communities that host them. Moreover the ICMM framework is silent regarding the participative process needed to ensure sustainable development.

Level III issues

Sustainable development, however, is not the same as the even larger expectation regarding the economic development and growth for the region under the mine's influence. An extractive firm's Level III impact therefore relates to its power to influence the *allocation of* mining profits and tax revenues for local development. Typically, a firm's attempt to get involved in the resource-allocation process will be rebuffed as political interference, putting its own franchise in peril.

For example, the key issue facing Shell in Nigeria is the investment in the development of the Ogoni people whose land provides the core resources for oil extraction and transport, yet the Ogoni have little voice in the Nigerian power structure and receive little in the way of the tax revenues generated from oil sales. Freeport McMoran's copper and gold mines in Irian Jaya, Indonesia, face similar challenges from the locals, who believe that the federal government is using their land to develop a profitable operation, while allocating few tax dollars to their own development. The Indonesian military has been accused of brutally putting down any rebellious activity from the locals; some would say with the connivance of the Freeport authorities themselves.[26] In both cases, in the face of hostility from host communities and intransigence from host governments, the companies have been forced to set up special trust funds for channelling their pre-tax revenues into dedicated local economic development projects.[27]

Thus, in the absence of democratic governance, companies increasingly find themselves adopting the surrogate governmental role. This problem highlights the larger question of how companies can work with host governments to ensure that the national wealth generated by their efforts are allocated in a manner that corresponds with the desires of local communities. Although international efforts like the British government's Extractive Industries Transparency Initiative (which pressures governments and companies to disclose payments and revenues from oil, gas and mining) are afoot to build increased transparency over resource wealth, there are as yet no international

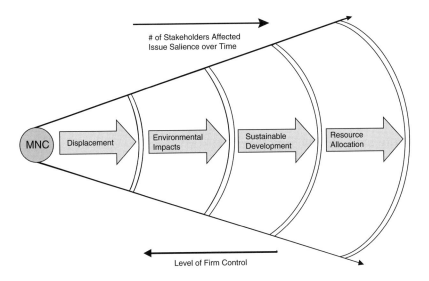

Figure 9.2 CSR in the extractive sector: the emerging frontier

standards on how companies should engage with governments to ensure appropriate distribution of revenues or, in the absence of viable democratic institutions, how to establish and run trust funds of their own.

In Figure 9.2 we map out the hierarchy of impacts just discussed and show how each level represents a *sphere of influence* that extends from an extractive MNC operating in a developing country. Each sphere of influence represents a series of impacts that are either directly (such as the displacement or resettlement of people living on or near the resource to be extracted) or indirectly (such as the long-term economic development of the host community) linked to the firm's core operations.

These spheres of influence have impacts that over time affect an ever-broader group of stakeholders with increasingly diffuse interests. Each successive sphere of influence touches a broader geographic area: initially the company's effects are limited to those people living directly on the land to be excavated (displacement). Within a short time, extractive operations begin affecting those living downstream or downwind of operations (environment), then influencing the economy of nearby towns (sustainable development) and finally affecting the welfare of the entire region or country with regards to export earnings and taxation (resource allocation). In order to exert influence over each sphere, thereby minimizing externalities and reducing the risk of losing their social license to operate, companies are forced to interact with an ever-wider group of stakeholders on increasingly complex issues over which they have less and less control and are guided by fewer international standards.

For many mining companies, as their CSR approach has grown more sophisticated, they have begun to internalize their most immediate impacts on the surrounding society (displacement and environmental damage) through policies and procedures that establish internal standards of environmental and social performance. These standards over time serve to broaden the scope of CSR issues over which a firm takes ownership. But, in order to respond to rising local stakeholder demands for economic growth and allocation of tax revenues, a firm can no longer dwell comfortably within its first level of influence; it must also begin to excel in operating further along the CSR frontier – that is, in the areas of sustainable development and resource allocation – and to do so, must engage increasingly sophisticated processes involving more issues and more people, while guided by fewer international standards.

At Tintaya, even though almost all of the company's actions in the first and second waves were taken in reaction to the actions of Oxfam and other civil society organizations, it is notable that it entered into the dialogue process using a bottom-up approach that ensured that grievances were aired, thoroughly investigated and addressed. Having such a process in place is crucial. Regardless of any existing global standards, ultimately the displaced people have to feel comfortable about the compensation and alternate settlement schemes. The issues addressed in the first and second waves pertain to what we have termed Level I and II issues. These are fundamental, and even though international and local laws provide benchmarks, the issues are best addressed through community consensus. It is people who feel the burden and the cost of the displacement, and their input in arriving at the compensation package has to be a key part of the calibration. While the management at Tintaya mine seem to have adequately addressed Level I issues, it is a bit early to tell whether similar closure has been gained on Level II issues. Part of the problem may be with a lack of agreement on what sustainable development means – whether it is sustainable 'for now' versus 'being sustainable after the mine shuts down'. As for Level III issues, clearly the mine had only begun to scratch the surface of the issues.

What is confounding about Level III issues is that, unlike the earlier phases, quite often the private investor would view the protests as uncalled for and politically motivated. The issues may not appear to be justifiable at a first glance. As for the protestors themselves, regardless of where the instigation came from, issues at all three levels will loom large, vested interests and representatives fanning the flames of their partisan agendas. Lacking an effective political governance structure, which is the norm in many emerging countries where the mining resources reside, the protests become a vehicle for venting public grievances in a private channel.

The tension in this model lies in the fact that most extractive firms are not equipped to deal with the latter two spheres of influence. International and even industry standards are not up to the task and local guidance is fraught with highly political tensions. Operating in this space requires a level of stakeholder responsiveness and bottom-up consultation that many companies find difficult to cultivate.

Conclusion

In many parts of the business world, CSR is seen as a series of activities that are ancillary to core operations and that rarely add to the bottom line. For the extractive sector, however, building strong community relations through the diligent application of CSR standards is essential to gaining and maintaining the goodwill needed to operate in the first place. Both multilateral and private investors recognize this and funding for extractive projects increasingly comes with strings attached; sponsors demand that projects be developed according to internationally accepted standards on environmental performance and resettlement. Even for companies that don't face these demands, it behooves them to operate according to these standards in order to avoid the scrutiny of civil society activists who will no doubt hold them similarly accountable.

But international standards have yet to be articulated for the two major issues facing extractive companies operating on the CSR frontier: sustainable development and resource allocation. The very context-specific nature of these challenges may be why such standards are lacking, but their absence, as illustrated by the Tintaya example, does not mean that a clear strategy for addressing them does not exist.

In BHP Billiton's case, the company inherited a series of social and environmental liabilities from the mine's previous owners. Poor community relations management by the company itself through its additional land purchases compounded existing problems. And while the company initiated dialogue with affected communities in response to an NGO threat, its initial reactiveness was soon transformed into an approach of consultation and problem-solving that built a foundation for mutual understanding and long-term partnership.

By building trust through a long-term dialogue process based on consensus-seeking and broad participation, the company was able to negotiate an agreement with the Dialogue Table communities that remedied their grievances and met their aspirations for long-term economic development. Later, by expanding its community development footprint through the creation of the Espinar Framework Agreement, BHP Billiton addressed the fact that local politicians and communities felt that the federal government had not adequately distributed mining revenues for local purposes in spite of the mining canon laws. Moreover, it has been reported that the provincial and national governments, even when disbursing the funds, usually dictate how it should be used rather than pay real heed to the needs of the local community.[28] The company's failure to engage the federal government on this issue early on meant that it took up the burden of meeting the growing expectations of local communities itself. Eventually, these growing expectations exploded with the protests of May 2005 and the shutdown of the mine. Nevertheless, unlike its counterparts in other regions of Peru (Newmont in Yanacocha and Manhattan Minerals in Tambogrande), BHP Billiton was not forced to abandon its operations. Thanks to the efforts it invested in building local relationships based on trust and mutual benefit, it ensured a safety net of support that buffered it against demands that, in their essence, were directed at the Peruvian government.

Such demands are bound to come up time and again in countries that are marked by weak governance and high levels of poverty. Nevertheless, the Tintaya case illustrates the positive opportunities that exist for those companies that choose to operate at the CSR frontier. By acknowledging and attempting to address the complex issues of sustainable development and resource allocation, and by doing so in a way that builds trusts and ensures joint benefit, extractive firms can both meet local stakeholder expectations and strengthen their license to operate. Our suggestion should not be viewed in vacuum. In conjunction with the appropriate transparency processes promoted by the Extractive Industry Transparency Initiative (EITI) and the internal regulatory processes that govern the allocation of mining revenues to the local government, the participative structure we advocate can enable a way out of the potential conflicts of resource allocation that many mining firms experience, over which they have no control.[29]

Notes

1 The term 'social license' is frequently used in the mining and oil industries to refer to both the legal permissions needed from host governments and the 'goodwill granted by communities based on perceptions of good citizenship'. See R. Sullivan and P. Frankental, 'Corporate Citizenship and the Mining Industry: Defining and Implementing Human Rights Norms', *Journal of Corporate Citizenship*, 7 (2002): 79–91.

2 PricewaterhouseCoopers, *Mine – Riding the Wave: Review of Global Trends in the Mining Industry* (2007). Available at: www.pwc.com/extweb/pwcpublications.nsf/docid/AD4DEFB47A20ED0A852572F9007200C7/$File/07–02111_mine2007.pdf.

3 PricewaterhouseCoopers (2007: 7).

4 Metals Economic Group, *World Exploration Trends 2008* (2008). Available at: www.metalseconomics.com/catalog/pages/pdac2008.pdf.

5 G. Whiteman and K. Mamen, 'Meaningful Consultation and Participation in the Mining Sector? A Review of the Consultation and Participation of Indigenous People within the International Mining Sector' (The North-South Institute, 2002). Available at: www.nsi-ins.ca/english/pdf/lit_rev/lit_rev_final.pdf.

6 *Fortune Magazine*, 'Fortune Global 500 2007' (2007). Available at: http://money.cnn.com/magazines/fortune/global500/2007/full_list/index.html.

7 *Fortune Magazine* (2007).

8 See R. Auty, *Sustaining Development in Mineral Economies: The Resource Curse Thesis* (London: Routledge, 1993); M. Ross, 'The Political Economy of the Resouce Curse', *World Politics*, 51/2 (1999): 297–322; J. Sachs and A. Warner, 'Natural Resource Abundance and Economic Growth', NBER Working Paper 5398, 1995.

9 Ross (1999).

10 See Paul Collier, *The Bottom Billion* (Oxford: Oxford University Press, 2007). In chapter 3 (pp. 38–52), Collier discusses in detail how oil wealth and corruption have co-existed in Nigeria to hamper economic development.

11 See Joseph E. Stiglitz, *Globalization and its Discontents* (New York: W.W. Norton, 2003), pp. 53–88.

12 International Council on Mining and Metals (ICMM), 'The Prize: The Challenge of Mineral Wealth', Spotlight Series 01, April 2006.

13 For a more complete description, see Keith Slack, 'Sharing the Riches of the Earth: Democratizing Natural Resource – Led Development', *Ethics and International Affairs*, 18 (2004).

14 J. Perlez and L. Bergman, 'Tangled Strands in Fight over Peru Gold Mine', *New York Times*, 25 October 2005.

15 Authors' estimate based on Newmont's 2004 average revenue per ounce of gold of $412.

16 *Gold Stock Analyst*, 'Priced for Perfection', No. 107, April 2003. Available at: www.goldstockanalyst.com/sample/Apr03.pdf.

17 This section of the chapter is based on V. Kasturi Rangan, Brooke Barton and Ezequiel Reficco, 'BHP Billiton and the Tintaya Copper Mine', Harvard Business School Case Study N9-506023 (Harvard Business School Press, 2006).

18 J. Aste, J. de Echave and M. Glave, 'Procesos Multi-Actores para la Cogestión de Impactos Mineros en Perú: Informe Final' (Lima, Peru: La Iniciativa de Investigación Sobre Políticas Mineras, 2003). Available at: www.iipm-mpri.org/biblioteca/docs/procesos_multiactores_informe_final.pdf.

19 Oxfam America, 'Tintaya Copper Mine'. Available at: www.oxfamamerica. org/whatwedo/where_we_work/south_america/news_publications/ tintaya/art6243.html.

20 Oxfam Community Aid Abroad, *Mining Ombudsman Annual Report 2003. Tintaya Case Notes*, 2003. Available at: www.oxfam.org.au/ campaigns/mining/ombudsman/2003/cases/tintaya/tintayafull.pdf.

21 Oxfam International website. Available at: www.oxfam.org/eng/about. htm.

22 The World Bank Operational Directive on Involuntary Resettlement is also referenced in the Global Reporting Initiative's Mining and Metals Sector Supplement, a public disclosure guideline developed by a multi-stakeholder working group and endorsed by the International Council on Mining and Metals, the main mining industry membership organization. Available at: www.icmm.com/sd_reporting.php.

23 A. Rosenfeld Sweeting and A. Clarke, *Lightening the Lode: A Guide to Responsible Large-scale Mining* (Conservation International, 2000).

Available at: www.celb.org/ImageCache/CELB/content/energy_2dmining/lode_2epdf/v1/lode.pdf.

24 BHP Billiton, *BHP Billiton Sustainability Report 2005*, 2006. Available at: http://hsecreport.bhpbilliton.com/2005/docs/BHPBilliton SustainabilityReport2005.pdf.

25 United Nations Environment Programme (UNEP), 'The Rio Declaration on Environment and Development', 1992. Available at: www.unep.org/Documents.multilingual/Default.asp?DocumentID=78&ArticleID=1163.

26 Project Underground: Report of the Australian Council for Overseas Aid, April 1995.

27 Brigid McMenamin, 'Environmental Imperialism', *Forbes*, 20 May 1996, p. 130.

28 For more detail, see World Bank, 'Peru: Restoring Fiscal Discipline for Poverty Reduction: A Public Expenditure Review' (World Bank, 24 October 2002).

29 Final note: BHP Billiton sold its Tintaya mine to Xstrata plc, another mining conglomerate headquartered in Switzerland in May 2006.

10 | Overcoming rural distribution challenges at the bottom of the pyramid

SUSHIL VACHANI AND N. CRAIG SMITH

Les bons pauvres ne savant pas que leur office est d'exercer notre générosité.[1]

Introduction

Recent thinking and practice in management has challenged the widely held view that the role of the poor, as Sartre put it, is to exercise our generosity. There are alternatives to charity where the poor help themselves and business plays a part by pursuing its economic interests and tapping the economic potential of the bottom of the pyramid (BOP) – the 2.7 billion people who live on less than $2 a day. Prahalad and Hammond, in their seminal article on 'Serving the World's Poor, Profitably', highlighted the potential of market forces in large-scale poverty alleviation: 'By stimulating commerce and development at the bottom of the economic pyramid, MNCs could radically improve the lives of billions of people and help bring into being a more stable, less dangerous world.'[2]

This was a particularly welcome message in light of the challenges of meeting the Millennium Development Goals and concern about the role of poverty in fostering terrorism. A literature has since developed that builds on the core argument of Prahalad and his colleagues.[3] However, while multiple case studies have provided further support for the idea of 'a fortune at the bottom of the pyramid', less attention has been given to the specific strategies and business models required.[4] In this chapter, we focus on distribution strategies for reaching the rural poor – the majority of the BOP that poses distinct distribution challenges relative to the urban poor, who in many respects are easier to reach. As Prahalad and Hammond point out, '[T]he critical barrier to doing business in rural regions is distribution access, not a lack of buying power'.[5] We call overcoming this barrier socially responsible distribution.

In the marketing literature, distribution is conceived as the provision of availability. Channels of distribution are the routes leading to customers and the associated marketing management considerations range from gathering and providing customer and product information to physical distribution.[6] However, this literature assumes a developed world marketplace of intense competition and a highly developed communications and distribution infrastructure. The developing world, particularly its rural markets, are almost entirely ignored. Nonetheless, the core question remains the same – how do customers get access to products and services?

We start by clarifying and quantifying the geographic spread of the BOP. We then turn to the challenge of distribution to the BOP and the fundamental reasons why large numbers of the rural poor cannot access basic and essential products and services. Next, we introduce the idea of socially responsible distribution strategies – innovative strategies that offer the opportunity to create access for the rural poor and enhance their welfare while making efficient use of scarce resources. Five case studies from rural India illustrate socially responsible distribution and highlight the importance of cross-sector collaboration among multinationals, non-governmental organizations (NGOs) and governments. However, we do not restrict our attention to MNC initiatives. Our interest is in the use of market mechanisms, be it by a private firm or a state enterprise, thus two of our cases look at innovative distribution strategies adopted by government departments while another is about an NGO. We identify key insights from the case studies and, in conclusion, highlight the major payoffs and insights from socially responsible distribution for the people at the BOP and MNCs, governments and NGOs.

Geographic spread of the BOP

The term bottom-of-the-pyramid, used in the economic context, refers to the poor. Sachs builds on definitions used by the World Bank to distinguish among poverty levels, categorizing them as extreme poverty, moderate poverty and relative poverty.[7] Households in extreme poverty, which occur almost entirely in developing countries, are unable to meet basic needs. They are:

chronically hungry, unable to access health care, lack the amenities of safe drinking water and sanitation, cannot afford education for some or all of the children, and perhaps lack rudimentary shelter – a roof to keep the rain out of the hut, a chimney to remove the smoke from the cook stove – and basic articles of clothing such as shoes.[8]

Those in moderate poverty manage to barely meet basic needs. Sachs refers to people in relative poverty (in developed countries) as those who meet basic needs, but whose income is so far below national average that they 'lack access to cultural goods, entertainment, recreation, and to quality health care, education and other prerequisites for upward social mobility'.[9]

The World Bank, which is the authoritative source of data on income distribution across countries, determined that people with daily consumption income of less than $1.08[10] (rounded off to $1) lived in extreme poverty.[11] A somewhat arbitrary number of $2 is used to estimate those living in moderate poverty, those 'more typical of [living in poverty in] low-middle income countries'.[12] World Bank data indicate that about 1.1 billion people lived in extreme poverty in 2001. They were concentrated in South Asia (39.5%), sub-Saharan Africa (28.9%) and East Asia (24.8%).[13] About 2.7 billion people, or nearly half the global population, live on $2 a day (see Table 10.1).[14]

The distribution challenge

Today, more than ever before, enhancing the ability of the rural poor to reach ... markets, and actively engage in them, is one of the most pressing development challenges.[15]

The market access disadvantages suffered by the rural poor are rooted in many factors, which affect the flow of goods and services both in and out of rural areas, and adversely affect the rural population's income and quality of life (see Figure 10.1).

Poor road, communications and electricity infrastructure

A large proportion of the rural population in developing countries live in remote villages that are inadequately connected by roads with the outside world and poorly served by appropriate and affordable transport, which poses a physical barrier to markets. The poor in Ghana regard bad roads as one of the 'major obstacles to more

Table 10.1 *Population living below $1 and $2 per day, 2001* (million)*

Region	Region's below-$1 pop. (m)	Percentage of region's pop. living below $1	Region's below-$1 pop. as ratio of total below-$1 pop. (%)	Region's below-$2 pop. (m)	Percentage of region's pop. living below $2	Region's below-$2 pop. as ratio of total below-$2 pop. (%)
Column #	(1)	(2)	(3)	(4)	(5)	(6)
East Asia	271.3	14.9	24.8	864.3	47.4	31.6
Of which China	211.6	16.6	19.4	593.6	46.7	21.7
Eastern Europe and Central Asia	17.6	3.7	1.6	93.5	19.7	3.4
Latin America and Caribbean	49.8	9.5	4.6	128.2	24.5	4.7
Middle East and North America	7.1	2.4	0.6	69.8	23.2	2.6
South Asia	431.1	31.3	39.5	1063.7	77.2	38.9
Of which India	358.6	34.7	32.8	826.0	79.9	30.2
Sub-Saharan Africa	315.8	46.9	28.9	516.0	76.6	18.9
Total	1092.7	21.1	100.0	2735.6	52.9	100.0

Notes: * the precise income used is $1.08 and $2.15 per day at 1993 PPP.

Numbers in column 2 are the ratio of the region's total population that lives on less than $1. For example, 14.9% of all East Asians live on less than $1 – so 271.3m is 14.9% of total East Asian population.

Numbers in column 3 indicate what percentage of the world's population of people living on less than $1 are accounted for by people in that region. For example, 24.8% of the world's population living on less than $1 (which is 1092.7m) are East Asians; i.e. 271.3m is 24.8% of 1092.7m.

Numbers in columns 5 and 6 are similar to those in columns 2 and 3 with $2 being the benchmark instead of $1.

Source: S. Chen and M. Ravallion, 'How have the World's Poorest Fared since the Early 1980s?', World Bank Policy Research Paper, 2004.

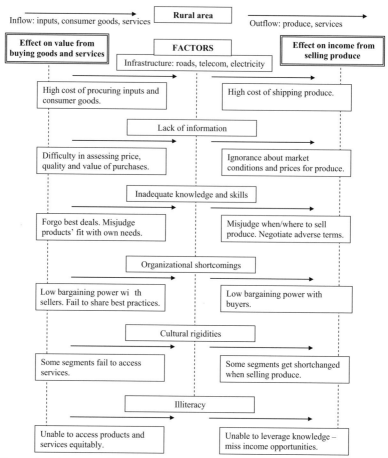

Figure 10.1 Factors affecting the rural population's income and quality of life

successful farming and food security in their communities'.[16] Small local demand combined with the high cost of transporting goods to and from remote villages depresses farmers' incomes, and results in higher prices of agricultural inputs and consumer goods they acquire from urban areas. For example, in Chile consumer goods prices in the remote north and south of the country, are 20–5 per cent higher than the more highly-populated central region of Santiago and Valparaiso.[17] Recognizing the disadvantages suffered by people living in its western and central regions on account of poor connectivity, the Chinese

Table 10.2 *Distance to primary school*

Country	Distance to the nearest primary school (km)		
	Poorest fifth	Richest fifth	Ratio*
Bangladesh 1996–7	0.2	0.1	1.6
Chad 1998	9.9	1.3	7.6
India 1998–99	0.5	0.2	2.3
Mali 1995–6	7.9	5.2	1.5
Nigeria 1999	1.8	0.3	5.5
Uganda 1995	1.4	0.9	1.5
Zimbabwe 1994	3.0	3.5	0.8

Note: * Ratio of distance for poorest fifth to distance for richest fifth.
Source: World Bank, *World Development Report 2004: Making Services Work for Poor People* (Washington, DC: World Bank, 2003b), p. 22.

government has pledged to build 85,000 km of road to connect those regions to other parts of the country.[18]

Poor roads can present a significant barrier to school attendance. Okunmadewa *et al.* report that in parts of Nigeria, '[s]choolchildren have to trek many kilometres daily, to and from the nearest school, and most cannot attend in the rainy season or other times the road becomes impassable'.[19] Physical location can pose a significant barrier for poor urban neighbourhoods as well. A number of poor children living in urban slums fail to attend school regularly owing to the distance from home to school, and an inability to afford or safely use public transport. In Papua New Guinea the average travel time to the nearest school is an hour.[20] Average distance to the nearest primary school is much higher for the poor than the rich in many developing countries (see Table 10.2).

Despite significant improvement in connectivity resulting from growth in mobile telephones, the information highway still bypasses many in developing countries. In 2004, less than 10% of Africans and only 17% of Asians were mobile subscribers compared to 71% of Europeans.[21] Internet penetration in Africa was a mere 2.6%, 8.1% in Asia, compared with 31% in Europe. The rural poor live in areas where communications infrastructure is worse, and even when it exists most are unable access information because they cannot afford mobile phones and computers.

Table 10.3 *Electrification rates, 2002*

	Electrification rate (%)		
Region	Overall	Urban	Rural
Sub-Saharan Africa	23.6	51.5	8.4
China and East Asia	88.1	96.0	83.1
South Asia	42.8	69.4	32.5
Latin America	89.2	97.7	61.4
Transition economies and OECD	99.5	100.0	98.2
World	73.7	90.7	58.2

Source: International Energy Agency, *World Energy Outlook, 2004*
(Paris: International Energy Agency, 2004).

Lack of electricity also shuts out much of the population at the bottom of the pyramid. Developing countries have far lower electrification rates than developed countries; in 2002, 76% of the population in sub-Saharan Africa (526m people) and 57% (798m) in South Asia lacked electricity.[22] As with other services, the rural population is less fortunate with a greater ratio of people without electricity than in urban areas (see Table 10.3).

Information problems

Inadequate infrastructure and lack of information providers result in unavailability of information necessary for the rural population to make informed choices about buying and selling goods and accessing services. A major challenge is information asymmetries in which small farmers are unaware of commodities' market prices and trends and see few options regarding when and where to sell their produce while those they trade with are better informed. The International Fund for Agricultural Development reports '[t]raders, especially if irregular or facing little competition, may be little concerned about reputation, and in such cases asymmetric information often forces the poor to accept low prices for products and to pay high prices for consumer goods'.[23] Rural consumers are also disadvantaged when it comes to purchasing agricultural inputs as they lack information on competing product prices, features and quality.

Lack of knowledge and skills

The availability of information is necessary but not sufficient for welfare enhancement. In order to extract the benefits of information, rural farmers must develop knowledge of how best to use it. For example, they must understand how to analyse information on trends to time their sales for maximum profit, or evaluate product lifecycle costs when comparing competing diesel pump sets to purchase, or decide what practices to adopt to tackle threats to agricultural crops and what pesticides are appropriate.

Those who are illiterate or poorly educated naturally suffer greater disadvantages in developing the knowledge and skills to derive value from information. Sub-Saharan Africa and South Asia are the regions with the lowest literacy, averaging 64% and 61%, respectively. The average years of schooling in India is only five years (7.8 years in urban areas and 3.9 in rural areas) compared to between twelve and thirteen years in developed countries where there is little difference in urban and rural areas.[24] The average is 5.8 years in Nigeria and two years in South Africa.

In describing the plight of the rural poor in India, the World Bank notes that 'illiteracy and malnourishment may prevent [the poor agricultural labourer] from breaking out of the cycle of poverty'.[25] Lower-caste labourers become heavily indebted to powerful upper caste landlords and '[e]ven if laws were in place that would allow him to challenge his landlord's dictates, being illiterate he would find it difficult to navigate the political and judicial institutions that might help him assert his rights'.

The World Bank reports 'there is growing recognition that consumers in even the poorest countries can suffer from the sale of counterfeit goods, as examples ranging from falsely branded pesticides in Kenya to the sale of poisoned meat in China attest'.[26] The illiterate are especially prone to being confused by counterfeits as they cannot read information on packages and rely entirely on package design to recognize and evaluate brands, while counterfeiters and imitators artfully design packaging closely resembling original products.

Organizational shortcomings

It can be difficult to fully realize the power of information and knowledge without organizational improvements. Many farmers live off small land holdings and, unless they are members of cooperatives, lack bargaining power when selling produce and buying agricultural inputs. They are unable to spread fixed costs over a large enough volume to be competitive. Furthermore, they lack access to valuable information on agricultural practices and experience with consumer products and services that might help enhance productivity and provide the basis for informed purchases.

Cultural rigidities

In many countries cultural norms and historical legacy discriminate against certain groups such as women, the indigenous population, minority ethnic or religious groups and lower castes. In Latin America the indigenous population, which is concentrated in rural areas, has higher poverty and lower literacy and lower access to land and credit.[27] Sometimes this is reflected in poor market access for their produce.

Socially responsible distribution strategies

We refer to socially responsible distribution to describe initiatives that provide poor producers and consumers with market access for goods and services that they can benefit from buying or selling, by helping neutralize the disadvantages they suffer from inadequate physical links to markets, information asymmetries and weak bargaining power. Governments, civil society, multinational and local companies, and small private entrepreneurs can all play a role in providing socially responsible distribution.

In order to understand how socially responsible distribution meets the challenge of distributing goods and services we looked at the strategies of five organizations drawn from all three sectors – government, the private sector and civil society. We decided to focus our research on India, which has the largest population living in poverty – 826 million in 2001, counting extreme and moderate poverty. India also has the highest concentration of extreme and moderate poverty (79.9%).

Table 10.4. *India's rural and urban population living below $1 and $2 per day, 2001***

	Total pop. (m)	Pop. with income below $1/ day (m)	Percentage below $1	Pop. with income below $2/ day (m)	Percentage below $2
Rural	744	311	41.8	658	88.4
Urban	289	56	19.3	175	60.5
Total	1033	367	35.5	833	80.6

Note: ** the precise income used is $1.08 and $2.15 per day at 1993 PPP.
Source: World Bank Povcal data source. Some numbers have been calculated using downloaded data.

The share of its population in extreme poverty, 34.7%, is also very high (though it is well below that of sub-Saharan Africa, which has the highest share at 46.9%). In 2004, India's billion people had per capita GNI (gross national income) of $620 ($3,100 at purchasing power parity, or PPP) compared to $32,040 for the billion who lived in high-income countries ($30,970 at PPP).[28]

About three-quarters of the world's poor live in rural areas and are expected to outnumber the urban poor for at least a generation. Unfortunately, per capita public expenditure on provision of rural services is half that in urban areas.[29] A staggering 88 per cent of India's rural population, 658m people, lives in poverty (see Table 10.4).

Notwithstanding the poverty, lower-income groups in India provide significant markets for certain products. Poorer consumers tend to purchase essentials: consumables such as tea, cooking oil, washing cake and powder, talcum powder, electric bulbs and casual footwear, and durables such as bicycles and transistor radios.[30] For some products, as early as the mid-1990s, rural demand exceeded urban demand (see table 10.5). In 2005, rural markets were responsible for 56% of the demand for the fast moving consumer goods (FMCG) category, which comprises food, beverage, household products, personal care products, confectionery and tobacco, and accounted for 80% of consumer spending in India.[31]

Table 10.5 *Rural share in purchase of selected consumable and durable products in India, 1993–4*

Consumables		Durables	
Product	Rural share (%)	Product	Rural share (%)
Washing cake	71	Portable radios	79
Casual footwear	69	Bicycles	78
Cooking oil	67	Mechanical wrist watches	76
Cigarettes	59	Sewing machines	64
Toilet soap	57	Table fans	62
Tea	53	B&W TVs	57
Washing powder	53	Cassette recorders	53
Talcum powder	44	Motorcycles	49
Toothpaste	38	Scooters	30
Electric bulbs	38	Mixers/grinders	25
Shampoo	25	Washing machines	12
Nail polish	24	VCRs	8
Lipstick	5	Hot water heaters	1

Source: S.L. Rao and I. Natarajan, *Indian Market Demographics: The Consumer Classes* (New Delhi: Global Business Press, 1996).

In order to study socially responsible distribution strategies, we chose two multinationals, an NGO and two government departments in India that have initiated programmes to bridge the gap in serving the bottom of the pyramid. We spoke with a number of managers, academics and government officials to identify the goods, services and organizations to focus on. ITC Limited and Hindustan Unilever Limited were mentioned by several as having more significant programmes for rural distribution than other companies, and so we chose them. In order to broaden industry focus, in selecting the NGO we looked at education, and picked Gyanshala since it is run by a professional manager and was financed by reputable agencies such as the Tata Foundation. Our choice of government departments was guided by conversations with senior bureaucrats, who recommended the Departments of Posts and Rural Electrification.

Data were gathered through twenty-six in-depth interviews with rural entrepreneurs, slum dwellers, managers, bureaucrats and NGO officials. Interviews were conducted in five villages in the states of Andhra Pradesh and Madhya Pradesh, and in the cities of New Delhi, Mumbai, Ahmedabad, Hyderabad and Mhow (see Figure 10.2 for interview sites). In addition to the organizations we focus on in our case studies, we gathered information from others directly or indirectly involved in promoting welfare at the BOP – the National Bank for Agriculture and Rural Development, the Reserve Bank of India, the Public Distribution Department and the Rural Development Department – with the objective of understanding the institutional nature of the rural BOP environment.

ITC Limited[32]

As noted above, small farmers suffer tremendous disadvantages when selling their produce. They lack accurate information on market prices, which is necessary to ensure that they sell their produce at the best prices. They are often bullied and cheated by buyers in the process of grading and weighing produce at the point of sale. ITC Limited, which trades in agricultural commodities, uses information technology to empower small farmers by providing them with real-time market information, and has set up a direct procurement system that gives farmers an alternative channel for selling their produce. In addition, ITC has begun setting up supermarkets to sell a range of goods and services to rural consumers.

ITC Limited was established in India as the Imperial Tobacco Company in 1910, as a subsidiary of what eventually evolved into British American Tobacco. It started out as a tobacco company and over the years diversified into unrelated businesses. In the early 1970s, when the Indian government passed laws requiring multinationals to dilute their foreign equity, some major companies like Coca-Cola and IBM exited India. However, some others like ITC, Ciba Geigy and Unilever, chose to remain in India and treated this as an opportunity to diversify and expand.[33] Today ITC is an associate company of British American Tobacco, which owns 31.7 per cent of its stock.[34] ITC's annual sales are $3.7 billion with a little over 50 per cent of the net turnover (after removing excise taxes collected) accounted for by cigarettes.[35] One of ITC's major growth activities today is export of agricultural commodities, which grew 68 per cent in 2005–6 to $390m.

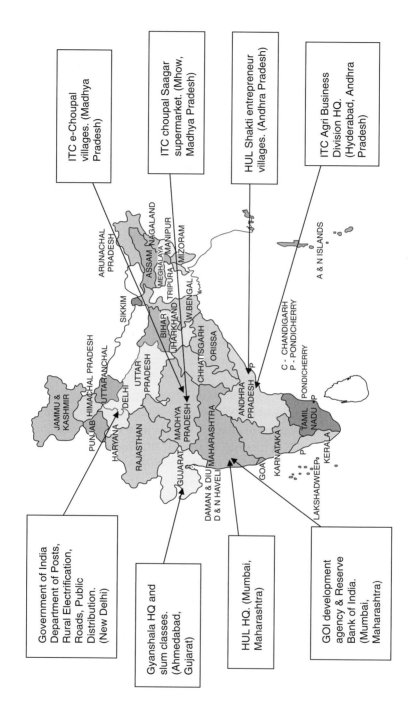

ITC e-Choupal villages. (Madhya Pradesh)

ITC choupal Saagar supermarket. (Mhow, Madhya Pradesh)

HUL Shakti entrepreneur villages. (Andhra Pradesh)

ITC Agri Business Division HQ. (Hyderabad, Andhra Pradesh)

Government of India Department of Posts, Rural Electrification, Roads, Public Distribution. (New Delhi)

Gyanshala HQ and slum classes. (Ahmedabad, Gujarat)

HUL HQ. (Mumbai, Maharashtra)

GOI development agency & Reserve Bank of India. (Mumbai, Maharashtra)

JAMMU & KASHMIR
PUNJAB
HIMACHAL PRADESH
UTTARANCHAL
HARYANA
DELHI
RAJASTHAN
UTTAR PRADESH
SIKKIM
ARUNACHAL PRADESH
ASSAM NAGALAND
MEGHALAYA MANIPUR
TRIPURA MIZORAM
BIHAR
JHARKHAND
W.BENGAL
GUJARAT
MADHYA PRADESH
CHHATISGARH
ORISSA
DAMAN & DIU
D & N HAVELI
MAHARASHTRA
ANDHRA PRADESH
GOA
KARNATAKA
TAMIL NADU
PONDICHERRY
LAKSHADWEEP
KERALA
A & N ISLANDS
C - CHANDIGARH
P - PONDICHERRY

Figure 10.2 Interview sites

Typically, small Indian farmers bring their produce, such as soya bean, to the 'mandi', a state-sanctioned wholesale marketplace where traders bid for farmers' produce. Farmers line up in front of a trader's kiosk at the mandi and each farmer is offered a price for the produce depending on its weight and grade (adjustments are made depending on moisture content, foreign matter, broken seeds, etc.). Farmers' bargaining position is weak. They lack accurate information on prices offered by other traders in that mandi and other mandis in the state (having to rely on word of mouth), are unable to verify if their produce is weighed accurately, and are discouraged from turning down an offer because they have already incurred the sunk cost of bringing their produce to the market and would need to incur additional cost to take it back and return another day. Essentially, farmers end up with lower income than would be possible if there were ways to ensure their produce was accurately weighed and graded and they had access to better information which allowed them better options on when and where to sell their produce.

ITC, which previously bought produce from intermediaries (traders who procured it from farmers), set up a system that empowers farmers in two ways: by providing them with real-time information on commodity prices so that they can obtain better prices for their produce, and giving them an alternative selling channel, direct to ITC. The company has set up an 'e-Choupal' in 6,000 villages (Choupal means village gathering place in Hindi). In each village it recruits a progressive farmer and sets up a computer in his home. Given that many of the villages lack Internet connectivity, ITC sets up a satellite dish on the roof of the farmer's home to provide connectivity. It also installs a solar panel and battery to generate and store enough electricity for twenty minutes of uninterrupted computer operation when power supply is unavailable.

ITC has a web portal through which it provides information on soya prices the previous day at each mandi in the state and at its own procurement centre. It also presents information on prices in international markets such as the Chicago commodities exchange, which are precursors of local prices. Each evening the portal announces the minimum price ITC will offer the following day at its own procurement centre.

ITC's procurement centres are large, clean and well-maintained. Farmers are able to wait in the shade rather than in the open sun and have access to cool drinking water and bathroom facilities. They use electronic weighing systems which reduce chances of inaccuracy. Farmers are given cash for their produce rather than deferred payment as sometimes happens at the mandi. If prices at the nearby mandi turn out to be higher that day, ITC raises its procurement price to match them. However, if prices at the mandi are lower it abides by the price commitment made the previous evening on its web portal, on which the farmers based their decision to bring the produce to market.

ITC has enhanced the value of its procurement system by turning it into a two-way distribution chain. In addition to assisting procurement of agricultural produce from farmers, its village representatives (or 'sanchalaks' as they are called) also sell a range of products and services to villagers, earning a commission on sales. These go all the way from insurance to motorcycles.

ITC has broadened the scope of products distributed to rural areas by building supermarkets (called Choupal Saagars) at some of its commodity procurement centres, to sell a wide variety of products and services, including packaged consumer goods, white goods, agricultural inputs, and health, insurance and banking services. ITC has entered into partnerships for these; for example, Apollo Hospital, which has a chain of hospitals around India, is a partner in providing health services at these 'choupal saagars'. An Apollo-affiliated general physician is available for consultation and to conduct basic diagnostic tests. The general physician can access specialists via the Internet and telephone as necessary. In March 2006, ITC had ten Choupal Saagars in three states and was planning to build another forty by the end of 2007.

Hindustan Unilever Limited (HUL)[36]

The unavailability of basic consumer goods such as tea and toothpaste, results in rural consumers either forgoing their consumption or purchasing poor-quality counterfeits or substitutes. HUL addresses that problem by extending the reach of its rural distribution by relying on women entrepreneurs to sell its products (the Shakti programme). It also delivers information about health and hygiene (via a programme called Shakti Vani) which, in turn, facilitates sales of its products, and partners with government to run a rural community portal that provides broader information with social benefits (iShakti).

HUL, Unilever's Indian subsidiary, is the largest seller of fast-moving consumer goods (FMCG) in India. In 2005, HUL had revenues of $2.5 billion and net profits of a little over $300 million. About 45% of its sales are derived from soaps, detergents and household care products, 28% from personal products and 25% from foods.[37] It also has the largest private sector rural distribution network in India. HUL has a strong interest in selling to rural consumers given its product focus and the fact that over half of India's total FMCG demand is in rural markets.[38]

HUL sees three major marketing challenges associated with rural markets: it is difficult to reach a significant percentage of villages through conventional business methods; low rural literacy and poor media reach create communication challenges; and it is difficult to influence rural customers owing to low brand awareness and low consumption levels. It has three programmes for addressing rural challenges:

(1) The Shakti Entrepreneur programme appoints women as agents to sell HUL products to homes in clusters of between three and five villages. The average entrepreneur earns about $16 per month in sales commissions, which helps supplement family income. (One of the women entrepreneurs we interviewed earned $65 per month.) A field force of 1,000 helps train the 20,000 Shakti entrepreneurs in twelve states. By 2010, HUL expects to have 100,000 Shakti entrepreneurs servicing 500,000 villages with a population of 600 million.

(2) Shakti Vani is a communication programme that provides valuable information on health and hygiene, which is also useful in promoting the company's products such as toothpaste. The programme trains village women to communicate with fellow villagers using specially designed communications materials provided by the company.

(3) iShakti is a more recent programme to provide broader information through a rural Internet community portal. Villagers register as users and access information via HUL's web pages on a variety of topics including agriculture, education, veterinary services and entertainment through kiosks installed in partnership with the state government. The web interface uses voice-over design to make information accessible to the illiterate. When the cursor is moved over an icon a voice announces the topic, and when the icon is clicked, a voice provides information in the local language.

HUL's strategy differs from ITC's in a number of ways. Given the larger breadth of its FMCG offering it does not need to carry others' products and, therefore, limits its sales to its own brands. So far it has focused on a one-way flow of products – out to rural areas. In addition to serving rural customers' needs for consumer products, HUL's strategy is laying the foundation for future rural market share – as incomes rise and consumption of consumer goods increases, HUL is well positioned to capture and retain rural customers, making it difficult for competitors to follow.

Gyanshala

Illiteracy is a significant barrier to enhancing welfare at the bottom of the pyramid. Public education programmes' reach is severely limited by paucity of resources, and thousands of children forgo the opportunity to attend school because the closest public school is too far to attend. Gyanshala is an example of a non-profit entrepreneurial start-up that has developed a scaleable model to provide low-cost, consistent-quality education to poor rural and urban children who are inadequately served by existing public education programmes. Its model provides very basic education using specially developed high-quality materials delivered by low-wage, well-trained teachers at locations close to the homes of under-privileged children.

Gyanshala, an Ahmedabad-based NGO, was set up in 1999 to create a radical low-cost design for delivering effective education for poor children in grades 1 to 3. In order to provide highly accessible education at low cost in a scaleable format, Gyanshala relies on several key design elements:

(1) Classes are located in the village, or in the urban slum, so that young children can easily walk to them.
(2) Costs are contained by hiring teachers who live in the community, or close by, have a grade-ten high-school education, and are willing to work at low wages.
(3) Teachers are given solid training, and are continually and closely monitored and assisted to ensure that they deliver quality instruction.
(4) High-quality materials are developed and used, and detailed teaching plans guide delivery of each class session in the year to ensure consistent high-quality education.

The net effect is that at the end of a three-year programme young children can read, write and perform basic arithmetic functions, and have developed the habit of reading the daily newspaper, all at an annual cost of $36 per child, which is a third or less of the typical cost in government schools. Moreover, given the teacher profile there is a large potential pool of teachers, which helps the model's scalability. Gyanshala has also developed a system of selecting, training and monitoring teachers, which helps ensure quality as it scales up. Gyanshala currently has 5,000 children enrolled in classes in Gujarat State.

Postal service

The rural population's ability to benefit from the growth, industrialization and development of the country is seriously compromised by poor communications links. The Indian Postal System has 155,516 post offices (POs) of which 89 per cent, or 139,120, serve rural areas, giving it the widest physical reach of any Indian organization. In order to build this large network the postal system has relied on collaboration with private entrepreneurs, and in order to enhance its economic feasibility and derive greater benefits for consumers it offers a wider range of services than is typical of postal systems.

As the postal network penetrates deeper into rural areas transportation cost increases and population sparsity reduces revenue potential. The Department of Posts has population, distance and income norms for setting up post offices. The urban population is expected to have a post office within 1.5 to 2 kms, and normal rural areas with populations exceeding 3,000, within 3 kms. In hilly, tribal and desert rural areas, clusters of villages with population exceeding 1,000 are eligible for a post office within 3 kms. The income norm restricts the permissible loss per post office to about $50 per year in normal rural areas and $100 per year in the other, more remote, rural areas. New urban post offices are expected to start out breaking even and earn 5 per cent on revenues after a year.

Given the difficulty in ensuring break-even operations in rural areas the Department of Posts has extended the reach of its network by relying on private entrepreneurs who serve as its representatives and offer a range of postal services from their own, private, premises; for example, from a small shop they might run in the village. They are paid a commission for managing these 'Extra Departmental Post Offices'. Nearly 130,000, or 83 per cent of India's post offices are managed by such entrepreneurs.

The Department has a strategy of extracting larger value from the investment in the postal network by offering a wide range of services. In addition to normal services such as delivering mail and money orders, it offers basic financial services such as savings accounts and insurance (some of which are also available in other countries, like Japan). Some of the products it carries are from the private sector; for example, it serves as an agent for general (non-life) insurance products of the Oriental Insurance Company and distributes mutual funds and bonds offered by ICICI-Prudential. The Department also offers retail services for the non-profit sector, such as application forms for universities and for other government agencies; for example, bill payment for utilities and distribution of passport application forms. The postal network is also used for gathering valuable information – for example, data for the Election Commission – and accepts applications from the public for government organizations under the Right to Information Act, 2005.

Technology is used to enhance service. With the advent of the Internet the Department of Posts has introduced services to bridge the gap between Internet users and non-users. The postal system enables customers to send e-mail messages to recipients who lack Internet access. The messages arrive at a post office close to the recipient, are printed at the post office and delivered to the recipient. Similarly, messages may be sent in reverse direction with the assistance of the post office.

In 2002, the Department introduced the Gramin Sanchar Sewa (Rural Communications Service) to bring valuable telephone service to areas not covered by conventional landline or cellular service. It uses Wireless Local Loop (WLL) technology, which relies on radio signals to connect with the wider Public Switched Telephone Network (PSTN), thus bridging the infrastructure gap. (The technology is sometimes referred to as radio in the loop, RITL, or fixed-radio access, FRA.) Today about 2,700 postal delivery agents provide the service.

Rural Electrification Department

Absence of electricity supply affects not just quality of life but the ability to enhance productivity and income using mechanized agricultural and industrial equipment. In 2005, 77.8 million rural households

(56 per cent of India's rural population) lacked access to electricity, making India the country with the largest number of households without electricity.[39] In recent years, the Indian government has launched ambitious initiatives that aim to extend electricity supply to the entire rural population by the end of the decade. A crucial aspect of these initiatives is the use of radically different business models to enhance the economic feasibility of power distribution and generation.

The major barriers to rural penetration of electric supply have been high cost of revenue collection, high cost of long-distance transmission losses and large burden of subsidies. State utilities lose money on rural distribution and lack incentives to extend its reach. Energy losses in India are as high as 25% while the OECD average is less than 10%.[40]

In order to improve the financial feasibility of distribution, the Indian government has launched a scheme to engage franchisees to manage the last mile of the distribution chain – from village transformer to household. The franchisee is in charge of signing on new customers and the utility assumes responsibility for connecting the home to the transformer and for installing and sealing the meter. The franchisee bills customers and collects payments, paying the utility for the power drawn from the system at an agreed rate that provides for standard transmission losses and a commission for the franchisee's services. The franchisee has a strong incentive to detect losses, or theft, and maximize collections. When customers default the franchisee can ask the utility to discontinue supply. Currently there are about 400 franchisees and the government plans to increase that number to 100,000.

The government proposes to overcome the challenge of large power losses from long-distance transmission by encouraging distributed power generation, and limiting the burden of financing and managing these by allowing private entrepreneurs to invest in capacity and sell power to the grid. Entrepreneurs will be encouraged to use renewable energy sources, such as biomass, for units generating as little as 2.5–5MW, which would usually be enough to serve up to a thousand households. The government will help entrepreneurs arrange special low-cost financing. The model under consideration carefully separates activities between the government and private entrepreneurs with the objective of allowing entrepreneurs easy entry and exit, facilitating competition. The land on which the generators will be situated, the transformer, and the power cables to the homes will be owned by the government. Entrepreneurs would own and maintain the generating capacity on the land leased from the government. This would allow private investors to exit easily if the project becomes unattractive. More than one private entrepreneur could supply power into the network.

At a 2000 conference of Indian Chief Ministers and Power Ministers the consensus was that the ability and willingness of rural consumers to pay for electric power is underestimated, suggesting that the barrier to rural electrification was not consumers' ability to afford it, but inadequate investment in efficient, well-managed, distribution systems. Initial experiments with distribution franchising have been promising. For example, in the north-east Indian state of Assam, which is famous for tea plantations and oil fields, an experiment in twenty-two villages in 2005 more than doubled electricity billing and raised collection from 12% of billing to 88%.[41]

Intervention strategies

As the cases illustrate, challenges to socially responsible distribution are addressed by all three sectors – government, civil society and private companies – through intervention in a number of ways. The poor benefit by earning higher income and deriving value from free services and from being able to choose among a greater variety of products available for purchase. Some of these benefits are the direct result of entrepreneurial opportunities, services and products provided by organizations. Part of the welfare enhancement results from strengthening bargaining power, which depends on availability of information and its transformation into knowledge.

Four sets of moderating factors significantly affect the availability of information, its transformation into knowledge and impact on bargaining power: illiteracy, cultural rigidities, market structure and organizational shortcomings. The effect of intervention strategies by the government, NGOs and companies at various stages is illustrated in Figure 10.3, which distinguishes between direct links and moderating factors in our model of socially responsible distribution.

The government adds value in many ways – by providing infrastructure for transportation, communications and electricity, and information and knowledge through government-controlled media and extension services,[42] and certain basic market institutions, such

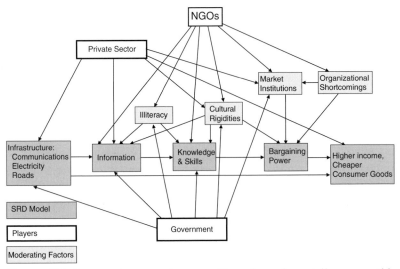

Figure 10.3 Intervention to enhance welfare through socially responsible distribution

as the mandi. The government's efforts can be leveraged by drawing on the other sectors. For example, the World Bank, in enumerating the key principles for design of effective extension programmes, suggested that '[e]xisting and new institutions such as NGOs, universities, private firms, and even public agencies can compete for delivery of publicly funded extension services'.[43]

The private sector plays a crucial role. Large companies help empower farmers with information and provide competition to traders who previously exercised monopsony or monopoly power. Private entrepreneurs serve to extend distribution deep into the bottom of the pyramid and earn better livelihoods in the process. Increased product competition at the BOP helps reduce prices.

NGOs assist by providing information and knowledge, alleviating illiteracy and cultural rigidities (such as constraints imposed by caste) and helping organize farmers to leverage knowledge into bargaining power. They supplement the efforts of the government by implementing scaleable models to provide social services and education where the government is unable to keep up with huge demand given its limited resources.

The types of intervention can be further distinguished by separating them into broad or targeted. In Figure 10.4 we provide examples

		Scope of Intervention	
		Broad	**Targeted**
Effect Type	**Direct Effect**	Govt. • Infrastructure development (e.g. Rural Electrification) • Information provision (e.g. govt. controlled media) • Knowledge provision (e.g. extension services) NGOs • Information provision (e.g. information/warnings of corporate negative externalities) • Knowledge provision (e.g. Gyanshala addressing illiteracy)	Private Sector • Specific infrastructure projects (e.g. ITC e-Choupal) • Information pertinent to particular tasks (e.g. ITC commodities data) • Knowledge provision specific to task (e.g. HUL dental hygiene practices) NGOs • Information provision specific to tasks (e.g. commodity prices to farmers) • Knowledge provision specific to tasks (e.g. educating farmers on timing of commodity sales) Govt. • Bridging infrastructure gaps (e.g. Post Office wireless local loop technology to provide phone service) • Information provision (e.g. Post Office dissemination of educational programme information) • Knowledge provision on specific social issues (e.g. HIV/AIDS prevention)
	Moderating Effect	Govt. • Institutional development (e.g. commercial code) • Addressing market abuse (e.g. anti-trust action) NGOs • Institutional development (e.g. advocacy of rights of vulnerable/marginalized groups) • Addressing market abuse (e.g. advocacy of microfinance as solution to credit abuse)	Private Sector • Measures to overcome illiteracy obstacles to the task (e.g. HUL e-Shakti web interface) • Increased competition (e.g. ITC) NGOs • Addressing market abuse (e.g. microfinance to support BOP entrepreneurs, such as Shakti) • Organizational shortcomings (via development of self-help groups) Govt. • Development of specific market institutions (e.g. set up and oversee mandi system)

Figure 10.4 Types of intervention

of the intervention by governments, NGOs and companies using this classification. The major difference in the strategies of the three sectors on scope of intervention is that the private sector's strategies are typically targeted whereas those of government and NGOs are both broad and targeted. Below, we discuss some of the learning about specific strategies that can enhance socially responsible distribution.

Bridge the infrastructure gap

Managers who are used to operating in conditions where infrastructure is taken for granted as being provided by the government, may shy away from entering the bottom of the pyramid, especially the rural part of it, when infrastructure limitations appear to pose significant barriers. Rural markets can actually present significant profit opportunities for certain products and services that are demanded by poorer consumers. Companies like ITC that are willing to bridge the infrastructure gaps, such as lack of Internet connectivity and reliable electric power, can extend distribution channels into the BOP. Such companies can set up formidable barriers for followers, who must contend with the prospect of defraying infrastructure investment over smaller volume of product distributed.

Multinationals' strategies of investing in infrastructure to build new BOP markets are not dissimilar to that of McDonald's when it entered the former Soviet Union in 1990. McDonald's recognized that in order to ensure its core competence would translate to the Soviet environment, where infrastructure made procurement of high-quality inputs a major challenge, it had to invest in production of quality inputs and assist suppliers in producing them and moving them to McDonald's in a timely fashion. McDonald's made a significant commitment to securing the supply of high-quality commodities and converting them into appropriate inputs in a $40m plant, which was not an activity it typically undertook elsewhere.

Differential, or layered, distribution

As organizations seek greater distribution depth, extending distribution networks outward to remote areas, transportation cost rises and population becomes sparse, rapidly inflating distribution cost. In order to extend reach, it becomes necessary to design differential distribution systems to serve urban and rural areas, with lower-cost distribution layers penetrating the outer extremities of the network.

Differential distribution is key to socially responsible distribution, just as differential pricing is key to socially responsible pricing.[44] Pharmaceutical multinationals could have saved lives through differential pricing of AIDS drugs in South Africa, but were deterred from doing so by a number of barriers including institutional risks to their developed-country profit margins from gray markets and price referencing. Governments and NGOs play an important role in reducing such risks and, thereby, facilitating differential pricing. Similarly, infrastructural and institutional shortcomings discourage differential

differentiation, and governments and NGOs can work with companies to help overcome these difficulties and encourage distribution,
bringing valuable products and services to BOP consumers and also
helping them raise their incomes.

Outsource the 'last mile' to BOP entrepreneurs: differential distribution requires examination of the distribution chain to select activities that can be outsourced to drastically reduce distribution costs. By
outsourcing the 'last mile' (in reality, the last several miles) to small
private BOP entrepreneurs, companies like HUL and ITC, and government departments like those for post and rural electrification, can
take advantage of talented and motivated local entrepreneurs at much
lower cost than company or government employees. This results from
their low opportunity cost and negligible overheads, given that they
live in the target market and operate from existing premises. So while
the transportation cost of delivering the product or service to the outer
reaches of the network is higher than delivering it to urban locations,
the fixed overhead is contained by outsourcing the promotion, selling
and collection tasks to franchisees.

Organizations treat urban and rural distribution channels differen-
tially in terms of economic benchmarks to evaluate feasibility. Unlike
urban channels, companies treat rural channels as longer-term investments that lay the foundation for larger future markets while making a social contribution today. Government departments use them
to maximize the reach of services with limited deployment of public
resources. With the burden of retail distribution shifted partly onto
BOP entrepreneurs, scarce public resources can be redeployed to provide a wider span at wholesale distribution to serve a larger array of
conduits into rural areas.

Leveraged distribution

Challenges of physical access and fragmented demand deter investment in distribution infrastructure reaching into the rural parts of the
bottom of the pyramid. For many organizations the task of extending access into the outer extremities of the BOP may seem simply
too expensive to undertake. Both the private sector (e.g. ITC) and
the government (e.g. the Department of Posts) provide examples of
leveraging the investment in rural distribution to enhance its value
and improve economic feasibility, first by broadening the distribution

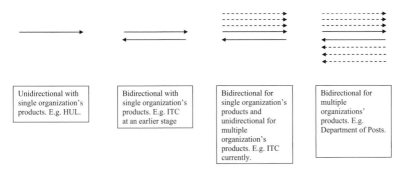

Figure 10.5 Degrees of leveraged distribution

network's scope by sharing it and, second, by increasing value generation by converting it into a bidirectional network (see Figure 10.5).

Bidirectional distribution: the feasibility of distribution can be further improved through additional economies of scope obtained by creating two-way flow of products and services. ITC's distribution strategy creatively enhances the value of its procurement system by turning it into a two-way distribution chain. Its sanchalaks serve the function of stimulating purchases from farmers as well as selling products to them. Similarly, the commodity procurement centres not only facilitate direct commodity purchase but build traffic to the company's supermarket located on the premises. Similarly, the network of the Department of Posts is bidirectional.

Bidirectional distribution has some similarities to the concept of 'reverse distribution' (or 'reverse logistics'). Reverse distribution systems typically are focused on the return of end-of-life products or the recall of faulty products. These systems often stem from regulatory requirements around recycling, but can provide additional value to manufacturers through, for example, re-manufacturing using the returned product and information that can be ascertained on product performance.[45] Reverse distribution systems ease the challenges around product recalls.[46] In contrast, our concept of bidirectional distribution refers to the two-way flow of different products using the same logistics. Bidirectional distribution also has an information component, not about returned products but about information on the consumer's needs for a wider range of products and services.

Shared distribution: once a distribution channel is in place and can carry additional products at low incremental cost, contribution earnings can be raised by widening product range to derive greater economies of scope. ITC has aggressively pursued alliances with a broad range of vendors, which allows it to offer a full range of goods and services in its rural supermarkets and spread recovery of its large fixed cost on that distribution platform across larger sales volume. Similarly, the Department of Posts is delivering greater value to the public and helping cover the cost of its Extra Departmental POs by carrying products of companies and educational institutions.

This strategy is somewhat similar to that of Amazon.com in e-commerce. Having established a powerful Internet distribution channel Amazon has significantly expanded contributions at low incremental cost by carrying a much wider range of products than its original narrow offering of books.

The network of the Department of Posts is the most complex, carrying products of multiple organizations in both directions.

Using information to empower the BOP

The rural poor suffer low incomes as a result of traders' market power. One of the ways in which governments can enhance rural incomes is through stronger market institutions; for example, through regulation that discourages adulteration, tampering of weights and market-rigging, and that enables the rural poor to acquire superior inputs and better prices for their produce.[47] Access to information on prices and the availability of alternate market channels, as provided by ITC, gives farmers the opportunity to capture greater value from sale of their products.

The role of the private sector in dissemination of knowledge is especially powerful in places where public rural extension services are inadequate, as in some African countries. The International Fund for Agricultural Development notes: 'New market routes or other mechanisms to reduce the time-lag before the poor adopt better technologies are badly needed if the poor are not to miss out on new opportunities.'[48] Both HUL and ITC provide valuable information on products and practices, supplementing government extension services. NGOs play a key role in organizing entrepreneurs at the BOP so that they can leverage information into knowledge and bargaining power, as evident from the thriving self-help movement in India. HUL's Shakti entrepreneurs are usually members of self-help groups in the villages they live in.

Leveraging technology

The poorest segments of rural populations may not benefit from technology that is embodied in expensive equipment (such as mechanized farm equipment). However, they can benefit a great deal from knowledge of other kinds of technology, such as agricultural practices, which may be applied without significant additional capital. The challenge is to find ways to bring these to the attention of potential users. By using technology, companies like ITC and HUL are able to set up channels to bring a wide array of useful information to rural users. Technology also allows them to make information accessible to the weaker segments, such as the illiterate. This service builds social capital that helps further companies' objective of selling products on which they can earn contributions today and set the foundation for future profits.

Cross-sectoral collaboration

When setting up business models that integrate activities of different sectors it is important to design the system so that responsibilities are clearly demarcated and performance easy to measure. The effectiveness of strategies for cross-sectoral collaboration, especially when significant private and public sector resources need to be combined, as required in rural power generation, requires careful analysis of activities that can be put in the hands of entrepreneurs and the infrastructural support and monitoring that government needs to provide. Easy entry and exit is helpful to facilitate participation by the private sector, so the government has to assume ownership of parts of the value chain that require longer-term commitment, especially in public goods.

Scalability

The challenge of socially responsible distribution is to serve an enormous population at the bottom of the pyramid in need of goods and services. This calls for solutions that can stretch scarce resources. A remarkable aspect of Gyanshala's model to bring basic education to the poorest children in villages and urban slums is that instead of striving to provide a rich educational environment using college graduates, it decided to strip out non-essential aspects of education and focus on providing high-quality essential education, which meant it could deliver valuable service using widely available basic resources, facilitating scalability while making education highly accessible to the target population by bringing school closer to childrens' homes.

In their decision to use BOP entrepreneurs to manage distribution's last mile, the Departments of Posts and Rural Electrification, and HUL and ITC have all opted for scalable models as these human resources are abundantly available. The use of technology platforms also helps in this regard. Having invested a fixed cost in developing or appropriating information and knowledge, organizations, using technology, are able to disseminate it widely at negligible marginal cost.

Payoff

Involvement in rural distribution provides a range of benefits for multinationals, as well as people at the bottom of the pyramid.

What's in it for multinationals?

Multinationals that have invested in rural markets are benefiting by earning contributions on current sales, laying the foundation for substantial future earnings, pre-empting future competition in rural markets and developing consumer information databases that can secure future competitive advantage.

Contributions on current sales

Given the cost structure of the rural distribution set up by HUL and ITC it is likely that they are earning positive contributions on sales through franchisees even at the outer extremities of their network. The franchisees get a small commission on product sales, and while shipping costs are higher, other variable costs are not much higher than selling in urban markets. Neither is there a large fixed overhead. On the new supermarket format set up by ITC, however, investment is large and requires substantial volume to break-even. While contributions are probably positive it is not clear if volume is large enough to cover fixed operating costs.

Future earnings

Reaching out to the bottom of the pyramid with valuable products and services in the face of little competition from other organized sector firms can help build a loyal customer base that will deliver future profits. As developing-country economies grow, some of this rural population will migrate to urban areas and as that happens familiarity with brands they have encountered in rural areas will help them transition to companies' products in urban areas, once again helping secure future earnings. Similarly, as urban BOP consumers become more affluent they are likely to purchase upscale products of companies whose products they have previously used.

An important factor in creating long-lasting customer loyalty is the creation of trust through provision of goods and services with higher perceived value compared to traditional traders with whom the BOP customers interacted. The free provision of information that empowers farmers by enhancing their bargaining power vis-à-vis traders, or allows them to improve agricultural methods or improve hygiene, can serve to create goodwill and build social capital.

Pre-emptive distribution

ITC and HUL are racing to pre-empt future competition from distribution heavyweights. The Indian government is under pressure from foreign governments to open up its retail sector to foreign competitors, and giants such as Wal-Mart are poised to enter the 'last frontier for hyper-markets'.[49] Large local companies, such as Reliance, have committed substantial resources to enter the retail sector. Reliance intends to invest $5.6 billion to grab a share of the rapidly growing organized retail sector, which is expected to triple in size to $15 billion by 2010.[50] These new players will provide formidable competition that will begin in urban areas and eventually roll out into rural markets. Reliance has announced plans to create fifty-acre 'rural business hubs' in each district of India in the third phase of its strategy, after it begins setting up 200,000 sq ft hypermarkets and 2,000 sq ft supermarkets in urban areas.[51] By moving early to blanket rural markets, whose fragmented nature provides logistical advantages to first-movers, ITC and HUL can hope to create entry barriers for some of the followers, or at least strengthen their position against the onslaught of giants like Reliance, much as Wal-Mart shut out competitors like K-Mart in US rural markets during its initial years.[52]

Consumer information databases

Companies that control the last mile of the distribution chain stand to gain from developing proprietary databases with valuable consumer information that can be used to sell market research services to new entrants, as well as to influence product and brand choices. Government departments are also aware of the value of such market information. They expect entrepreneurs who manage electricity sales as franchisees of the Rural Electrification Ministry will benefit from market information they can provide to companies selling a host of electrical gadgets.

Payoff for the bottom of the pyramid

Intervention by government, NGOs and private companies delivers valuable payoff for the BOP. People are better informed and, given assistance on how to use information, can raise their incomes and derive higher value from purchases of agricultural inputs and consumer goods. Knowledge of better agricultural practices raises productivity and income, and appreciation of health and hygiene factors improves quality of life. Entrepreneurship opportunities build self-esteem and loosen cultural constraints. Better communications with urban areas create stronger awareness of rights and opportunities.

Risks

As companies extend their reach into the BOP, bringing goods and services to areas inadequately served by the majority of their competitors, there are naturally opportunities for exercise of monopoly power, and exploitation of consumers and labour, because institutional mechanisms and government oversight are weak in rural areas. These concerns are already being raised by NGOs. Thus, it is important to concurrently create governance mechanisms, perhaps using coalitions of government, civil society and companies that have demonstrated their commitment to enhance the welfare of the BOP.

Conclusion

Management scholars and development economists have provided a compelling case for greater attention to the bottom of the pyramid. However, few contributions have examined specific strategies for reaching the bottom of the pyramid. We have introduced the term 'socially responsible distribution' (SRD) to describe initiatives that provide poor producers and consumers with market access for goods and services that they can benefit from buying or selling by helping neutralize the disadvantages they suffer, from inadequate physical links to markets, information asymmetries and weak bargaining power. This has been illustrated by five case studies. In doing so, we have identified the role the private sector, governments and NGOs can play in promoting SRD, the different kinds of intervention strategies they use and the benefits for various parties, including the people at the bottom of the pyramid.

The chapter highlighted the obstacles to higher earning potential and access to cheaper consumer goods for poor consumers, identifying direct and moderating factors. The direct factors identified were infrastructure shortcomings, lack of information and knowledge and skills, and low bargaining power. The moderating factors identified were illiteracy, cultural rigidities, (inadequate) market institutions and organizational shortcomings. The strategies of organizations tackling these obstacles used broad and targeted interventions. These strategies included bridging the infrastructure gap, use of empowering information, leveraging technology and cross-sectoral collaboration as well as differentiated distribution and leveraged-bidirectional and leveraged-shared distribution. Managers who are interested in reaching into the BOP could well learn from the strategies adopted by the organizations discussed here, which are in many respects at the forefront of efforts to serve and engage with the BOP.

Acknowledgements

We thank the various managers, bureaucrats, NGO officials and rural entrepreneurs who shared valuable insights with us, and Aparna Pande, doctoral student in international relations at Boston University, for assisting with the research.

Notes

1 J.-P. Sartre, *Le Mots*.
2 C.K. Prahalad and A. Hammond, 'Serving the World's Poor, Profitably', *Harvard Business Review* (September 2002): 48.

3   C.K. Prahalad, *The Fortune at the Bottom of the Pyramid* (Upper Saddle River: Wharton School Publishing, 2005); Prahalad and Hammond (2002); C.K. Prahalad and S.L. Hart, 'The Fortune at the Bottom of the Pyramid', *Strategy+Business*, 26 (2002): 54–67.

4   See H. Chesbrough, S. Ahern, M. Finn and S. Guerraz, 'Business Models for Technology in the Developing World: The Role of Non-governmental Organizations', *California Management Review*, 48 (2006): 48–61, for a notable exception.

5   Prahalad and Hammond (2002: 50).

6   See, for example, P. Kotler, *Marketing Management* (New Saddle River: Prentice Hall, 2000).

7   J. Sachs, *The End of Poverty: Economic Possibilities for our Time* (New York: Penguin, 2005). For World Bank, see S. Chen and M. Ravallion, 'How did the World's Poorest Fare in the 1990s?', World Bank Policy Research Working Paper, WPS 2409, 2000; S. Chen and M. Ravallion, 'How have the World's Poorest Fared since the Early 1980s?', World Bank Policy Research Paper, 2004.

8   Sachs (2005: 20).

9   Sachs (2005: 20).

10 1993 dollars at purchasing price parity.

11 Chen and Ravallion (2000).

12 Chen and Ravallion (2000: 7).

13 Chen and Ravallion (2004).

14 Prahalad and his colleagues count a much larger number (four billion) in their definition of the bottom of the pyramid; that is people earning below $1,500 per year at purchasing power parity (Prahalad and Hart, 2002; Prahalad, 2005). We choose to work with the more widely-accepted number of poor people, which is around 2 billion as discussed earlier.

15 International Fund for Agricultural Development, *Rural Poverty Report 2001: The Challenge of Ending Rural Poverty* (New York: Oxford University Press, 2001), p. 161.

16 E. Kunfaa, T. Dogbe, H. MacKay and C. Marshall, 'Ghana: Empty Pockets', in D. Narayan and P. Petesch (eds.), *Voices of the Poor: From Many Lands* (Washington, DC: World Bank, 2002), p. 24.

17 F.G.H. Ferreira and J.A. Litchfield, 'Calm after the Storms: Income Distribution in Chile, 1987–1994', *World Bank Economic Review*, 13/3 (1999): 509–38.

18 F. Guerrera, 'IHG Plan to Ride China's Boom in Infrastructure', *Financial Times*, 6 June 2006, p. 29.

19 F. Okunmadewa, O. Aina, G. Ayoola, A. Mamman, N. Nweze, T. Odebiyi, D. Shehu and J. Zacha, 'Nigeria: Illbeing and Insecurity', in D. Narayan

and P. Petesch (eds.), *Voices of the Poor: From Many Lands* (Washington, DC: World Bank, 2002), p. 101.

20 J. Gibson, 'Who's not in School? Economic Barriers to Universal Primary Education in Papua New Guinea', *Pacific Economic Bulletin*, 15/2 (2000): 46–58.

21 International Telecommunications Union, *World Telecommunication/ ICT Development Report, 2006: Measuring ICT for Social and Economic Development* (Geneva: International Telecommunications Union, 2006).

22 International Energy Agency, *World Energy Outlook, 2004* (Paris: International Energy Agency, 2004).

23 International Fund for Agricultural Development (2001: 168).

24 World Bank, *World Development Report 2006: Equity and Development* (Washington, DC: World Bank, 2005).

25 World Bank (2005: 21).

26 World Bank, *World Development Report 2005: A Better Investment Climate for Everyone* (Washington, DC: World Bank, 2004), p. 85.

27 Q. Wodon, 'Poverty and Policy in Latin America and the Caribbean', World Bank discussion draft, Washington, DC, 1999.

28 World Bank (2005).

29 World Bank, *Reaching the Rural Poor: A Renewed Strategy for Rural Development* (Washington, DC: World Bank, 2003a), p. 6.

30 S.L. Rao and I. Natarajan, *Indian Market Demographics: The Consumer Classes* (New Delhi: Global Business Press, 1996).

31 KPMG International, 'Consumer Markets in India – the Next Big Thing?', KPMG International, publication number 213-405, September 2005.

32 For other case data on ITC Limited see: D. Upton and V. Fuller, 'The ITC EChoupal Initiative', Harvard Business School Case Number 9-604-016, 2004; and Prahalad (2005).

33 D.J. Encarnation and S. Vachani, 'Foreign Ownership: When Hosts Change the Rules', *Harvard Business Review* (September–October 1985): 152–60.

34 Tassel and Turner 2006.

35 ITC, *ITC Report and Accounts*, 2006.

36 For other case data on HUL see: V. Rangan and R. Rajan, 'Unilever in India: Hindustan Lever's Project Shakti – Marketing FMCG to the Rural Consumer', 2005; and Prahalad (2005).

37 Hindustan Lever Limited, *Annual Report*, 2005.

38 KPMG International (2005).

39 Ministry of Power, Rajiv Gandhi Grameen Vidyutikaran Yojana: Scheme for Rural Electrification & Household Electrification (New Delhi: Ministry of Power, Government of India, 2005).

40 International Energy Agency, 'Energy and Poverty', in *World Energy Outlook, 2002* (Paris: International Energy Agency, 2002).

41 Assam State Electricity Board, *Empowering Rural Consumers: A Study of the Impact of Single Point Power Supply Scheme (Franchisee Scheme)* (Guwahati: Assam State Electricity Board, 2005).

42 'Extension services' refer to programmes run by government agencies, universities and cooperatives to provide information, training and education via workshops, classes and events.

43 World Bank (2003a: 47).

44 S. Vachani and N.C. Smith, 'Socially Responsible Pricing: Lessons from the Pricing of AIDS Drugs in Developing Countries', *California Management Review*, 47/1 (2004): 117–44.

45 J.D. Blackburn, V.D.R. Guide, Jr., G.C. Souza and L.K. van Wassenhove, 'Reverse Supply Chains for Commercial Returns', *California Management Review*, 46 (2004): 6–22; M.W. Toffel, 'Strategic Management of Product Recovery', *California Management Review*, 46 (2004): 6–22.

46 N.C. Smith, R.J. Thomas and J.A. Quelch, 'A Strategic Approach to Managing Product Recalls', *Harvard Business Review*, 74 (1996): 102–12.

47 International Fund for Agricultural Development (2001).

48 International Fund for Agricultural Development (2001: 10).

49 A. Jain, 'A Dramatic Change in Shopping', *Financial Times*, 28 June 2006.

50 K. Merchant, 'Reliance Spends $5.6 Billion on Retail Foray', *Financial Times*, 28 June 2006.

51 Jain (2006).

52 P. Ghemawat, 'Wal-Mart Stores' Discount Operations', Harvard Business School Case Study, 9-387-018, 1986.

Index